"Katherine Woodward Thomas brings a gentle but fiercely powerful approach to what can otherwise be such a painful experience. Through Conscious Uncoupling, we can transform the deepest disappointment into a sacred journey from sorrow to peace."

—Marianne Williamson, *New York Times* bestselling author of *A Return to Love*

"During a breakup—a time that normally brings out the worst in us, Katherine Woodward Thomas takes us by the hand and helps us live in ways that are aligned with the highest and the best we have within us. With amazing clarity and depth, she'll take the splinter out of your soul and support you to end your relationship in a way that leaves you, and those you care about, whole and complete rather than broken and damaged. I absolutely love this book!"

—Marci Shimoff, *New York Times* bestselling author of *Happy for No Reason*

"*Conscious Uncoupling* is a kind and compassionate guide on how to overcome breakup grief and use it to transform and enrich your entire life. The process Katherine Woodward Thomas provides will not only help make your heart whole again, but will also ensure a positive, hopeful future for all involved. A paradigm-shifting book that promises to uplevel how we collectively do breakups moving forward."

—Jo... Gr... *New York Times* bestselling author ... *Are from Venus*

"There is so much wisdom, heart, and humor in this book you'll want to sleep with it under your pillow. Katherine communicates the real deal—you'll see it immediately and breathe deeply for having such a friend on the path. Full of head, heart, body, and relational wisdom gathered from years of deep exploration, *Conscious Uncoupling* is the book that you've been looking for to guide you to true freedom. I loved it!"

—Kathlyn Hendricks, Ph.D., *New York Times* bestselling coauthor of *Conscious Loving* and *Conscious Loving Ever After*

"Before *Conscious Uncoupling* we didn't have a road map for how to turn the pain of a breakup into a genuine opportunity to re-create our life for the better. Now, thanks to Katherine Woodward Thomas's brilliant and beautifully written manifesto, anyone going through the ending of a relationship has an opportunity not only to heal from heartache but to evolve human relationships, and thus humanity, to a new level. With her trademark wisdom and deep kindness, Katherine shares her well-tested 5-step process that will guide you through the storm to a brighter future than you ever imagined possible."

—Claire Zammit, founder, FemininePower.com

"Katherine Woodward Thomas is my relationship guru. Her wisdom and guidance helped me clear all blocks to romantic freedom. *Conscious Uncoupling* will help you embrace the true meaning of forgiveness and restore your faith in love."

—Gabrielle Bernstein, New York Times bestselling author of *Miracles Now*

"*Conscious Uncoupling* is a powerful and groundbreaking process that provides a proven path to healing and wholeness from the devastation of heartbreak. From her decades of experience as a therapist and her personal story of divorce, Katherine Woodward

Thomas reveals the transformative steps back to a life of love, freedom, and happiness."

—Arielle Ford, bestselling author of *The Soulmate Secret*

"The book *Conscious Uncoupling* presents a sensible and very helpful five-step approach toward turning the tragedy of a breakup into a new healthy beginning instead of a wound that keeps festering."

—John Gottman, author of
The Seven Principles for Making Marriage Work

"Katherine Woodward Thomas is as wise and intelligent as she is empathetic and brave. Her knowledgeable, visionary, and clear teachings have consistently represented empowerment and healing to so many, myself included. Her seer-like insight and her gentle yet unwaveringly leading-edge and applicable guidance holds our hands as we traverse the often debilitating territory of breakups and endings. I am so happy Katherine is on this planet."

—Alanis Morissette,
Grammy Award–winning singer-songwriter

"In *Conscious Uncoupling,* Katherine Woodward Thomas has created the definitive blueprint for how to complete a relationship in a way that leaves everyone honored and empowered. If you're considering uncoupling, I suggest you run—not walk—to the nearest bookstore and start reading it today. You'll discover that a graceful parting of the ways is doable even under the most extreme of circumstances. I find Katherine to be always on the leading edge of thought—and we are once again the beneficiaries of her brilliance."

—Debra Poneman, bestselling author and
founder/CEO of Yes to Success, Inc.

conscious uncoupling

conscious uncoupling

5 STEPS TO LIVING
HAPPILY *EVEN* AFTER

Katherine Woodward Thomas, MA, MFT

Published in Great Britain in 2015 by Yellow Kite
An imprint of Hodder & Stoughton
An Hachette UK company

1

First published in the United States by Harmony Books, an imprint of the Crown Publishing Group, a
division of Penguin Random House LLC, New York.
www .crownpublishing .com

Harmony Books is a registered trademark, and the Circle colophon is a trademark of Penguin Random
House LLC.

Library of Congress Cataloging-in-Publication Data
Thomas, Katherine Woodward.
Conscious uncoupling / Katherine Woodward Thomas.
pages cm
1. Divorce. 2. Separation (Psychology) I. Title.
HQ814.T428 2015
306.89—dc23 2015009538
Copyright © Katherine Woodward Thomas 2015

A CIP catalogue record for this title is available from the British Library

ISBN 978 1 473 61932 6
eBook ISBN 978 1 473 61933 3

Printed and bound by CPI Group (UK) Ltd, Croydon, CR0 4YY

Jacket design by
Jacket photography

Hodder & Stoughton policy is to use papers that are natural, renewable and recyclable products
and made from wood grown in sustainable forests. The logging and manufacturing processes are
expected to conform to the environmental regulations of the country of origin.

Hodder & Stoughton Ltd
Carmelite House
50 Victoria Embankment
London EC4Y 0DZ

www.hodder.co.uk

To all social artists, agents of change, and
pioneers of new possibilities between us
who with great heart, deep goodness,
and keen intelligence
are leaning in to find a better way . . .

and to Mark and Alexandria,
who make living
happily **even** *after*
a joy

contents

Introduction: Landing on the Wrong Side of Love
1

PART ONE: A BETTER WAY TO BREAK UP

Chapter 1: Shame, Blame, and the Failure of Love
15

Chapter 2: Bitter Breakups, Nasty Endings,
and the Art of Living *Un*happily Ever After
28

Chapter 3: A New Possibility Between Us:
Introducing Conscious Uncoupling
44

Chapter 4: How and When to Do This Program
62

PART TWO: THE 5 STEPS OF CONSCIOUS UNCOUPLING

Step 1: Find Emotional Freedom
83

Step 2: Reclaim Your Power and Your Life
115

contents

Step 3: Break the Pattern, Heal Your Heart
137

Step 4: Become a Love Alchemist
169

Step 5: Create Your Happily-*Even*-After Life
210

Postscript: Evolving Love
255

The Conscious Uncoupling Creed
259

Deep Gratitude Goes To . . .
263

Online Resources
267

Notes
273

Bibliography
287

Index
299

landing on the
wrong side of love

*Every intimacy carries, secreted somewhere below its
initial lovely surfaces, the ever-coiled makings of
complete catastrophe.*

ELIZABETH GILBERT

None of us think, when walking down the aisle to stand open-hearted before our one true love, that we will one day wind up on the wrong side of that tenacious 50 percent divorce divide. Nor do we assume impending heartache when basking in a newly forming union that is filled with hope and the promise of lifelong happiness. For we are the believers in love, resolute in our fervent stand for forever, and willing to risk it all in our pursuit of happily-*ever*-after.

As the author of the US bestseller *Calling in "The One": 7 Weeks to Attract the Love of Your Life,* and teacher to hundreds of thousands of students throughout the world who've used my principles to clear away their inner obstacles to love and create happy, loving relationships, I would be lying if I told you I wanted to write this book as the sequel to my last. I did not want to be writing this book any more than you want to be reading it.

In fact, when I realized that my husband of nearly ten years and I were going to end our marriage, my prayer was a little less than pious. Lying flat on my back in the grass at a nearby park, and looking up at the vast blue sky, searching for meaning in this unwelcomed twist of events, I murmured out loud the only prayer that made sense to me at the time. "You've *got* to be kidding me," I said, seething. I was beyond irritated at the unseen forces of life and love that seemed hell-bent on entertaining themselves at my expense—forces that seemed determined to create unwanted mischief with my happily-ever-after ending to a rather tumultuous childhood. A happy ending that was documented so beautifully, and *publicly,* in my first book.

It was awkward, at best.

Yet, once past the shocking realization that this was indeed happening, I turned my attention to making sure it happened well. For I, like many thousands of my peers, had been the product of a nasty and terribly *unconscious* uncoupling when I was a young girl. So nasty, in fact, that there were two rather brutal custody fights that led to my eventual alienation from my father, at the age of ten, when he finally threw in the towel and surrendered his parental rights altogether due to his inability to get on at all with my infuriated mother. While I did not know a lot of things as my marriage unraveled before my eyes, the one thing I did know was this: I was *not* going to do that to our daughter.

> *You may not control all the events that happen to you, but you can decide not to be reduced by them.*
> MAYA ANGELOU

Yet, as our separation unfurled, I discovered that I had

worried in vain. For not only was ours a very civil uncoupling, it was also deeply kind, respectful, humane, and characterized by an unexpected spirit of generosity and goodwill, with gestures of friendship and mutual support woven throughout. My former husband, Mark, and I did everything in our power to minimize the damage done to one another and, of course, to our young daughter, whose primary concern was that she not lose contact with her father, as she'd seen happen to two of her friends. United in our stand to create cohesion and well-being for our daughter during and after our transition out of the marriage, we readily reassured her she would not.

It was a far cry from the horrible breakups I'd had in the past—those months on end when I'd be unable to eat or sleep, and when I was so consumed with rage that I could barely get through the day without snapping the head off some poor, innocent stranger who was unfortunate enough to get in my way. Or the time when I was so distraught that I started smoking again after nearly a decade, and when half the hair on my head fell out from the stress of it all. Or the mother of all my bad breakups, the heart-wrenching and terribly dramatic, and traumatic, severing I'd had from my high school boyfriend, Frank, which held me captive with an unresolved and prolonged grief that haunted me for years. For nearly two decades he continued to show up in my dreams, frequently shaking me out of a restless sleep to relive the horrible realization that he was indeed gone forever, and was living happily ever after with his intimidatingly beautiful wife and their three perfect children thousands of miles away from me.

I, like you, am well acquainted with the shadow side of love. Which is why, once I had dealt with my own shock and pain, I immediately began to look back to see if I could decipher the process of the rather unique way in which Mark and I had managed to transition out of our union with such goodwill and grace. Because I recognized that we had fallen upon something incredibly valuable, my awareness made more acute by those in our inner circle who would shake their heads in dismay, to declare that they had never seen any couple let go of their marriage with as much thoughtfulness and care.

As much as I had yearned for a happy ending to my less than happy childhood, in an odd twist of fate I seemed to have stumbled upon a new *kind* of happy ending. A way to end a romantic union with dignity, goodness, and honor, and where no one was left shattered or destroyed by the experience. And, being the gourmet lemonade maker that I am, I realized that I could even make something beautiful of this. For we'd actually undergone what I eventually was able to identify as a five-step process for leaving each other, and all those impacted by our separation, whole, healthy, and complete rather than wounded, walled off, and significantly broken by the experience.

As a believer in love, and an ardent supporter of marriage and long-term committed relationships, breakups are probably one of my least favorite things. Right up there with global warming, elder abuse, and high child-poverty rates. Given my disdain for breakups and divorce, why then would I choose it as my own life path? How horrible was it between Mark and me that I would venture into the swampland of dividing hearth and home, and the dismantling of long-held hopes and dreams?

There are a million little ways that a marriage grows apart, most too mundane to mention. Yet what happened to Mark and me, in a nutshell, is that I changed. And I mean, I radically and in many ways quite unfairly, changed. It's kind of an occupational hazard—the downside of being a teacher of growth and transformation. My husband didn't cheat on me, he didn't abuse me, and he was not an alcoholic or a chronic gambler.

Yet, as the years went by, the core values by which we lived grew further and further apart. Where I am a change junkie, ever pushing the edge of my own and others' evolution in pursuit of fulfilling the potential we hold in all areas of life and love, Mark, gentle-hearted man that he is, aspires to the spiritual ideal of total acceptance and appreciation of things as they are, without the need to change anyone or anything. Where I am ever fascinated to dig into the darker recesses of our psyches to discover and purify our inner motives, he believes in minimizing the focus on flaws to simply value the goodness and beauty of all living beings. It's not like someone is right and someone is wrong here. They are both perfectly gorgeous paths to be on. And often when couples are polarized like this, they find a way to balance each other out, complementing one another and filling in the blank spots for each other in the most lovely of ways. Yet, with Mark and me, conversations about those things that mattered most and that we each held sacred in our hearts just kind of fell flat, in a way that left us little room to grow together toward a shared vision or goal, something we both admitted to needing deeply in our lives. As much as we cared for one another, it became apparent that the place where we were most aligned was in the love we shared for our daughter.

Now, if we had been born fifty years earlier, we would have easily stayed together for the sake of our child, without thinking much about it. Although yet again, if we'd been born fifty years before, we probably wouldn't have ever gotten married in the first place, as interracial marriages were illegal throughout much of America, until the Supreme Court declared otherwise in 1967. As I am Caucasian and Mark African American, we would have had to risk everything, our very lives included, to choose one another back then—further evidence of the ever-evolving nature of culture. However, this little detail aside, I, like many millions of others in the Western world, have come to expect more of my primary partnership than staying together for the sake of the children. As author and marriage historian Stephanie Coontz points out, relationships have changed more in the past thirty years than in the three thousand years before. And I, like so many of us, aspired to a union that was far beyond the ones my mother, and my grandmother before her, expected to have. It's not that Mark and I weren't wholeheartedly and doggedly devoted to raising a well-adjusted, healthy, happy daughter. Of course we were; our lives revolved around this shared commitment. But did that really mean that we had to be bound together with the bonds of matrimony and morally required to have sex with each other for the rest of our lives in order to do so?

I mean, Mark's a sexy guy but . . . *seriously*?

As someone who is an evolutionary at heart, meaning that I believe in the noble pursuit of consciously making the effort to become a wiser, more enlightened, and more evolved human being in service to helping build wiser, more enlightened, and more evolved human societies, I am ever-fascinated with new and emergent possibilities for loving connections that are a little left of center—and perhaps even a whole lot outside of the box. I'm quirky that way. As a "cultural creative," and there are millions more like me throughout the world, I'm prone to pioneering new possibilities on the vast frontier of human relationships. My orientation as a licensed marriage and family therapist is strongly rooted in humanistic psychology with a particular devotion to the human potential movement, which

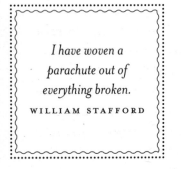

I have woven a parachute out of everything broken.
WILLIAM STAFFORD

is about the purposeful striving toward the realization of our highest potentials, on both individual and societal levels. So, it's not really my nature to stay married simply because of current cultural assumptions about what's best for the kids. Assumptions that, while certainly well informed by research that is worthy of deep discussion and reflective thought, seems to fundamentally lack the creative effort toward solving the problem of how we can form a balanced, stable, and loving family life in the aftermath of divorce. When I thought of it this way, my curiosity got the best of me, and I became deeply interested in discovering how we might collectively begin to do this better.

The Journey Ahead

I will be sharing with you, in the pages ahead, the results of that curiosity. You are invited to join me on what became a profound inner journey of healing, transformation, expansion, and re-invention. To begin, I will challenge you to rethink our collective long-held assumptions about breakups and divorce, and ask you to reconsider the very common knee-jerk conclusion that a relationship has failed if it ends for any other reason than that one or both people have died. I will also attempt to raise our awareness about how, inside of this collective assumption of failure, we have never really evolved beyond primitive and destructive ways of separating, yet at great cost to well-being and wholeheartedness—and in many incidences, severely handicapping ourselves, our children, and each other from successfully moving forward in life. And finally, I will offer a new possibility between us, that of Conscious Uncoupling, which allows for a healthy and humane way of ending a romantic union.

At that point, Part Two will move you into your own,

personal Conscious Uncoupling process, offering intimate guidance and support for each of the five steps along the way. Starting with the first step, Find Emotional Freedom, and leading you through to the final one, Create Your Happily-*Even*-After Life, you will find the practical tools and skills you'll need to navigate the tender transition you're in, all the way home to wholeness.

If you are in a tremendous amount of pain right now, you may prefer to go straight to Part Two of this book, coming back to read Part One later, once your oxygen mask is firmly in place and you're able to breathe again.

My Own Moral Dilemma

Now, I have to confess that I hesitated a long time before writing this book, dragging my feet to put this all down on paper. This was largely because I didn't want to encourage anyone to be casual about the critical decision to dissolve a long-term committed partnership. What happens when you take away the social shame associated with a "failed" relationship, or the terror that you will absolutely mess your kids up for life, coming as they now do from a "broken" home? I certainly don't want to be even partly responsible for tipping the scales further in the direction of marriages that end before one or both people die.

I am a strong supporter of committed, long-term unions, and I do my best to empower couples to stay together whenever possible. In fact, when clients come into my office saying they want to have a Conscious Uncoupling, I'm apt to spar with them a bit, trying to poke holes in their certainty and reveal it to be a bit premature. Because I'm such an ardent advocate of committed love, I'm thrilled with the recent twists and turns on the marital landscape of America, as we now invite our gay and lesbian friends to join us in forming lifelong, stable, *and legal* partnerships that can further contribute to the strengthening of American society. So, it's important to understand that I did not create this process to make light of the choice to separate. In fact, a bit later on, in the "How and When to Do This Program" chapter, we are going to have a serious discussion about why staying together might actually be the better path to take.

Life's not always fair. Sometimes you can get a splinter even sliding down a rainbow.

CHERRALEA MORGEN

Here's what I really want us to understand, however. In a world where more people divorce in any given year than buy new cars or eat grapefruit for breakfast, I think it's time that we learned how to do this better. And that is the heart and soul of what the book is all about.

Who This Book Is For

The Conscious Uncoupling process is not just for those who made it all the way to the altar. It's for anyone whose heart is heavy with the unspeakable grief of lost love. All breakups, in addition to being crazy painful, are also a critical crossroads. The loss of love is a definitive moment in life that will demand a grave decision of you. From the dung heap of your despair, you are either going to throw in the towel and contract from life in order to protect your heart from this kind of hurt again, dooming yourself in the process to living a lesser life, or you are going to find a way to use this tragic experience as the opportunity to cultivate greater wisdom, depth, maturity, and a deeper

> *If life gives us rocks,*
> *it's our choice whether*
> *to build a bridge or*
> *a wall.*
> ANONYMOUS

capacity to love and be loved. In a nutshell, a breakup is nothing short of a once-in-a-lifetime opportunity to have a complete spiritual awakening. One that catapults you to a whole new level of authenticity, compassion, wisdom, depth, and—dare I say it?—even joy. The only way the searing agony of your breakup is going to become the latter, though, is if you set your heart and mind in that direction, and make a conscious and determined effort to get there.

If you have the courage to rise and take on heartache for all it's worth, then this book is for you. If you're willing to use the pain you're in to flush out the falsehoods you've been tolerating for far too long, and emancipate yourself from the painful patterns you've been unable to face until now, it's for you. If you will use this setback as the opportunity to liberate yourself and others from the many ways you've been dimming down, and showing up as less than who you are in life, it's for you. If you're ready to use this shocking loss to break your heart open, expanding and enlarging your capacity to authentically love yourself and others in the process, it is for you. If you have the fortitude to make something beautiful of this, for yourself and all those you love, then this book is for you.

I wish I could promise that if you engage in a Conscious Uncoupling process you will have a pain-free breakup, but I can't. For we human beings are biologically predisposed to bonding, and there is simply no way not to bleed at least a little (and maybe a whole lot) when the ties that bind us are cut, even if we do it ever so gently. Yet, having taken thousands of students successfully through the process, I'll be sharing with you over our next few days, weeks, or months together what I can promise you is a safe passageway to wholeness for yourself and those you love. I can promise you that your life will not just be tolerable on the other side of this dark night of the soul, but it will actually be even better and more beautiful for all you have been through. I can promise you the hope of loving again, with a wide open, happy, and trusting heart that is confident you will not make the same mistakes again. And finally, I can promise that you will one day look back on this disastrously difficult moment in your life and speak a prayer of gratitude, having turned the worst thing that ever happened to you into the absolute best.

If love is the answer, could you please repeat the question?
LILY TOMLIN

a better way
to break up

CHAPTER I

shame, blame, and the failure of love

We who have experienced it know that romantic love is a fall-in, crawl-out proposition.
MARTHA BECK

Much of the horror of a breakup is the insult to our expectations of how this story was *supposed* to unfold versus how it actually *did*. Falling short of the happily-ever-after goal to which we all aspire is considered such a terrible failure, it may feel as though you'll never recover. Not from the shock of it, not from the sorrow of it, and certainly not from the shame of it.

As saddened as I was by the loss of my marriage, I must confess I was equally mortified by the loss of face I was about to endure by making it public. We have a collective story about how romantic love is supposed to work, and it's a pretty straightforward one. It goes something like this: If it lasts, then it's real. If it doesn't, then it wasn't. Either that, or someone screwed it up really badly.

Upon telling people that Mark and I were breaking up, I could look forward to a covert and automatic devaluing, either of our entire relationship, or of one of us, or of both of us. I could almost hear how people would respond. Not overtly, of course, but in the inner chambers of their private thoughts, which are never quite as private as we think. *Hmm, it must not have been very real to begin with,* or *Hmm, I never thought much of him* (or her, depending upon whom I was speaking with). It was enough to make me want to stay home, wrapped up in a comforter and in my flannel pajamas, and do nothing but eat chunky peanut butter from the jar while watching classic movies in bed. Films in which in the end the girl gets her guy and . . . yep, you got it, they all live happily ever after.

Most of us assume true love will last a lifetime, particularly when a couple has stood before friends and family and taken vows. "Till death do us part" has been a part of marriage ceremonies since it appeared in the Book of Common Prayer in 1549, and perhaps long before. From the ancient Indian tradition that obliged a woman to hurl herself onto the burning funeral pyre of her dead husband, to the practice of binding the feet of a young Chinese girl to make sure she'd be unable to run away from her husband later in life, the idea that marriage is forever has been around for . . . well, just about forever.

We even assess the value of our unions based on the length of time we've been together, with each milestone anniversary surpassing the previous one in the hierarchy of suggested gifts. Tin for your tenth, silver for your twenty-fifth, and gold for your fiftieth. Even as I write this, I find myself wondering what tin gift I might have gotten Mark had I hung in there just a little longer: a handsome tin keychain perhaps, or a pair of classy tin cuff links? Years ago, long before I married Mark, I recall being curled up on the couch late one night, reading articles related to the master's degree I was pursuing in clinical psychology, and I found myself startled by what one respected psychologist had to say about long-term marriages: "Don't celebrate the union of two people who've been married for fifty years until you understand what that relationship has done to their souls." Before that, I'd never heard anyone say anything that might dampen our ideal of longevity as the best way to determine the value of an intimate union.

Which brings us smack back to our collective story about the end of love: *If a romantic relationship ends for any reason other than one or both people die, we assume that relationship to be a failure.*

What love stories can we even point to where living happily ever after included a kindhearted, honoring breakup, and where the love that was shared changed forms and was blessed and celebrated by all? A breakup where neither party was blamed or shamed, yet where both people were left valued and appreciated for all that they'd given one another, and to the community, as a result of their union?

Say what?

In a culture that assumes that *breakup* is just another word for *failure,* it's hard to not drop down into the gutter of disgrace at love's end. Feeling dishonored and humiliated is a normal part of breakup pain, particularly if you are the one being left. Yet, the loss of love is hard enough on the heart, without the added loss of social status and shame that can come along with it.

> *Failure is just another name for much of real life.*
> MARGARET ATWOOD

The root of the word *shame* means "to cover," and it's characterized by the need to run and hide from the eyes of the world. This was certainly true for a former client of mine, Leslie, whose husband of only seven months decided he'd made a terrible mistake by marrying her. While hiking one morning near their home in the Hollywood Hills, he announced that he was leaving her and returning home to England alone. Stunned, she could barely speak, yet still managed to eke out a few questions to try to wrap her mind around what he was telling her. Was he having an affair? No. Did he miss England? No. Was he sexually unhappy with her? No. He simply realized that he did not like being married. In some ways that was worse. Shame flooded her from every direction. She must have been a bad wife. She must be unlovable for her own husband to reject her.

She began to worry obsessively, "What will people think of me?" "How will I tolerate the humiliation of being single again?" So filled with shame, she could not bring herself to tell anyone what was happening. Rather than call her friends for support, she stopped answering her phone. Instead of asking family members to stay with her while she adjusted to her loss, she closed her curtains and became a recluse, isolating herself for months afterward to save face and not reveal the shame of her rejection. Just at the time we need support and connection the most, we're apt to crawl under the covers and cower, consumed with feelings of social inadequacy.

> *Shame derives its power from being unspeakable.*
> BRENÉ BROWN

According to former Columbia University professor and cultural anthropologist Ruth Benedict, shame differs from guilt in that guilt is something we're more likely to feel when we violate our own core values, disturbed that something we have *done* is fundamentally bad and wrong. Shame is what we feel when violating external rules and expectations that society imposes upon us, and it leaves us feeling that *we* are fundamentally bad and wrong. When we feel vulnerable to the negative judgments of others because we believe they're covertly assessing our "defects," even if they do it ever so nicely and with pity in their eyes, we can easily slip into a deep, dark sea of shame.

> *Among the problems with shame was that it in fact did not make you shorter or quieter or less visible. You just felt like you were.*
>
> J. R. WARD

Expectation has been called "the root of all heartache," and certainly, failed expectations are often the root of deep confusion and inner chaos, as well. For our minds lose their footing when our reality doesn't live up to the way we thought things should go. Just as surely as if we were lost in the woods with no clear path in sight, we can become disoriented and even paralyzed with panic about what to do next to find our way back to safety. Our brains much prefer it when we're able to predict the future with accuracy, and so we're inclined to create cultural stories and patterns that allow us to do that. Living happily ever after is one such collective pattern that grants us a sense of predictability and certainty in life and holds the standard for societal harmony.

In her studies with the Neuroleadership Institute, my good friend, brain-based executive coach Dr. Karey Pohn, discovered that when our expectations are in line with reality, our brains receive a hefty dopamine hit to reward us. We feel good when life matches our vision of what we think could and should happen. Yet when our expectations are not met, our stress levels shoot through the roof, shifting our brains into a threat state. Our cortisol levels rise, our immune system function drops, and our limbic brains—the seat of our emotional reactivity—go into fight-or-flight mode as our dopamine and oxytocin levels take a nosedive, spiraling us downward into a morass of misery and morbidity.

The Once Upon a Time of Living Happily Ever After

At heart, I've always been a bit of an amateur anthropologist. As such, I will often relate to my own personal experience in an impersonal way. Meaning that in many ways, I'm my own guinea pig, and my thoughts, assumptions, feelings, and tendencies often serve as information for me about what might be going on for us all. Imagine, then, how curious I became in response to the sense of inferiority and shame that engulfed me as my marriage was coming to an end. I noticed it at first by the profound feeling of being exposed and unprotected after taking off my wedding ring and walking around in the world without it. Frequently, I had the impulse to slip my hand into my pocket to defend against the vulnerability of my glaringly naked ring finger. I also noticed, and rather unhappily I might add, that I now felt slightly inferior to others who seemed happily coupled, as well as fearful that others might be looking down on me now that I was single again.

> *I have not failed. I've just found 10,000 ways that won't work.*
> THOMAS A. EDISON

Although my mind rebelled against such an idea, on an emotional level I felt as though I'd lost status in my now single state. Having had the advantage of teaching so many students over the years, I knew enough to not relate to these feelings as a personal pathology but, rather, more as a collectively shared experience. The emotional vulnerability resulting from a breakup can feel as screeching as fingernails on a chalkboard, particularly if you are a highly sensitive person, as many of us are.

It started me on a Nancy-Drew-like quest to see if I could discover the source of these collective ideals that were holding so many of us hostage, and that I and millions of others had so dismally failed to fulfill. I began with the phrase itself, "and they all lived happily ever after." A quick search on the Internet allowed me to discover that several hundred years ago, living happily ever after was simply one way to end a story as people sat around the community campfire telling tales late into the night. There were many variations on the theme, as well. In Persia, one might know it was the end of the story when the teller clearly announced, "This story has come to an end, but there is still more to be told," offering a precursor to the cliffhanger that any devotee of a weekly television drama knows and loves so well. In Norway, one might have said the very astute "And if they're not dead, then they're still alive." And my personal favorite, offered by the Hebrews, "And they lived in happiness and luxury to this very day," which is my way to end a story.

Digging a little deeper, I discovered that while fairy-tale motifs can be found throughout ancient Indian, Chinese, Greek, Hebrew, and Roman literature, fairy tales themselves only emerged as a popular form of storytelling in the late sixteenth century in Venice, Italy. Wouldn't you know that the aspiration to live happily in the arms of your one true love forever would originate with those romantic Italians paddling around in their gondolas on the canals of Venice? Fairy tales were different from the more well-known and established folktales of the day, uniquely characterized by their wish-fulfilling tales of magic, adventure, and a happy ending that always included coming into great wealth along with finding true love.

Yet, it made me wonder. Why then? What was life like in Venice in the late sixteenth century that would create the conditions in which the happily-ever-after myth would so quickly take root and begin to flourish and thrive? So much so that this new aspiration in love would come to dominate the majority of love seekers throughout the world within a relatively brief period of time? We're only talking about a little over four hundred years in which this one idea has transformed our world in really significant ways. On an evolutionary scale, four hundred years is but a hiccup on the timeline. Before this time, mating and marriage wasn't about *love.* It wasn't about *happiness.* It was still about forever, yes—but that's only because it was largely about land, trade, commerce, and power dynamics, not things you shift around too quickly. Before this time, mating and marriage were all about survival, and the deep human need to be safe and secure in life.

The Unfortunate Origins of Ideal Love

In my mission to understand what had given birth to our current expectations of romantic love, I discovered two extreme life conditions that were profoundly impacting the Venetians of the day. The first was a life expectancy of less than forty years. Now, that doesn't mean that everybody up and died when he or she turned forty. A lot of folks lived well into their fifties, sixties, and seventies. Yet, the lion's share of Europeans who lived at that time—60 percent of them, actually—died before their sixteenth birthday.

Wow. I don't know if you can put yourself in the shoes of those who lived in Venice a mere four hundred years ago, to even try to imagine the unspeakable sorrow and grief they lived with, as half of the children you gave birth to, half of the children your friends and neighbors brought into the world, half of the children your siblings had, half of your children's friends, were doomed to die before they even had a chance to grow up. And when I pause long enough to really let that touch me, I suddenly become aware of the part where we say "and they *all* lived happily ever after" like I'd never actually heard it before. In a world where the kids have such a narrow chance of survival, it's probably a really great idea to support the parents to stay together through thick and thin, to give those babies the best possible shot.

The second thing I was fascinated to discover had to do with the rigid and oppressive class structure of the day. While there existed a thriving noble class in Venice at the time, the majority of city dwellers were quite poor, with economic realities providing hardworking Venetians little hope of improving their lots in life. Their sense of futility is likely to have further been solidified by a law that took effect in the 1520s, making it illegal for a noble person to marry outside of his or her social group. Remember, this is before "love match" times, when marriage was all about the preservation of wealth. The oppression of their economy, along with this rather rigid law, created for the poor people of Venice an ironclad sense of being locked into their current life circumstances, with no possibility of ever getting out of the daily grind of poverty.

Luckily, however, in post-Renaissance times, even the poor were a literate bunch, and were able to take flight in escapist books that delivered the miracle of upward mobility in their fantasy life. Can we blame them, then, for eating up the delicious new literary offerings of fairy tales, offered by the man considered to be the creator of this new form of literature, Italian writer and publisher Giovanni Francesco Straparola? While originally much less refined than the French would eventually make them a century later, fairy tales offered the respite of magic, enchantment, and romance, where in the end the hero or heroine could be counted on to gain a better life, and where they all lived happily ever after in some faraway and distant land (because, remember, it couldn't actually happen in Venice, given the laws preventing a royal from marrying a commoner).

I found it startlingly moving to discover the fertile soil in which fairy tales grew to be such a beloved part of our culture. And I was deeply inspired by the indomitable spirit of those robust Venetians, who refused to give up in the face of the impossibly oppressive circumstances into which they were born. I even began to see the myth of living happily ever after as the beginnings of the human potential movement, as it encourages us to be undeterred by our current life conditions, to nobly strive toward the possibilities of an abundant and flourishing life, no matter what evidence we might be experiencing to the contrary. I'd always thought that the human potential movement began with greats such as William James, Viktor Frankl, Abraham Maslow, Carl Rogers, Jean Houston, and Milton Erickson. Yet, maybe I'd not paid enough attention to the strong shoulders upon which they stood, for it was the unstoppable Giovanni Francesco Straparola who was responsible for popularizing the highly transformative practice of imagining a better way.

> *I've been married three times and each marriage was successful.*
> MARGARET MEAD

A Case for Consciously Evolving Love

As inspiring as all this is, it's time to consider that the myth of *living happily ever after* may have outstayed its welcome and should now be up for review and revision. For the mores of dating, mating, and marriage have never stayed the same for long. From the radically novel idea of romantic love as the reason for marrying in the mid-eighteenth century, to the "traditional" idealized stay-at-home mom and breadwinning dad of the 1950s, to the two-daddy household, where birth mommies visit two weekends a year, the customs of love have always been, and remain, a moving train.

Dr. Helen Fisher, professor at Rutgers University and re-nowned relationship anthropologist, reports that serial mo-nogamy has now become the norm, suggesting that most of us will have two or three significant relationships in our lifetimes. The implication being, of course, that most of us will also go through one or two significant romantic endings as well. Just as it was once the norm to meet and marry your one true love, it's now just as common to *not* mate for life. With over 40 percent of first marriages, over 60 percent of second marriages, and over 70 percent of third marriages ending in divorce, maybe we should begin to consider it normal to change our primary part-ners? The bottom line is this: the majority of us will not, in fact, have one lifelong partner to whom we will remain faithful for better or for worse and until death do us part. In an age when we recognize the need to up-level just about every aspect of life to keep pace with our ever-evolving life conditions—our work environments, sleeping habits, child-rearing practices, diets, and computer programs—maybe we should also consider retiring our outdated and overly simplistic model of romantic love. Setting aside the escapist fantasies we have of the lives we wish we *could* live and move toward a more wholehearted vision that's relevant to the lives that we *do* actually live.

A recent *New York Times* article reports that for the first time in recorded history, more people over fifty are now divorced than widowed, the rate of uncoupling after a long marriage having nearly doubled since 1990. And why not? The wonders of Viagra and the miracles of hormone replacement therapy offer to keep us sexually vital long beyond what Grandma and Grandpa dreamed possible. Where Grandma was lowering her expectations and settling down to enjoy some pleasant bridge playing as she entered her sixth decade of life, we're just getting started, looking to get a makeover, maybe to run a marathon or two, and gearing up for our next big love. "Silver Seekers" over sixty are reported to be one of the fastest growing demographics of Internet dating sites. Those of us who are "retirement age" want more out of life than weekly playdates with our grandkids. We want weekly playdates with our main squeeze.

> *Failure is just another way to learn how to do something right.*
> MARIAN WRIGHT
> EDELMAN

It is my hope that we might begin a conversation that will allow us to expand our capacity to more wisely hold the nuances of modern-day living and modern-day loving, particularly around the end of love. Rather than define the value of our relationships by the overly simplistic question "How long did it last?" that we instead begin to ask questions like "What wisdom have I gained?" and "What have I learned about love that I can now apply moving forward?"

I believe with all my heart that love does indeed prevail against all odds. And apparently I'm not alone. For Andrew J.

Cherlin, author of the highly regarded *The Marriage-Go-Round*, tells us that Americans, in spite of having one of the highest divorce rates in the Western world, have one of the highest marriage rates as well. In fact, close to 90 percent of us are predicted to marry at least once in our lives, in spite of the uncertain odds that that marriage will last a lifetime. So, our attempt to redefine a "happy ending" is not evidence that we no longer believe in love. To the contrary, we are the relentless believers in love and lifelong union. Yet, given the realities of our time, which include the postmodern tensions between the stability of marriage and the American ideals of individual freedom, self-expression, and personal growth, we must accept the choice to unmarry by the many who make it. For learning to live happily *even* after, finding a way to forgive the unforgivable, and to move forward in life graciously with hope in our hearts and goodwill in our gestures and in our words, may very well be the essence of what it is to truly love each other.

> *Even divorce might be seen as one kind of fulfillment of love. Love asks many things of us, including actions that seem to be utterly counter to feelings of attachment and loyalty.*
> THOMAS MOORE

Yet before moving too quickly toward the evolution and expansion of love, let's first take a moment to peer a little deeper into love's shadows, as we take a quick detour to meet Shame's sordid sisters, Hatred and Rage. Fasten your seat belt, as we take a little spin through the dangerously unpredictable and primitive hells of hatred, revenge, and the disturbingly darker sides of love.

CHAPTER 2

bitter breakups, nasty endings, and the art of living *unhappily* ever after

If you prick us, do we not bleed? . . . If you poison us, do we not die?
And if you wrong us, shall we not revenge?

WILLIAM SHAKESPEARE

I t was a beautiful fall day in New York in the year 1959. A young, handsome, and well-dressed attorney turned his brand-new powder blue Cadillac down a street he rarely visited, immediately spotting a beautiful raven-haired young woman sitting on a park bench. Turning to his friend, he declared, "Look at that girl! I've got to have her," quickly pulling his car to the side of the road so that he might approach her. Thus began one of the more infamous love affairs of modern times—the passionate, and deeply disturbing, obsessive romance between Burt Pugach and Linda Riss.

Linda had no idea when their courtship began that Burt was already married, with a young disabled daughter at home. Smitten at first, she allowed herself to be swept off her feet, hopeful that perhaps she'd met the man she'd marry and with whom she'd create a family. Certainly Burt suggested such a future as he took her shopping for an engagement ring and home they might purchase. Yet, once she discovered the truth, she did what any decent woman of her time was expected to do: she broke it off immediately. Or she tried to, anyway. Burt, who wanted what he wanted when he wanted it, would not take no for an answer and he began stalking, threatening, and harassing her—all in the name of love. When he heard from Linda's father that she was getting engaged to another man, he lost it. Hiring three men to help him, Burt had lye thrown into Linda's face, blinding and maiming her for life.

In an ironic twist to the story, though his hateful rage abated, Burt's love apparently did not. Burt spent the next fourteen years in a federal prison, writing love letters to Linda, begging for forgiveness and proclaiming undying devotion. Within a year of his release from prison, the two were married and remained together for nearly forty years, before Linda died at the age of seventy-five.

Upon hearing such stories, we become voyeurs, rubbernecking to peer into the shadows of love, seemingly immune ourselves to such deep confusion between love, hate, passion, and revenge. Yet what separates us from Burt Pugach is solely our character. For while you and I have consciences that forbid such a despicable act of revenge, our biology, much like Burt's, might actually encourage it. While we would never do such a thing in the aftermath of being cast aside by the one we love, we are biologically predisposed to want to.

In a recent TED Talk, Dr. Helen Fisher describes the unfortunate irony of what happens in our brains after being spurned by the one we love. For the part of the brain that became activated when we fell in love is the exact same part of the brain that becomes even more stimulated when we are rejected by a lover. Rather than allow us to do the sensible thing and turn our attention toward starting a new life, our brains are hard-wired to increase our desire for the one we are losing, keeping us torturously entangled, as we desperately try to turn the *Titanic* around in a frenzied and highly focused state of craving, want, and longing. As the poet Terence once said, "The less my hope, the hotter my love."

During this initial protest stage we are on full alert and in a heightened state that is similar to the one found in baby animals who've been abandoned by their mothers. Frantic and distressed, we are driven to extremes to try to win back the affections of our beloved, doing almost anything to abate our anxious desire. For being rejected by the one we love sparks activity in the brain that is similar to the experience of a cocaine addict agitatedly seeking that next fix. Love withdrawal perfectly mirrors drug withdrawal, and is often accompanied by the same reckless and destructive impulses as the ones that land drug addicts, desperate to get high, behind bars.

Soul Mate to Soul Hate

In literature, a story without a happy ending is considered to be a tragedy. Sadly, many a relationship that fails to find its pot of gold at the end of the rainbow will become one as well. The circuits in our brains that control both reward and rage are deeply intertwined, and once we recognize the futility of our efforts to win back the object of our affections, all hell can break loose.

Consider Christina Reber, a forty-three-year-old woman from Muncie, Indiana, who gained national attention in the aftermath of her vicious and hateful act of revenge against her fifty-seven-year-old boyfriend after he'd ended their relationship. Seething with a rage of the "hell hath no fury" caliber, Christina stormed into her former lover's home uninvited and in a drunken stupor. She ran over to the computer where he sat quietly working and began striking him in the head repeatedly with her bare hands before she reached down to grab his scrotum and started squeezing as hard as she could. In agony, he tried unsuccessfully to pry her hands from his body. They wound up in a bloody brawl on the floor, where Christina, so fiercely intent on hurting the man she seemingly loved just days before, half ripped his testes from his body, leaving them precariously dangling once he finally tore himself away from her vengeful grip, and ran to the phone to frantically dial 911. Within minutes help arrived, and paramedics quickly transported him to the closest medical facility, aptly named Ball Memorial Hospital, where he promptly received treatment.

Obviously there are psychological factors that make some of us more vulnerable than others to lose it like this. Yet, self-destructive tendencies, lack of impulse control, and poor judgment aside, who among us doesn't know what she was feeling that drove her to act like such a crazy girl? I mean, we'd never actually do it—but we've thought about it. We've felt it. We've fantasized about it, right? I can't be alone here. I mean, somebody bought those 33 million and counting copies of my friend Alanis Morissette's song "You Oughta Know." A song that you can scream at the top of your lungs, spitting each word out as if it were a punch to the groin, as you're cruising along the freeway at 65 miles per hour when no one can hear you. "Did you forget about me, Mr. Duplicity?/I hate to bug you in the middle of dinner./It was a slap in the face how quickly I was replaced./

Are you thinking of me when you f— her?"* Damn, it's almost as satisfying as a good, swift kick in the you-know-where. Come on, admit it. It's just you and me here, and I won't tell. We're all closeted crazy girls at heart.

Heaven has no rage like love to hatred turned. Nor hell a fury like a woman scorned.
WILLIAM CONGREVE

But don't feel bad. For it seems to be nature's design that hurt people hurt people. Just like those baby animals that get hypervigilant in response to being abandoned by their mothers, we too go a little insane when our primary attachment figures start to disappear. Our relationships are our homes, and when they're threatened, our brains go a little haywire and start signaling for the secretion of fight-or-flight hormones, causing our thinking brain to slow down just at the time when our impulse toward movement is speeding up. Not always a good combination. And even the nicest of us can be held hostage by our biology and behave in the strangest of ways.

Rita, a truly lovely thirty-six-year-old elementary school teacher from Kansas, who spent her life trying to mold good citizens by teaching children right from wrong, came to see me one spring. With eyes cast to the ground and tears streaming down her face, she reluctantly confessed how her despair over a breakup had compelled her to drive to her former boyfriend's house late one night, only to confirm her suspicions that she had already been replaced. For there it was. "Her" green Honda Accord parked neatly next to his brand-new dark blue Mercedes-Benz in the driveway in front of his home.

---

* Special thanks to the extraordinary Alanis Morissette and her brilliant co-writer, Glen Ballard, for generously granting me the rights to quote their lyrics.

Overcome with grief and a blinding rage, Rita quickly jumped out of the driver's seat, and before she could think about it, she ran her key down the side of his car, digging her hurt into the paint job and leaving a huge, unmistakable gash for all to see. She felt liberated and empowered for all of twenty seconds, before the horror set in and she ran back to her car to speed away, terrified of being found out. Yet, of course, he knew who did it. Who else would it

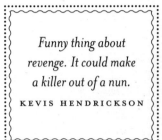

Funny thing about revenge. It could make a killer out of a nun.
KEVIS HENDRICKSON

be? Her retaliatory actions certainly didn't cause him to leave his new sweetheart. Most likely, they just further validated his instincts to get as far away from Rita as possible. She would now go down in his personal history as the deranged nutcase who keyed his brand-new car. By the time she came to see me, she'd been suffering with paranoia for months, completely humiliated and ashamed, and unable to gauge how many people might be whispering about her behind her back and laughing at how disturbed she was. She was mortified by her own behavior and simply did not know how to forgive herself for such a terrible lapse in judgment.

It can be really hard for us to accept these primitive parts of ourselves, as we may find ourselves doing and saying things that we would never have thought we could do or say. Dr. Fisher comes to the rescue once more to help explain to us our lunatic selves, suggesting that the rage and hatred we can feel for someone who we recently loved with all our hearts is actually "an evolutionary relic from the past," and it is simply nature's way of helping us to separate from that person and disengage from the relationship. Wow. Talk about overkill.

Most of us know to call a friend before allowing ourselves to get this out of control. And the Good Friend Code of Honor will require our friend to join with us in our victimization

An eye for an eye will only make the whole world blind.
MAHATMA GANDHI

and rage by saying things like "He's an idiot. He's not even worth crying over," "I never liked her anyway. Forget about her, she's just a gold digger," or "He's such a loser, and completely unworthy of you," insisting upon devaluing, diminishing, and dismissing your former love, and your relationship in the process, to try to help you move on. Which, at first glance, seems helpful. Yet, fanning the flames of disdain in an attempt to disconnect from the one we love will not ultimately bring us the relief that we seek. It's a Band-Aid, yet only a temporary fix. Hating someone you've loved to try to remove them from your psyche is akin to the primitive medical practice of giving someone a lobotomy to help rid them of depression. Maybe it will work momentarily to steel your heart against the former object of your affection, but then you are left with . . . well, a steely, closed, and hardened heart. Made solidly so by the decision to hate.

The Cost and Consequences of a Negative Bond

Love's opposite is not hatred, it's indifference. Hate is just as strong a bond as love, and will quickly make a negative bond of a positive one, keeping us just as tied to our former love as we have ever been. The bonds we form are a continual exchange of energy that keep us interested, invested, and engaged with one another, whether that engagement be positive or negative. They are the underlying emotional synergy we share that goes way beyond speaking with or seeing one another. Haven't we all had the experience of thinking of a friend we've not spoken to in a while, only to have the phone ring five minutes later to discover it's that person on the line? Composer Claude Debussy once said, "Music is the space between the notes," and much like music, a relational bond is the connection we share between the words. The influence we have on one another does not die simply because we've given someone back the key to their condo. And any attempt to disconnect by disdain will ultimately serve to root down heartache and make a home of it.

Recently, I met with Dr. Louis Cozolino, author of *The Neuroscience of Human Relationships: Attachment and the Developing Social Brain* and professor of psychology at Pepperdine University, to learn what's happening in the brain when our hearts are being put through a shredder. At the start of our discussion, he shared that the brain has but one primary mission: to keep us safe and ensure our survival. It doesn't really care that much about our spiritual aspirations, our noble ideals, or our self-image of being nice and loving people. And, as the brain is a social organ and hardwired to stay connected, it's not necessarily prone to letting go easily of a primary attachment. In the brain's world, better to have a negative bond than the existential death of no bond at all. And so, even if you know deep down inside that leaving is the right

> *Stronger than lover's love is lover's hate. Incurable, in each, the wounds they make.*
> EURIPIDES

thing to do, even if you have five times as many bad days together as good ones, even if the lies between you are making you physically sick, the brain still doesn't want to let the relationship go.

In a study done at UCLA not long ago, Drs. Naomi Eisenberger and Matthew Lieberman discovered that being rejected by someone we love triggers the same alert in the brain as a primal threat. Reminding us that in earlier times, being part of a tribe was essential for survival, and expulsion from the clan could signify a most certain death. You and I know this as the intense sense of panic that can grip us and cause our hearts to begin racing when our lover threatens to leave; we're terrified we will die if rejected by the one we love. Yet once the pain of staying in the relationship has surpassed the fear of leaving it and the decision to break up has been made, the brain can still hold on for dear life in a number of ways.

One way the brain may try to do this is through a highly contentious and nasty separation, where both people feed each other a steady diet of hostility and disdain, upping the ante on lowlife behaviors, and where one or both people become obsessed with winning and/or getting revenge. This negative engagement can go on for a lifetime if the brain is left to its own devices. One former wife of a man I knew had never gotten over the fact that he'd left her for another woman some seventeen years before. Catholic by upbringing, she'd always assumed that when she married, it would be for life. Having given birth to their three children, she felt entitled to the entirety of the money he made both before and after their divorce, and she made it her life's mission to make sure she got as much of it as she could. Even all these years later, she sat diligently at the computer night after night doing research on his latest business dealings, calculating how much profit should be hers. There was always some hungry attorney who was willing to file a lawsuit on her behalf, and when I met him, he'd never been without the burden of her hounding since the night he left nearly two decades before. Having never re-created her life in any meaningful way, she'd become a shadow of her former self. Without friends, and with no means of support other than the money she managed to wrangle out of him, her life was consumed with keeping alive their negative bond.

Another way we can keep a connection festering in our psyches is, ironically, by cutting it off too quickly. Acting from the raging impulse to purge a connection, you may be tempted to try to violently vomit someone right

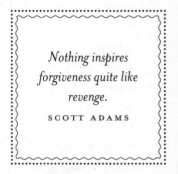

Nothing inspires forgiveness quite like revenge.
SCOTT ADAMS

up and out of your heart and soul. This may be the cruelest and most unkind way of ending a romantic union. In severing the bond this brutally, the person who has been cut off can feel as though she will surely lie there until she bleeds to death. These are the kinds of nasty breaks that can induce what's called "Broken Heart Syndrome," which is when the physical heart is literally stunned into behaving in ways that simulate a heart attack. There are even rare cases where people have up and died from the profound shock and sting of the sudden loss of love. In blowing up the relationship, often without warning or against great protestations, the abandoned lover can feel as though she is left as an empty shell, who has been given the morbid task of trying to come to terms with the sudden death of love, all on her own. It can leave her obsessively sorting through the shock, and repeatedly ruminating over and over again on each little detail, leading up to the dreaded moment of severing.

A client of mine had one such experience. Janet was in her midforties when her boyfriend of three years, a married man who'd rigorously pursued her, promising her on multiple occasions he would soon leave his wife, had a dramatic change of heart once his wife discovered the affair. Yet, rather than kindly explaining his choice to repair his marriage as one might hope he'd do, he turned on Janet instead. He called her up and, in an ice-cold and heartless tone of voice, accused her of having seduced and manipulated him into their affair, completely distorting what had actually happened. Projecting his flaws onto her, he made Janet out to be an evil temptress, throwing her under the bus to protect his self-image as a good and honorable man and to rebond with his wife. Deeply traumatized and left feeling like the victim of a crime, Janet was saddled with the burdensome task of picking shrapnel from her psyche for many months afterward. For frozen deep inside of her were not the happy memories that they shared, but the horrible, dreaded moment of impact: that wretched conversation that held her captive to the most abusive and ugly parts of love. Making it hard for her to breathe, eat, or sleep for well over a year, and souring her on the idea of ever opening herself up to love again.

Such are the dangers of an *unconscious* uncoupling that many of us know all too well. Where the primitive, self-protective ways we're tempted to behave at the end of love to help shield our hearts from hurt end up calcifying them closed instead.

The Risks of Waiting for Time to Heal Your Broken Heart

If you've truly breathed a person deep down into the core of your being, entwining your very identity with theirs, you will be hard pressed to purge them too quickly, simply because you suddenly now may want to. The external breakup may be quick, but the inner one rarely is. If you have ever tried to untangle matted hair, it may feel much the same way. So tangled together is your psyche from theirs that it seems nearly impossible to get it all straightened out. What opinion belongs to you, what belief might be theirs, and what goal is yours to keep or to give back—all can be hard to unknot. As though you were moving out of a home filled to the brim with ragged, dog-eared books, unique knickknacks, and custom furnishings, every item in your psyche now needs to be sorted through in order to reclaim your autonomy and reinvent your life.

I spent my twenties living in the heart of Greenwich Village, working as a waitress and singing in local cabarets, hoping to be discovered as the next Edith Piaf. One of my favorite songs of all time was written by Jerry Herman and made popular by the

> *Before I built a wall*
> *I'd ask to know*
> *What I was walling in*
> *or walling out.*
> ROBERT FROST

great Barbara Cook. It was called "Time Heals Everything," and I loved caressing each velvety lyric as though it were a sacred ode to longing. A lament that concluded with the sad recognition that time heals everything . . . "but loving you."

I knew of what I sang. Suffering with a broken heart for years, having gotten stuck in the prolonged and unprocessed grief from a rather chaotic and confusing childhood that was filled with a multitude of losses, I wore sorrow around me like a thick and heavy cloak. People would often comment on the sadness they could see in my eyes, despite my many attempts to hide it. I know from personal experience that until we get busy with the very proactive task of healing heartbreak, and take steps to initiate the alchemy of making something beautiful of it, the agony of lost love can and often will steal

> *They always say time changes things, but you actually have to change them yourself.*
>
> ANDY WARHOL

years of happiness from our lives, just as surely as severe illness or acute physical pain can do.

A poorly navigated loss, and its resulting poorly healed heart, can make you a lifelong victim to the darker side of love, and keep you locked into a lesser life with a diminished capacity to love and be loved moving forward. There is a movement in the therapeutic community to have Prolonged Grief Disorder, also referred to as Complicated Grief, added to the *Diagnostic and Statistical Manual of Mental Disorders (DSM)*. Complicated Grief is described by the Mayo Clinic as a chronic, heightened state of mourning characterized by numbness, intense longing, irritability, purposelessness, depression, and a lack of trust in others. It's being stuck in the quagmire of lingering regret, sorrow, and shame, with life as void of joy as it is of hope that things will ever get better. You will be vulnerable to experiencing Prolonged Grief to the extent that you have previous tendencies toward anxiety and depression, or your breakup shocked and took you by surprise. It can also hit you if the way things went down between you and your former partner validates your worst fears about yourself, or your grief is compounded by previously unresolved losses you've suffered along the way. While some of us are more vulnerable than others to this experience, we're all a little at risk, for the loss of love can break your spirit every bit as much as it can break your heart.

Contrary to popular belief, time does not heal all wounds. We do. You want to treat your broken heart with the same amount of care that you might offer your broken leg. Imagine

for a moment having just fractured your femur; lying on a gur-
ney, unable to get up, writhing in pain and groaning with the
unspeakable ache of it, your doctor looks on, your X-ray in
hand, cocking her head to the side and saying ever so kindly,
"Well, now, let's just give it some time. You'll feel better soon
enough." Broken hearts, like broken legs, need a lot of tending
to in order to properly heal. Unless, of course, you don't mind
the possibility of your heart's healing a little too crooked, a little bit closed, a whole lot defensive, and way too easily bruised
moving forward from here. That's the heart's equivalent of
walking with a limp for the rest of your life and feeling pain
every time it rains.

You may feel as though you will die from this pain. I assure
you, however, if you have the presence of mind to have picked
up this book and read this far, that you won't. Yet, if you shut
down and give up on life, using this disappointment as an excuse to hide from love, dimming down your hopes and walling
yourself off from ever being hurt like this again, you could, for
all intents and purposes, join the ranks of the living dead. It's
one thing to lose your beloved, and another thing entirely to
lose yourself.

What's Good About a Bad Breakup?

I recognize that, given the excruciating pain you are in, offering you a pep talk about transforming your breakup into a
breakthrough—or turning your trauma into triumph—might be
a bit of a slippery slope. There is nothing light about the crazy,
big emotions that may be washing over you in this very moment
like terrifying tidal waves—hopelessness, hatred, despair, de-

pression, and sorrow turning you upside down and backwards, and slamming you into the rocks over and over again.

Yet, here is the lifeline that I'd like to hold out to you, and I ask you to consider grabbing on. Even though this is one of the more excruciatingly painful experiences you've had in life, it also holds the most promise for a wholehearted awakening that is bigger than any you've ever known. Now, if you are in the very center of the storm, that may seem like the booby prize, and not at all what you care a rat's you-know-what about. I assure you, however, that as you move forward in life, this will matter to you.

What's good about this breakup is that you have been brought to your knees by the great leveler of life. Heartache has you upside down and is furiously shaking loose from the crevices of your psyche every lie you've ever lived with. Every fear you've ever swept under the rug, minimized, or denied is now staring you straight in the face. Every way that you've given away your power, denied your own deeper knowing, put someone else's feelings and needs before your own, stayed embedded in a victimized story, or settled for less in life—all of it is now up for review. You have nowhere to hide. Life has broken you open and it is violently, mercilessly forcing you to evolve, to develop, and to grow. In the immortal words of the great Leonard

> *You know when you come across one of those empty shell people and you think, what the hell happened to you? Well, there came a time in each one of those lives where they were standing at a crossroads. Some place where they had to decide to turn left or right. This is no time to be a chicken shit.*
>
> SANDRA OH AS PATTI, IN
> *UNDER THE TUSCAN SUN*

Cohen, "There is a crack in everything./That's how the light gets in."

The only way to outrun the sorrow of losing the attentions and affections of the person you have loved is to use the fierce and fiery pain of it to catalyze your own awakening and propel you to become the person you were born to be. Whether you were the leaver or the left, whether your breakup happened five minutes ago, five months ago, or five years ago, this book is going to help put it all into perspective, and deliver you safe, sane, and sound to the new and beautiful life that is waiting for you on the other side of this.

CHAPTER 3

a new possibility between us: introducing conscious uncoupling

It is with hearts full of sadness that we have decided to separate. . . .
We have come to the conclusion that while we love each other very much
we will remain separate. We are, however, and always will be a family,
and in many ways we are closer than we have ever been.

GWYNETH PALTROW AND CHRIS MARTIN

onscious Uncoupling shot into the lexicon of global awareness in the aftermath of an announcement offered by a beautiful actress and her talented musician husband, who used the term to make public their intention to separate. I will forever be grateful to them for doing so. Within twenty-four hours, millions were talking about how we might more consciously complete our unions, and improve upon the antagonistic and contentious ways of breaking up we'd come to accept as the norm.

At the time, I was deep in the jungles of Costa Rica on a self-imposed writing retreat to work on the proposal for this book. The book (which has since become *this* book) would share the Conscious Uncoupling process I'd been developing and teaching to thousands since 2009, on how to honorably end a romantic union. For years I, along with many professional colleagues, had been wrestling with the awareness that a paradigm shift in this area was not only possible but also desperately needed.

Though I'd gone to the most remote place I could find in order to minimize distractions, in our virtual world there are few places to hide. Within hours of the announcement, I found myself camped out in a tiny room that was little more than a closet, talking on the only landline the retreat center had available to guests, with reporters from around the globe who, one after another, all wanted to know the answer to one very simple question:

What the heck is a Conscious Uncoupling?

This is what I told them: a Conscious Uncoupling is a breakup or divorce that is characterized by a tremendous amount of goodwill, generosity, and respect, where those separating strive to do minimal damage to themselves, to each other, and to their children (if they have any), as well as intentionally seek to create new agreements and structures designed to set everyone up to win, flourish, and thrive moving forward in life.

Conscious Uncouplings are most known for their bountiful acts of kindness, big-hearted gestures of goodness, and the genuine efforts made to do the right thing for the right reasons. In short, it's a breakup that manages to surmount, defy, and even triumph over the unconscious, primitive, and biologically based impulses we may have to lash out, punish, get revenge, and/or otherwise hurt the one by whom we feel hurt.

Granted, it's easier said than done.

For, as we have been discovering, the brain is not necessarily a big fan of reconfiguring our primary partnerships. In my recent meeting with Dr. Louis Cozolino in his homey Beverly

Hills office, whose walls are lined with books and whose desk overflows with papers and periodicals, I had the opportunity to ask what's going on in our brains that would push even the sweetest of us to suddenly turn into spiteful predators. The good doctor, who's a dead ringer for actor Harry Hamlin, right down to the hip spike haircut, leaned in to explain. Unlike our pancreas, kidneys, or livers, our brains are actually social organs, having developed over millions of years as though purposely designed to connect with the brains of those around us. This attachment circuitry causes our brains to link up to become one interactive system that, in addition to other functions, serves to regulate our moods and emotions. In the world of neuroscience, this is called "sociostasis," and it is the reason we can become so deeply dependent upon, and even somewhat addicted to, our lovers. In other words, at the heart of all attachment is fear regulation, and our closest relationships serve the purpose of calming us down when we're in danger of spinning out of control.

Dr. Cozolino demonstrates how this works by sharing a story of two chimps fighting, explaining that chimps will often fight to the death. When it becomes clear that one chimp is clearly losing the battle, the beta chimp, in order to save his life, will often run to a nearby mama, snatch her baby from her arms, and thrust it into the face of his enraged enemy. Immediately upon seeing the baby, the testosterone of the alpha chimp plunges and he calms down, reducing the chances that the beta chimp will be killed. In that moment, the baby chimp has regulated the emotions of the alpha.

I think to myself, Wow, well, this explains why even after a lover has been abusive and cruel, the one face we most yearn to see is theirs, desperate for their presence in much the same way a heroin addict is pining for a fix. Unfairly, nature seems to have designed it so that the one person in the whole world who can best calm us down when we're terrified is unfortunately the same person who is terrifying us. I am also beginning to understand why we go crazy during a breakup, with tornadoes of terrifying emotions sweeping through us, threatening to empty us of all common sense and sanity. The rupture of attachment throws us into a high state of fear, with a lessened ability to regulate our own emotions, as we have not yet adjusted to our new circumstances by finding new ways to self-soothe that would prevent us from having a meltdown.

We all know that once we allow fear to hijack us and step into the driver's seat of our lives, that we're apt to say and do some really dumb, pretty destructive things. Fear just makes us plain old stupid. Right at the moment when we need our thinking brains the most to help sort through some incredibly important decisions, the consequences of which we will be living with for many years to come, our brains are programmed to not be thinking much at all.

In understanding this, I gain an even deeper respect for a person's decision to remain conscious while uncoupling. To strive to overcome the limbic-brain-induced impulses to burn the house down, smash all the china, or give his expensive suits away to Goodwill—choosing instead to take sound actions and make wholesome choices that are more in keeping with our conscience and which are centered in the cortex, the rational part of the brain. This is the part of us that can keep our compulsion to behave like a crazed wounded animal in check, and ensure that we show up in ways that make the triumph of our ethics over our emotions even possible.

The Conscious Uncoupling of Dianna and Brian

To realize the ideal of a conscious, peaceful parting of the ways, I've developed a five-step process to help navigate our way through the thorny terrain of lost love, and safely deliver us to the other side of separation with hearts, psyches, and souls intact. The developmental task of heartbreak is to harness the huge amount of pain we are in, and to use it to evolve beyond our old painful patterns in love, as well as to awaken us to the power we hold to re-create our lives to be even more beautiful than they were before. In being hurled into a well of unspeakable suffering, we are given a terrifying choice. Will we sink, or will we now learn how to swim?

Dianna learned to swim. Though at the beginning of our journey, I was uncertain as to which direction she might go.

The first thing I noticed about Dianna, an attractive real estate attorney in her midforties, as she impatiently flipped through *People* magazine in my waiting room, was the handsome dark blue wool suit she wore. The second was the anger in her eyes when she looked up to greet me. It was not until we were alone in my office, with the door closed behind us, that her face softened into a deeply sad expression of pain and confusion. Her story began tumbling out almost before I had the chance to sit down. Her husband, Brian, an aspiring filmmaker and primary caregiver to their four-year-old daughter, Stephanie, was having an affair. He'd informed her days before that he was leaving her for his new love. He was clear he wanted a divorce.

Dianna was both shocked and seething. For years she'd financially supported Brian as he plugged away at his "nonexistent film career" by working long hours as an attorney. She was unprepared for the intensity of her fury as the injustice and insult of it consumed her. She was having intrusive fantasies of throwing bleach on all of his clothes, hacking into his computer to delete and destroy his scripts, and driving over to his lover's house to break all of her windows. She felt terrified to be having these feelings, and on some level deeply unsafe with herself—as though if provoked further, she might actually lose control and start behaving this way. Initially, she acted on these feelings by putting an aggressive attorney on retainer who assured her Brian would get little beyond what he brought into the marriage. Yet, pausing to take a deep breath, she looked into my eyes and confessed that she did not want to behave in the same hostile and hateful ways her parents did when they divorced some thirty years before—behaviors that seasoned her childhood with periods of deep depression and despair.

Together, we began sorting through the pain, and thinking things through to try to gain some perspective. How might it impact Stephanie if she were torn between two enraged parents? If Dianna behaved vindictively as was her impulse, how might her angry actions impact any romantic relationship she might hope to have in the future? Did she really want to give Brian and his lover the power to determine the kind of human being that she herself would become? Given the circumstances, which looked unlikely to change, what might be the best possible outcome for all involved?

Thus began our work. We started with the first step of the Conscious Uncoupling process, Find Emotional Freedom, which taught her how to harness the intensity of the wildly difficult emotions she was feeling and transform them from a *destructive* impulse to do harm into the *constructive* energies of lasting, positive change. These constructive energies could help catalyze her own growth beyond the woman she had been in her relationship with Brian—insecure, people pleasing, self-abandoning, and chronically overgiving as a way to try to prove her value.

In letting go of her festering rage, Dianna softened into a sorrow so deep she thought she might drown in it, admitting after a long and pregnant silence that this sadness was nothing new. It had been there long before she'd even met her husband. Having grown up with an alcoholic mother who'd barely spoken to her, no matter how well behaved she was, how much she tried to please her mother, or how well she performed in school, Dianna knew well the pain of being chronically undersupported and left to fend for herself in life. She decided to set an intention to use this breakdown to evolve beyond her old, painful patterns of feeling so alone in life, and became determined to use this breakup as the catalyst for a whole new life.

We then moved on to Step 2, Reclaim Your Power and Your Life, to help Dianna stop obsessively ruminating on everything offensive that Brian had done by turning her attention instead toward herself, to discover what role she may have played in what happened between them. This was not at all easy to do. Yet, Dianna recognized that if she ever hoped to have love in her future, she'd need to understand her role in how things went down, in order to prevent something like this from ever happening again.

> *I do not want the peace which passeth understanding. I want the understanding which bringeth peace.*
> HELEN KELLER

Dianna sheepishly confessed that Brian had been asking to go to marriage counseling for two years before this happened, complaining of deep frustration with the long hours she worked. At the time she'd been too busy to consider counseling. Dianna began connecting the dots between the neglect she suffered as a child and the negligent ways she'd been behaving toward her husband and daughter. While painful to admit, ultimately, facing this truth freed her to begin making some serious changes in her life. It also helped her to understand the complexities of what had happened rather than settle into the half-truth of a victimized story that risked leaving her mistrustful of future love.

We then dove into Step 3, Break the Pattern, Heal Your Heart, where we looked to discover Dianna's "source-fracture wound"—the original break in her heart, which happened during her parents' divorce and left her emotionally homeless with a deep sense of having been displaced. Together, we made conscious the story she'd constructed in response to that experience: "I'm alone," "Men always leave," and "I can never really get what I truly need from others." Stepping back, as though watching her life as a movie, she tried to uncover how she might have inadvertently been duplicating this sad story ever since. She was surprised to see the many covert ways she'd been thinking and behaving that made it hard for others to find their way into her world. She prided herself on being self-sufficient. As a person who enjoyed being independent, she rarely asked for help, and often did not accept it even when offered. She was uncomfortable sharing her feelings, and presented herself as having everything together, as though she needed nothing from anyone. Once she saw herself as the source of her disappointing love story, Dianna discovered there was no shortage of evidence that she was the author of her own deep aloneness in life.

Dianna determined to graduate from this painful pattern and started by challenging her old beliefs. She recognized that she had a deep capacity and desire for closeness and love. She decided that the losses of her past would not determine what was possible in her future, and she began identifying new ways of relating to others that held the possibility of creating a different story. She began to take actions that were aligned with the creation of happy and healthy relationships with everyone in her life—co-workers, family, and friends, including Brian, because, after all, he was the only father Stephanie would ever have.

Moving on to Step 4, Become a Love Alchemist, Dianna learned how to clear the air of any residual resentment by taking responsibility for how her neglect of Brian had impacted him when they were together. While she could not hold herself accountable for the destructive choices he made in response to her neglect, she could acknowledge with a tender heart how her behavior must have caused him deep suffering. The bigheartedness of her amends inspired Brian to follow suit by taking responsibility for the immature and hurtful ways he mishandled their separation. With true regret, he was able to acknowledge the negative impact on her and on Stephanie.

Dianna realized she no longer wanted Brian's betrayal to characterize the connection between them. Rather than punish him for choosing another woman over her, she chose instead to further generate goodwill by giving him a financial gift as a thank-you for their years together, and for the beautiful daughter he'd given her. She wrote a kind note telling him she was forgiving him and hoped he'd do the same for her, suggesting that perhaps he might want to use her gift to help finish the short film he'd started that had gotten pushed aside in the turmoil of their separation. Stunned, he gratefully accepted, using the money

Lost love is still love. It takes a different form, that's all.
MITCH ALBOM

as she'd suggested. It was that film that launched his career as a filmmaker.

Brian, humbled and moved by her kindness, looked for ways to reciprocate. He rearranged his schedule to care for Stephanie each afternoon to spare Dianna the expense of a nanny. This routine of being picked up from school each day by her father created a greater sense of cohesion for Stephanie, as she got to spend time with him at least five days a week. This was the first of many positive and good-hearted exchanges that have since come to characterize the relationship between Dianna and Brian.

Because of these gestures and others suggested in Step 5, Create Your Happily-*Even*-After Life, which helps restore a sense of well-being to one's extended community of relatives and friends, Stephanie now moves freely between both of her homes with a feeling of warm friendliness, as well as an expanded sense of family, which is the outcome we aspire to in a Conscious Uncoupling.

While not all such stories must end with a new love interest to qualify as a happy ending, I am glad to share that Dianna's efforts were well rewarded with the affections of a kind and loving man who brings her much joy. She's become more deeply present, awake, and aware as a result of her heartbreak, and now understands the attention and care all relationships need to stay vibrant and strong. As simple as that sounds, it is not something she understood before. She has also learned to tend to her own deeper feelings and needs, and given up overgiving as a way to prove her value to others. Rather than work around the clock to support the dreams and creative aspirations of others, as she did with Brian when they were married, she prioritizes her own creative aspirations, and is currently working on

> *If we are willing to walk fearlessly and tenderly into the crucible of a painful ending, we will find gifts waiting for us there that we never could have seen had we continued clinging to the safety of the familiar.*
>
> CRAIG HAMILTON

her first novel. Dianna is living a much more true and well-rounded life than she was before, and for that she is deeply grateful.

The lessons of love can be costly and the price of wisdom steep. Yet, these initially unwelcomed tutorials hold seeds of great potential to liberate us to live more authentic and meaningful lives. Dr. Ginette Paris, Jungian psychologist and author of the lovely book *Heartbreak,* reminds us that "the only pain that can be avoided is the pain that comes from living with a captive heart." While we cannot protect ourselves from being hurt in life, we can certainly escape becoming captivated by loss by choosing to make something beautiful of it. Such is the opportunity of a broken heart.

The Practice of Generosity, Goodwill, and Grace

Buddhist teacher Ken McLeod speaks about the concept of karma, which many spiritual seekers assume to be the cause and effect of our actions. If I step on the gas pedal, my car will go faster. If I assault someone, they, in turn, may hit me back. Either that, or life will find a way to even the score, perhaps by arranging a fender bender later that evening, or by having my wallet stolen when next at the market. Often we will be motivated to behave ourselves simply because we don't wish to create "bad karma" and be punished for our selfish and immature actions. This interpretation of karma, however, leaves out nuances that are easily lost when translating one language into another, and one culture's belief system to another's.

In the Tibetan language, the word *karma* is literally *las.rgyu. abras,* which means "action-seed-results." Ken explains that Tibetans often put together two or more words to define abstract ideas, such as joining the words *near* and *far* to explain the concept of distance, or *large* and *small* to represent the notion of size. Karma, as it was originally defined, means that each action we take is like planting a seed that will grow into a particular result. More than cause and effect, karma is the idea that

> *I would rather have eyes that cannot see, ears that cannot hear, lips that cannot speak, than a heart that cannot love.*
>
> ROBERT TIZON

the actions we take will, over time, begin to grow our lives in a particular direction. During a breakup, when our biology may be pulling on us to take rash actions, the challenge is not to give in to the temptation to plant seeds of ill will and revenge— actions that could eventually grow into bitter fruits that we may be forced to eat for many years to come. Instead, we want to plant seeds of forgiveness, goodwill, and generosity, so that in time our actions will grow to be a cornucopia of riches for ourselves and for those we love. Each action you take, each choice you make, will grow something in your life and in our world. Conscious actions and choices may not give you the euphoric high of revenge, but neither will they grow poison oak in your backyard. They can, however, grow you a bountiful and beautiful life.

The goal of a Conscious Uncoupling is not necessarily the restoration of justice, the attainment of restitution, or the vindication of being right. The goal of a Conscious Uncoupling is to be free. And to move forward from here empowered to create a happy, healthy, and fundamentally good life for yourself and those you love. As such, we strive to take all that is ugly and rotting, and turn it into compost to grow beautiful lives. In response to the toxic downward spiral created by two interlocking limbic brains, we consciously look to see how we might interrupt and redirect the snowballing momentum of angry and reactive words and deeds. And there is no more powerful action to turn things in a harmonious direction than a gesture of authentic generosity. For a generous gesture is like pouring cool, clear water onto the festering embers of hurt and resentment, often averting a blazing fire that could easily burn the house down, and course-correcting everyone back into the cortex brain, which is where we need to be to ensure the safety and well-being of all involved. While most are unable to offer a big financial gift as Dianna chose to do, we can all offer a tender and sincere gesture of kindness to our departing love, to set us in the right direction.

The best of who we are can be discovered in the choice to be generous in the face of great suffering and loss. The word *generous* shares the same root as *genesis* and *generate—gen,* which means "to give birth." A generous gesture initiates new life, giving birth to beautiful beginnings and liberating us from the cycle of reactivity and retaliation. That's not to be confused with co-dependently motivated giving, with its covert agenda to get something back, whether it is approval, validation, safety, or love. An act of generosity asks for nothing in return. It is a wholesomely motivated love offering to the universe, a simple act of goodness that affirms the sweetness of life, even in the face of sorrow and disappointment.

One way to be generous is through the simple gesture of offering a blessing to our former partners. As breakups often end with a curse of anger both on our lips and in our hearts, to say goodbye while also extending a heartfelt blessing can be incredibly moving.

Doju and Lucio had been married for thirty years when Doju confessed to her husband that she wanted a divorce. It was difficult for her to explain why exactly. In many ways theirs was the ideal marriage. At the center of their relationship was a shared devotion to Buddhism, as together they practiced non-attachment and the letting go of self-cherishing with great commitment and unwavering faith. Lucio was crushed. To lose his wife after all these years was not the life he'd planned. It was the ultimate challenge of his faith. Yet, Doju felt that the constraints of marriage itself were holding her back. Although Lucio had been a loving husband, the role of wife no longer suited her and she could not bear to continue on in a structure that felt oppressive to her. Reluctantly and respectfully, Lucio accepted her desire to be released from their marital vows and agreed to set her free. The day she left, Lucio drove Doju to the airport so she might return to her family's home many thousands of miles away. After checking her bags and walking her to the security gate, Lucio looked deeply into Doju's eyes. Tears streamed down both of their faces. Yet Lucio smiled, took a step backward, and with deep love and honor, bowed before his wife, blessing her decision to leave the marriage and wishing her well on her journey. She returned his bow to receive his blessing, turned, and soberly walked away to begin her new life. Even now, some ten years later, tears well up in her eyes as she shares her story with me, still so deeply moved by his generosity, goodness, and kindness.

There are flowers everywhere for those who bother to look.
HENRI MATISSE

Sufi poet Hafiz, who lived in the fourteenth century, wrote one of my favorite poems. It is called "The Sun Never Says."

> Even after all this time,
> the sun never says to the earth
> "You owe me."
> Look what happens with a love like that.
> It lights the whole sky.

By encouraging you to be generous, I am not suggesting you foolishly refuse to take a stand for what is rightfully yours, as you painstakingly start the sorting and divvying up of your life and assets. However, with all of the darkness you may be walking through right now, it's good to remember that where there is no light, you have the choice to become it.

A New Narrative for the End of Love

> I just think of things as beautiful or not. . . . I don't think of good or bad. Just of beautiful or ugly. I think a lot of nice things are ugly and a lot of nasty things are beautiful.
>
> JOHN FOWLES

Futurist Buckminster Fuller once said, "You never change things by fighting the existing reality. To change something, build a new model that makes the existing model obsolete." Conscious Uncoupling is not about how we can fix an old, ailing system, as much as the suggestion that we begin building a new one that empowers us to have healthier, wiser, and even happier endings. Many bright and dedicated people in the therapeutic and family law fields have been laboring for this evolution for decades, and I would be remiss to not credit their pioneering efforts. An idea whose time has come will always arrive through a tribe of people, rather than just one individual, and there are many of us who have been working for years, patiently tilling the soil for this day to come.

If we're to now start changing the narrative of breakups and divorce to be a more life-affirming one, we might even consider creating new language. My good friend Kit Thomas, filmmaker and founder of CircleOfWisdom.org, recently pointed out to me the negative bias of language when it comes to the end of a relationship. Phrases like *breaking up, splitting up, on the rocks, dumped, finished,* and *kaput,* with our poor children now coming from *broken homes,* perhaps because of some shameless *home wrecker,* leave a lot to be desired. And of course, there's also the offensive title of ex, which rhymes with *hex, ejects, wrecks,* and *vex,* and is reminiscent of x-ing something out to delete it forever from our lives. However, the phrase *conscious uncoupling* in and of itself opens up a world of possibility for breakups moving forward, and it's my theory that this is why it took off the way it did once it was introduced to the world. For language is generative, informing and inspiring us as to what's possible. New phrases and words like *wevorce, expanded families, wasband, sister-out-law, binuclear families,* and *stepwives* begin to make sense in helping to usher in softer, gentler ways to describe our matrix of relatedness in a post-breakup world.

Although this book is largely about the dissolution of romantic unions, heartbreak and loss are not reserved for lovers. I was pleasantly surprised when, in the aftermath of its introduction to the world, Conscious Uncoupling cartoons began popping up in newspapers and magazines around the globe. Rather than focus on romantic love, the majority of them were commenting on professional, political, and other kinds of endings. In a mobile society, where most of us will change jobs, the cities we live in, our professional networks, our circle of friends, and our spiritual communities almost as often as we change the oil in our cars, we are constantly uncoupling. As we continually find ourselves in a state of letting go of the lives that we have for the possibility of gaining the lives we might create, it behooves us to learn the art of healthy completion, in order to reap the benefits in all areas of our lives.

The most beautiful people we have known are those who have known defeat, known suffering, known struggle, known loss, and have found their way out of the depths. These persons have an appreciation, a sensitivity, and an understanding of life that fills them with compassion, gentleness, and a deep loving concern. Beautiful people do not just happen.
ELISABETH KÜBLER-ROSS

While many have aspired to the friendly ending of love, few have been able to overcome the biology of our brains' tendency to see a breakup as a life-threatening event. The five-step process offered in this book will serve as a blueprint that can bring out the best, rather than the worst, of who we are during one of the more stressful and challenging periods in our lives. It is my hope that these steps will become guideposts in the process of healthy separation, in much the same way that Elisabeth Kübler-Ross's five stages of grief are a roadmap to help us understand the emotional process of loss and grieving. As Ms. Kübler-Ross's model offers a flashlight that can help us make our way through the woods, so too Conscious Uncoupling can support us to make healthy, wholesome decisions at a time when clear thinking may be just out of reach.

Like it or not, a breakup is a time when we're stranded

between worlds. You are no longer the person you once were, and not quite the person you have yet to become. I encourage you to use the guidelines of Conscious Uncoupling as the candelabra you'll need to help you find your way through this dark night of the soul, and deliver you safely to the enhanced, expanded, and enriched new life that will soon be available to you. Not just in spite of your breakup, but paradoxically, in many ways, because of it.

CHAPTER 4

how and when to do this program

When they have reached their term, take them back in kindness,
or part from them in kindness.

KORAN

A rriving at this chapter, you may feel as if you're suddenly being asked to walk the plank. It's one thing to talk about consciously separating. It's another to confront how you can actually do it. Yet, the alternative, to simply let the chips fall where they may or wait for time to do your dirty work, leaves too much to chance. With your future happiness at stake, as well as the health and well-being of your children if you have them, I invite you to identify with the strongest, wisest, and most courageous parts of yourself, and resolve to do the right thing by wholeheartedly committing to a Conscious Uncoupling.

Bad endings have an unfortunate tendency to linger, tainting life and love moving forward. Of all my regrets in life, it is

the unkind partings that have stayed with me the most. I find I
can painfully recall the caustic barbs and gloomy sullen silences
long after fonder memories have
faded. Studies show that, no matter
how many good times you may have
shared before your breakup, a hellish
end will soil your recollection of the
entire relationship and color your
perspective on love in the future.
And though you may be far from
considering your *next* relationship at
this moment (consumed as you are
with the loss of this one), I caution
you that your next love affair will not

> *The setting sun, and music*
> *at the close,*
> *As the last taste of sweets,*
> *is sweetest last,*
> *Writ in remembrance*
> *more than things long*
> *past.*
> WILLIAM SHAKESPEARE

begin when you meet your next lover, but with how you end this
one. For baggage left buried, wreckage unresolved, and a heart
that has not healed don't just go away; they lie in wait, ready to
pounce on an unsuspecting potential new partner. Either that
or they leak out in toxic and destructive ways into other relationships, including the one you have with yourself.

Good endings, while never easy, are well worth the climb.

Conscious Uncoupling is not a quick and easy fix to heartbreak. Nor is it a spiritually superior path that will magically
spare you from any and all suffering. Suffering is appropriate
when facing the loss of love. As much as I wish I could promise you that this process will erase your pain in a few simple
steps, nothing can shortcut the organic rhythms of grief. Yet,
grief, that most dreaded of teachers, does not come empty-
handed. Though she may violently be sweeping away much of
what you've known and loved, she also comes bearing precious
gifts. As she offers to carve greater depths of kindness, compassion, wisdom, and courage into the core of who you are, it's

sometimes best to just surrender yourself to her agenda. You might even invite her to stay for a while and at least try to become friends, recognizing that something beautiful is seeking to wake up in your life as a result of her presence. When you are walking through the blackest of nights, and journeying through the thick of the woods, all there is to do, really, is to learn to love the silent softness of the moonlight, as Life miraculously finds a way to light your way home one step at a time.

Is This Program for You?

This program is for anyone who has a sincere desire to move through the ending of a relationship with integrity, truth, goodness, and honor. It is for you whether you were with your partner for thirty days, thirty months, or thirty years; whether you are in the midst of a breakup now, recovering from one that happened a while ago, or contemplating the possibility of one in your future. This program is for you if you are the one who is leaving or the one being left; if you're gay, straight, or some variation on the theme. It matters not if you were monogamous or polyamorous; if you were in a committed union or simply hoping to have been in one. Young, old, rich, poor, healthy, or sick, a rupture in attachment is agony for us all, and no one gets a free pass out of hell at the end of love. Although, if you have finally found the nerve to leave after a long time of secretly knowing the relationship was over, you may actually be feeling a bit euphoric to finally be free. If that's your experience, then this program is still for you, to ensure you not repeat toxic or disempowering patterns with someone new.

There is only one exception to this inclusive, equal-opportunity-for-all. And that is this: if you are making a hasty and somewhat premature decision to end a relationship that still holds hope for happiness, and/or deserves to at least be given the dignity of one final give-it-all-you've-got try.

Should You Stay or Should You Go?

Claudia and Andrew had been married a little over twelve years when Claudia resolutely walked into my office one Thursday afternoon, sat down, and asked me how to best tell her husband she wanted a divorce. I'd not seen her since they'd gotten engaged some thirteen years before, while still in the blush of love. Apparently, a lot had happened between now and then, and Claudia was eager to catch me up. They'd had three boys, ages five, eight, and eleven. Her eldest had been diagnosed with ADHD, and she spent a tremendous amount of her time teaching him the skills he'd need in life to succeed in spite of this challenge. Yet, it was not her son's ADHD that was burdening her the most; it was her husband's. Though he had never been officially diagnosed, Claudia was positive he had it. She began recounting all the evidence she'd gathered over the years to support her conclusion, culminating with a detailed account of the many ways she was overfunctioning in the relationship—managing his schedule, taking care of all of their bills and business matters, and making sure he was performing well at work—acting more like his mother than his wife. She was burnt out, overwhelmed, and exhausted—and at this point just wanted out of the marriage.

> *The older you grow, the more you realize that one half of you can firmly believe what the other half equally firmly refuses.*
> CONSTANCE HOLME

In more carefully examining how it had come to this, we discovered that one stone had been left unturned in her endless hours of obsessively trying to figure out her life. While Claudia was certain Andrew had ADHD, he'd never actually been tested, and therefore never treated for his chronic inability to focus on the task at hand. We decided, given the high stakes involved, to give it one last try before she took the drastic step of deconstructing their family.

That evening, after the children had gone to bed, Claudia made a fire, poured two glasses of Merlot, passed one to her husband, and told him she had a confession to make. She shared her feelings of overwhelm and despair, managing to do so without accusing him of being insensitive or uncaring as she'd done in the past. She candidly revealed how close she'd come to leaving him that day, giving him the opportunity to understand how dire their situation was. Although she'd been asking for a while that he get tested for ADHD, her direct candor spurred him to schedule an appointment with his doctor the following week. When we spoke several months later, Claudia told me that Andrew had, of course, tested positive and was now in treatment for ADHD. They'd also begun couples counseling with a therapist who was an expert in the family dynamics of ADHD, and their relationship had gotten markedly better since last we spoke. Andrew was taking greater responsibility for his deficits and not leaning on her as much to compensate for his challenges, releasing her from the very unsexy role of being his mom. While the jury was still out as to whether or not the marriage would last, they were taking solid steps to improve their relationship, and both felt more hopeful about their future together than they had in years.

For those of you at your wits' end who, like Claudia, are considering throwing in the towel, the initiation of a Conscious

Uncoupling process should be the last of many steps taken to try to find peace with your partner. I'd like to share with you three powerful actions Claudia took that I recommend you do as well.

First, she sought professional help. Although she felt quite certain that she wanted to leave her husband, she scheduled an appointment with me to discuss it before telling him so. Coming into the session with a conclusion already formed, she was open-minded enough to put it aside and explore the possibilities of working out her marital problems rather than breaking up the family prematurely. Before calling an attorney, she called a counselor, and that proved to be a very wise choice.

SAVING YOUR RELATIONSHIP RECOMMENDATION #1

When not sure whether to stay or whether to go, it's best to first work with a professional counselor to help you make a wise decision.

The second powerful action Claudia took was to share her feelings without shaming or blaming her husband, before coming to a conclusion that did not include his input. Rather than dumping her feelings onto him, blaming him for their problems, and then self-righteously announcing her departure, Claudia gave her husband the chance to hear what was in her heart, and to respond in a way that would eventually save their relationship. A lot of us skip this step, only letting someone know how serious things are by announcing that the relationship is over. Up to that point, we may have been quietly seething, nagging and complaining, thinking that we were communicating. Yet studies show that over 90 percent of communication is actually nonverbal. Meaning that your nasty, condescending tone of voice and your hostile, contorted facial expression will register long before the words you're saying, leaving your partner feeling belittled and badgered, and often throwing him into a defensive state so he's not hearing a word you say. Nagging and complaining are not to be confused with the initiation of an authentic, serious dialogue, and it doesn't usually get the results we're hoping for.

SAVING YOUR RELATIONSHIP RECOMMENDATION #2

Before you up and leave, find the courage to share your feelings with your partner without blaming or shaming them, and do so prior to coming to a decision, so that he or she has a chance to address and/or rectify the problem.

Finally, when her husband took steps that demonstrated his investment in their relationship, Claudia responded in kind by matching his efforts with her own. Relationships in which only one partner is continually striving to make changes are not sustainable. However, if in response to your heartfelt sharing, your partner begins taking concrete actions in a positive direction to make things better, I suggest you at least try to match that commitment with your own. Many couples do a painful push-pull dance, taking turns pursuing and distancing. When you move toward him, he backs up from you. When he moves toward you, you retreat from him. When Andrew extended himself to meet Claudia's needs, she did not back up or push him away. She let herself be supported and loved. I invite you to do the same and see if something new emerges between you.

SAVING YOUR RELATIONSHIP RECOMMENDATION #3

If your partner responds to your concerns by taking concrete actions to improve your situation, demonstrating that he or she is taking your distress to heart, do your best to match that effort with your own and really give it your all before initiating an uncoupling.

An oft-quoted study called "The State of Our Unions" from Rutgers University suggests that only 38 percent of married people in America describe themselves as happily so. Apparently, we don't leave our relationships all that easily. We tend to tough-out the hard times, rolling up our shirtsleeves when things get rough to try to make a good go of it. Yet, after doing all we can to make the relationship work, many of us will eventually choose to terminate the union.

Here are the three most common reasons. First, people choose out because one or both of them have behaved badly. Someone has stolen money from the family bank account, they've cheated, or they've started doing drugs or drinking excessively. These behaviors damage the fundamental safety of the connection and violate the agreements the relationship is founded upon. If this describes your relationship, I recommend you see a marriage counselor to help determine if your relationship holds the possibility of healing and breakthrough after such a betrayal.

The second reason is that after trying, sometimes for years, to navigate incompatible or just plain ineffective or destructive communication styles, one or both parties can't take it anymore. After months or years of walking on eggshells for fear of upsetting their partner, chronically being misunderstood or not heard, or feeling diminished each time one opens his or her mouth, one or both people simply stop talking. Maybe they have tolerated living in a war zone for so long that they've come to think that it's normal to argue over every little detail of life. These relationships run the gamut from being excessively disengaged, where one or both partners have given up trying to get their needs met and are emotionally shutting each other out, to being overly enmeshed, whereby both parties are easily reactive, defensive, and quick to initiate a fight. Whichever end of the spectrum you may be on, these relationships are characterized by a fundamental disregard for the feelings and needs of each other, and the residue of built-up resentments and hurts are triggers just waiting to be pulled at any given moment. At some point, someone gets plain old tired and disgusted and just wants out. Before ending such unions, however, I recommend studying with some of the great teachers out there who are offering advanced communication skills. They may help you evolve beyond toxic old patterns by providing new tools and techniques that have performed miracles of love, healing, and reconciliation. You can find some of them listed in the Online Resources section at the end of this book.

The third most common reason we end our unions is that we grow in different directions. Most people see this as a matter of changing interests, or "falling out of love." But I'd like to suggest that what sometimes happens is that, over time, people's core values begin to shift. It used to be that people were born into a certain worldview that was shared by the entire community, and they lived their whole lives within that perspective. Yet, the world you and I live in is far more complex and nuanced than the world our ancestors knew. We are a culture that loves change. Unlike previous generations that valued steadfastness, constancy, and fidelity to one core set of values, we now aspire to continually broaden our horizons, up-level our games, and realize our full potential. In a world where so many of us feel called to become all that we can be, relationships are going to be much less stable. In the best possible scenario, we grow together. But this is not always going to be the case.

The bottom line is this: Staying together through the hard times can be a noble and beautiful choice, demonstrating high levels of integrity, commitment, and character. However, if your partner is consistently saying to you in words and deeds, "I don't care about your feelings," "I don't give a crap about your needs," and "I especially don't give a hoot about your changing values, and have little to no interest in learning about who you've become," then it may be time to consider moving on. And, one important warning: if domestic violence is involved, then please run, don't walk, to the nearest exit. Sort it all out once you are safely out of danger. A fist is nothing to negotiate with, and the threat of physical harm is nothing to minimize.

If, after considering all of this, you're still swimming in a sea of uncertainty and ambivalence, and trying to force the matter one way or the other by doing this program, that's actually a good thing. By engaging a Conscious Uncoupling process, you'll see more clearly what can—and what can't—be changed. You'll learn not only how to lower your reactivity, let go of being a victim, and discover your role in the difficulties you've had in order to access your power to change the dynamic, but you'll also be liberated of baggage that doesn't even belong to this relationship. In addition, you'll learn new communication skills and tools that promise to deepen understanding and generate more harmony between you. The risk you run, of course, is that as you explore your own deeper knowing, you may discover that it's time to move on. You may find you've changed too much. Or come to care too little. One thing is certain:

> *If you love somebody,*
> *let them go, for if*
> *they return, they were*
> *always yours. If they*
> *don't, they never were.*
>
> KAHLIL GIBRAN

doing this program will stir the pot and help get you unstuck. I do, however, recommend that as a prerequisite going in, you try being 100 percent willing to let the relationship go if it's revealed to be the right thing to do. You may also need to modify the exercises a bit, as they may not reflect exactly where you are in the moment. If that's the case, you have my blessing.

What If You're Hoping You'll Get Back Together?

It's hard to give up on love. One sweet-spirited client of mine, Amanda, a pediatrician in her midfifties, had been steadfastly holding on to the hope of getting back with her former girlfriend, Benita, for six long years. In all that time, Amanda had not had so much as one date, faithful to the possibility of reconciliation with her beloved. However, Benita, who was significantly younger than Amanda, had long ago moved in with another woman and was helping her raise her two children. Yet, whenever Amanda contemplated letting go of hope, as though she could read her mind across the miles, Benita would text or call to reengage, rekindling the fires between them and validating the strength of their bond. Through our work together, Amanda realized she was loving Benita in a parental way, providing an emotional home for her prodigal daughter without any expectation that one would be provided for her in return. While releasing the hope of ever getting back together again felt as if she were betraying an unspoken contract between them, Amanda made the sober decision to move on. True to form, for the next two days, Benita frantically texted Amanda. "How are you?" "What's happening?" "I miss you." Amanda did not respond, and instead simply extended a blessing from her heart to Benita's, fully aware that if she were ever to be free to love someone new, she would have to disengage.

The letting go of hope can feel like a funeral dirge, initiating a cascade of grief just as surely as if you broke up yesterday. That final release of possibility can feel to some like unplugging someone you love from a ventilator. It's a somber and lonely-to-the-bone experience. Yet, if you ever hope to love again, you will have to face your loss head on, and surrender to reality: as of this moment, you are broken up. Even if there is a bit of push-pull and in-out going on, the truth is that the commitment between you has been compromised and right now, you are not, in fact, "a couple."

Yet assuming you have to let go of your relationship *before* doing the Conscious Uncoupling program is a little like cleaning the house before the cleaning woman comes (or since we're evolving beyond sexist stereotypes, the cleaning person). While it's unclear whether or not the two of you will ever get back together, the one thing we do know for sure is that the relationship you once shared—the one that was clearly *not* working for one or both of you—has to die. We do not yet know if a healthier and happier new one will be born in its place. Yet your best shot for getting it right next time, if you do get that coveted second chance, is to bring conscious closure to the relationship you've had to make way for a whole new possibility between you.

Many of the techniques, skills, and tools you will learn by engaging this program will dramatically help improve any relationship you hope to have in your future. Including, but not limited to, a rekindled romance with the current focus of your longings. If you're holding on to hope for reconciliation, your biggest challenge will be to let go of the covert agenda to re-claim your beloved as your motivation for doing this work. Yet if you can manage to set the healthy goal of simply striving to do the right thing for the right reasons, whatever that may be, then your journey through the program will be that much more powerful.

Doing the Program with Your Partner

Whether you do Conscious Uncoupling alone or as a paral-lel process with your soon-to-be-former partner, let's not lose sight of what's happening here: you're separating. While the program is designed to help you do that with a minimal amount of blame, shame, damage, and distress, it can't help but be a process of individuation, as you focus on leaving your rela-tional home and returning to a serene sense of solitude within yourself.

Breakups are a messy business, and even the best of them can be fraught with a lack of clarity and cohesion. And even those couples who consciously choose to uncouple together will tend to do so at a pace that's somewhat out of sync. When you need to share from the deepest part of your heart, he needs to unplug all communication and just be alone. When you need to get some distance between you, he suddenly needs to cling for comfort. Such is the imperfect process of parting ways. Yet the benefit of doing the Conscious Uncoupling program to-gether is that you'll have shared language for how to navigate your loss, as well as clarity on how to move forward without the residue of festering resentments between you. You'll be able to align on an agreed-upon vision for your future that can serve as the new North Star to which you both aspire, providing guidance for the many decisions you face as you move forward. By doing this program together, you'll be given the opportunity to create new agreements that will offer clarity on what you can expect from each other from now on. All in all, the opportunity to separate together promises to create a sense of safety, cohesion, and containment that is uncharacteristic of a more typical breakup experience, which will prove to be particularly valuable if there are children involved. To help you do this well, I offer instructions at the end of each step to address the specific concerns and questions that might arise for those of you who decide to do the program together.

Doing Conscious Uncoupling Alone

It only takes one to consciously uncouple. Your ability to use this breakup as a catalyst for your profound awakening does not rest in the hands of your former partner. Even if he or she is behaving like a beast, you are not bound to behave in kind. And if you think you are, you may want to look at your habit of giving your power away to other people to determine who you're going to be in life.

Breakups will bring out the best or worst in who we are. And if your former partner is leaning toward the latter, you want to remember that kindness is contagious, and that you have more power than you may think to influence the direction this breakup takes. As tempting as it may be to become obsessed by someone else's poor behavior, ultimately this breakup is

> *Anyone who has lost something they thought was theirs forever finally comes to realize that nothing really belongs to them.*
>
> PAULO COELHO

about *you*. By keeping your primary attention on yourself, you'll get to use this experience as a springboard for a whole new life. You will outgrow old painful patterns, you will discover your true value, and you will learn how to disengage in a way that is going to allow you to love and be loved again in your future.

Truthfully, most people do this program alone. The two of you are breaking up for a reason, and most likely you have different ideas about how things should be done. This is nothing new. If your former partner is not choosing to do this program with you, it may be that he or she doesn't value growth and development in the same way that you do. Or, if you're the one being left, your former partner may have secretly been planning their exit for a while now. At this point, he probably just wants out, and fears if he engages this program with you, it would only pull him back in. Perhaps he's willing to take the basic tenets of goodwill and respect to heart as the guidelines of how this will go between you, but isn't necessarily interested in doing the deep inner reflection that the program provides opportunity for. If that's the case, let's just be grateful he's willing to align with a separation that is characterized by goodness and decency. Let go of needing anything else from him. I promise, you will get everything you need here, with or without the other person's participation. Remember, the patient on the operating table is you.

On the other hand, you may be the one who doesn't want to do the program with your former partner, feeling that it's in your best interests to minimize or even end the connection between you. There is enough evidence to suggest that a clean break is a wise way to go, particularly as our hormones are shown to reengage every time we hear his voice, or see her face across a crowded room. If this is you, you have my full support. Conscious Uncoupling does not necessarily advocate for staying friends after the end of the relationship. Rather, it stands for clear completion so that you are free to move forward in life unencumbered by false hopes, ambivalent attachments, and/or dimmed down dreams.

*Eventually, everything
goes away.*
ELIZABETH GILBERT

There are those of you who are doing this program because you have never quite recovered from a love lost long ago. While your former partner may have long ago moved on, leaving you a mere footnote in his or her memory, something froze the moment things ended between you. If this is you, you are more than welcomed here, as I hold a special place in my heart for the long-suffering casualties of lost love, having once been one myself.

How Long Will It Take?

It's hard to say how long one should take when going through a Conscious Uncoupling program. Some, prompted by a tremendous amount of pain, have hunkered down for a long weekend and gone through the entire program within seventy-two hours, barely stopping to sleep or eat along the way. Some have taken an entire year to thoroughly engage each of the five steps, gestating and integrating the nuances of the program by putting each principle they learn into action before moving on to the next step.

For most, the pacing of this program will lie somewhere in

between. For those who have the time and wherewithal to commit at least a half hour a day, I suggest going through one step a week. Yet, I also honor your own deeper knowing as to what will work best for you, and encourage you to do the same.

Shoring Up Support

You may find you need extra support to help process the material and/or to help manage the feelings that come up for you in the program. If that is the case, you may wish to consider hiring a Conscious Uncoupling coach who is well trained in supporting people to move through the material. Either that, or you can enlist the support of a good therapist, counselor, divorce coach, or spiritual adviser. As I said before, there are many exceptionally compassionate, well-credentialed, and wise human beings who have been diligently developing support structures for those experiencing heartache, and I cannot encourage you enough to avail yourself of their services. To find a list of certified Conscious Uncoupling coaches, please go to www.ConsciousUncoupling.com/CUCoachDirectory.

> *Losing is the price we pay for living. It is also the source of much of our growth and gain.*
>
> JUDITH VIORST

Supplies You May Need

Finally, there are a few supplies you may need. The most important of these is a dedicated journal you can be sure is for your eyes only. Throughout this book, I offer a series of self-reflective questions that you may wish to write answers to in your journal. You will need to feel free to write your rage, tell the absolute truth, and make startling confessions you may never choose to speak out loud to another human being. The program will at times also suggest listening to music or creating art to help you release some of the wild energy that may be coursing through your body as you work through some very challenging emotions. So you may need an iPod or some other kind of stereo system as well as some art supplies of your choice.

And then, of course, don't forget the tissues.

> *Give sorrow words. The grief that does not speak whispers the o'er-fraught heart and bids it break.*
>
> WILLIAM SHAKESPEARE

PART TWO

the 5 steps of conscious uncoupling

STEP 1

find emotional freedom

New life starts in the dark. Whether it is a seed in the ground,
a baby in the womb or Jesus in the tomb, it starts in the dark.

BARBARA BROWN TAYLOR

The first step in your Conscious Uncoupling program is to learn how to harness the energies of the wildly dark and difficult emotions you may be experiencing, such as rage, hatred, fear, and despair, and transform them from *destructive* impulses to hurt yourself or others into *constructive* drivers of positive change. In this step, you will create the conditions that can take you beyond painful old patterns in love, and awaken you to the power you hold to use this shattering to radically evolve how you live and how you love.

In Step 1, Find Emotional Freedom, you will:

• Discover how to have an empowered relationship with your feelings by learning to use your very big and overwhelming emotions to inspire and fuel unprecedented change in your life.

- Awaken to this breakup as a life-altering opportunity to transform your disappointing and destructive patterns in love at the deepest level.
- Create an Inner Sanctuary of Safety that can help you hold and contain the intensity of your emotions from a deeper, wiser center within that is able to provide you with an endless supply of strength, stability, and support.
- Initiate your wholehearted recovery by setting your intention to make something beautiful of this sad parting.

Something has been broken and it is more than just your heart.

It may be your feeling of being safe in the world, your ability to make sense of your life, or even your very faith in life and love. Whether you made the difficult decision to leave, or you are in the devastating position of having been left, the losses you're facing are most likely many, deep, and multidimensional. The heart connection you called home, the shared rituals and routines that shaped your daily life, the "you" you knew yourself to be in your relationship, your standing and position in the community, the clear certainty of your life, and the future you were so carefully striving and saving for—all are gone. In their place are a plethora of raw and wildly painful and unpredictable emotions, perhaps a huge dose of wounded pride or cavernous guilt, and the dreaded drudgery of deconstructing and then reconstructing your entire life.

Yet, many who live through the loss of love discover how to use their pain as the catalyst they've needed to transform their lives in deeply meaningful ways. Having learned to harness their tsunami of emotions as a force for positive change, these are the ones who will one day look back to see their heartbreak as the golden opportunity they seized upon to create a brand-new, enlarged, and liberated life.

The Shock of Separation

Breakups can knock the wind out of us faster than a sucker punch to the heart. In the aftermath of lost love, you may be experiencing symptoms of trauma just as surely as if you had been the victim of a crime. Dr. Judith Herman of Harvard Medical School, author of the groundbreaking book *Trauma and Recovery,* acknowledges the "rupture of attachment" as one of our more serious shocks, putting it on a par with the horror of a bad car accident or the death of a family member. In fact, studies indicate that those in the midst of a painful breakup show the exact same brain patterns as those undergoing the death of a loved one.

We are relational creatures, born for bonding and deeply dependent upon the connections we form. Contrary to our self-image of being fiercely independent and self-sufficient (thank you very much), the latest findings in neuroscience show that we human beings are actually a pretty needy bunch—biologically and psychologically predis-

> *Ever has it been that love knows not its own depth until the hour of separation.*
> KAHLIL GIBRAN

posed to bond in ways that make us strikingly reliant upon those we are close to, and particularly helpless when it comes to regulating our own emotions independent of each other. For this and other reasons, the rending of a relationship can be, for some, no less traumatic than the severing of a limb, and can send us into a tailspin of terrifying proportions. The loss of love is no small matter for the tender human heart and the highly reactive human brain, which is prone to sending urgent signals of distress that trigger dramatic inner experiences. Acute anxiety, an obsessive impulse to connect with your lost love ("just to talk," of course), the vigilant scanning and blind hope of seeing him or her almost everywhere you go, and the desire to curl up and die, as well as the confusing and frightening impulse to lash out and hurt yourself or others.

> *And Silvia is myself:*
> *banish'd from her*
> *Is self from self: a deadly*
> *banishment!*
>
> WILLIAM SHAKESPEARE

And that's all within the first ten minutes of rising each morning.

Whoever coined the phrase "burned in love" knew well of what they spoke. Because the brain does not distinguish between psychic and physical death, and registers rejection in the same area that activates bodily pain, the early stage of a breakup may also be accompanied by disturbing physical symptoms. There's an increase in body temperature that can make your skin feel like it's on fire, a frighteningly fast heart rate, and the release of hormones that can cause sleeplessness, lack of appetite, and hypervigilance, as well as send your immune system plunging. Should your breakup have happened a while ago and you have since moved on to the latter stages of mourning, you may be suffering from a decrease in heart rate and body temperature, leaden inertia in your body, with a continued aversion to eating and the inability to sleep. After doing all you could to convince your love to return and to no avail, you may be living in a bottomless abyss of depression, resignation, and despair with all of the physical sensations that accompany such a state.

Of course, if you're the one leaving, you have the distinct advantage of having prepared yourself for this time. Most likely you've been clandestinely "uncoupling" in your heart and mind for a while before finally gathering the courage to announce you were ending the relationship. Perhaps you've even built bridges of new interests and connections elsewhere in preparation for your departure, to help make your transition smoother. Yet no matter which side of the fence you fall on, the end of love can be crushingly hard on the heart.

A breakup is one of our more underrated traumas, and there are surprisingly few resources for those suffering from the bone-crunching shock of it. To not be chosen by the one you've chosen, to be abandoned by the one who kept you safe against the world, to be unwanted and rejected by the one who knew you best, or to have the one you chose not show up in ways that would have al-

Sorrow was like the wind. It came in gusts.
MARJORIE KINNAN RAWLINGS

lowed your relationship to work—these are often alarming and overwhelming experiences. They can unleash storms of sorrow that threaten to engulf you. Caught in the quicksand of despair, it can seem as though these larger-than-life feelings have taken over, leaving you helpless to simply "move on" as others might suggest.

Rating Your Trauma

As there are different levels of trauma for the survivors of car crashes, so too are there for those undergoing a romantic split. To take this metaphor to the extreme, the mild Fender

Bender Breakup might be where the relationship ends after a few months of dating. With a bright beginning and high hopes for the future, the relationship fizzles out or simply fails to take hold. Perhaps she starts dating someone new. Or maybe he stops calling as often, slipping out the back door and underfeeding the connection until it just kind of flatlines and falls away. This is a 2, 3, or 4 out of a possible 10 on the Bad Breakup Scale of traumatic events.

The second type we might call a Single Car Collision Breakup, where a subtle yet pervasive lack of emotional attunement comes to characterize the connection. This misalignment characterizes the relationship more than accessibility, responsiveness, and engagement, which are the elements needed to sustain a loving union. The critical question "Are you there for me?" that holds couples together over time is answered more often than not with a vague and somewhat distracted "Not really." Usually the eating away of engagement happens when one partner undergoes a shift in core values. He or she grows to care about things that are foreign, and perhaps even somewhat threatening, to their partner, widening the gulf between them until eventually it is too cavernous to cross, leaving one or both too alone to be inspired to continue. The multiple mini rejections leading up to this split make it on some level predictable, lessening the shock factor a bit yet making your loss no easier to endure. Let's call this a 5, 6, or 7 trauma on the Bad Breakup Scale, dependent on the financial and social implications of cutting the ties that bind.

Then there's the more typical Head-On Collision Breakup, where the intensely contentious conflicts in communication finally get the best of one or both of you. Characterized by power struggles, unresolved conflicts, and highly reactive and enmeshed dynamics that easily spiral downward into the hurling

of hurtful words and wounded, sullen silences, these relationships are like battlefields. Both parties have done too many
tours of duty and have been living for long periods of time with
continual traumatic and disturbing events. At some point, one
of you finally gives up and throws in the towel. You may have
years invested in this relationship and much that you have co-
created. Sorting through the spoils of all you've built together
seems like a momentous task, and one that can be filled with
fear and the impulse to hoard and withhold. This may rank on
the Bad Breakup Scale of trauma anywhere between a 6 and a
10, depending upon all the implications of your loss, as well as
whether or not you saw it coming.

And finally, there is what I call the shattering Hit-and-Run
Breakup. This is for sure a 9 or 10 on the scale, because you
just didn't see it coming. Or if you did, you were too busy trying to avert impending doom to see things as they really were.
Unwilling to face the red flags, and in the unfortunate habit of
minimizing the evidence that life was not as it appeared, this
breakup is the betrayal that blindsides you, the lies that drop
the bottom out of your world, or the deceitful destructive behaviors that seem to turn your love into a laughingstock.

Whichever category your breakup falls into, all of them deliver a traumatic blow, and you need to be lovingly tended to in
order to ensure a robust recovery. For what happens at the end
of love will define life moving forward, either leaving your life
dismally contracted and diminished, or beautifully expanded
and enhanced. I think it's obvious which direction we're hoping you'll choose to go in.

ASK YOURSELF:

On a scale of 1 to 10, with 1 being hardly at all and 10 being completely and totally, rate your own level of trauma by asking yourself, "How traumatized am I by this breakup?"

The Alarming Absence of Safety

If love provides us shelter from the storms of life, where can we turn when our most intimate relationship *becomes* the menacing threat? Our romantic relationships are the sun we orbit around, the air we breathe, and the very home of our heart. When that home is compromised, it can be as if a thief stole into our bedroom late at night while we lay sleeping, and maliciously ransacked our most private and treasured possessions. On some level, all breakups are a violation; in the midst of love's meltdown, we are evicted from our emotional home, which can leave us feeling deeply unsafe, vulnerable, lost, and afraid.

Normally, under such trying circumstances we might turn to our faith to help us find a way through the briarpatch of grief. Yet, the end of love often includes a deep spiritual disorientation, as everything we thought we knew about how life is supposed to go is now upside down and sideways. In a breakup, the very framework of how we make sense of our lives is seriously shaken, leaving many unable to seek solace in the faith-based practices that once brought clarity and comfort.

I recall Dara, a thirty-two-year-old devout Christian who'd suffered a particularly traumatic breakup from the man she'd given her virginity to after many years of waiting for "the one," and who dismissed her soon afterward with a mere text message. She recounted her inability to pray or attend church services for an entire year. While intellectually she knew it was her former boyfriend who had disappointed her, she could not help but feel betrayed by a God who did not protect her from this brutally unkind man. At the very moment Dara needed her faith the most, she was unable to access it. Feeling so terribly let down by life, all she believed to be true had fractured into a million little fragments that she could not piece together again. Psychologists call this a "schema fracture," when our worldview is found to be insufficient to deal with the trauma at hand; when we experience a schema fracture, it feels as though the very ground beneath our feet has crumbled, leaving us in free fall.

Experts tell us that in the aftermath of a traumatic event, our first task will be to restore a sense of safety. Yet in the days, weeks, and months after a bad breakup, we've not only lost our safe place in the arms of our beloved—and in a friendly, fair, and ordered universe—but we may also be struggling with scary impulses to hurt ourselves or others, leaving us also strangely unsafe with ourselves. Our fears are not unfounded. Even the most psychologically sophisticated among us can look back at things we've said or done in a moment of upset that horrify us now. Behaviors that cause us to cringe years later as we ask ourselves, "What the hell was I *thinking*?" The truth is, we weren't.

In his book *Emotional Intelligence,* author Daniel Goleman explains what happens when we're hijacked by the reactive part of our brain during a life-threatening event, which the brain can perceive a breakup to be. As alarm bells go off, urgent messages initiate the release of fight-or-flight hormones that mobilize movement before rational thought. With radically impaired judgment that can render us unable to gauge consequences clearly, we're apt to act without conscience and/or respond without regard to normal ethical considerations. Consider my normally principled student Tania, who spends her days doing statistical research on high-profile psychological studies at a major university. In the aftermath of her husband's affair that led him to leave her, she used her sharp analytical mind to figure out the password to his e-mail account and began obsessively cyberstalking him, desperate to understand how this happened. In describing it, she says she lost any sense of an internal compass, and she felt unable to manage her overwhelming emotions, which would compel her to spend hours each evening at the computer reading and rereading his e-mails, past and present.

You, too, may be feeling overwhelmed and a little out of control right now. Having lost your emotional home, disoriented and abandoned, you may be flooded with big emotions driving you to act out, perhaps even compelling you to self-medicate with alcohol, drugs, casual sex, or binge shopping. What can support us in de-escalating such live-wire emotions in a healthier way is a surprisingly simple practice: *labeling our feelings.* Research shows it is highly effective at helping us respond rationally when in the midst of stressful life experiences.

Social psychologist Dr. Matthew Lieberman of UCLA spearheaded a study where he and his colleagues scanned the brains of thirty people who were shown pictures of faces expressing strong emotions, such as sorrow and despair. Initially, activity in the amygdala, a part of the brain that is associated with fear, panic, and other intense emotions, increased dramatically. Yet, when people were able to connect a word with a facial expression, such as the word *anger* to describe an angry face, brain activity decreased significantly. Dr. Lieberman concludes that the ability to label our feelings "seems to dampen down the response in these basic emotional circuits of the brain. What lights up instead is the right ventrolateral prefrontal cortex, the part of the brain that controls impulses." Apparently, the unassuming act of putting a label on each of our feelings, called "affect labeling" by psychologists, lowers arousal and puts us back in the driver's seat of our lives. To the extent that you can name your big and overwhelming feelings, you will begin feeling safe in your own skin again. You will be home again.

To help you to "contain the crazy" and talk yourself off the ledge when needed, thus ensuring you don't do anything you may later regret, I offer the following practice. It will help you return to a saner, *safer* part of your brain. Once there, you can respond with the intelligence, dignity, wisdom, and grace you'd hope to embody in life. Rather than your feelings having *you*, you instead can have your feelings.

··

Creating an Inner Sanctuary of Safety with Tonglen

This simple yet potent practice is designed to help you hold and contain your own inner experience when you feel emotionally overwhelmed. It was co-developed with my colleague and teaching partner of nearly a decade, Claire Zammit.*

In this version of the practice, I've added a component from the ancient Tibetan Buddhist exercise of Tonglen that is incredibly useful when the emotions you're experiencing are more than you can bear.

1. **Become Still.** Find a quiet space to sit for a few minutes. If it is safe to do so, close your eyes and take a deep breath, as though you could breathe all the way down into your hips. Moving into a place of deep listening and receptivity, become aware of the feelings

---

* Originally called the "Daily Power Practice," this was offered as part of the curriculum for the Feminine Power Transformative Courses for Women (see www.FemininePower .com). The practice has its roots in the teachings of Dr. Stephen Gilligan's Self-Relations Psychotherapy.

and sensations in your body and release any tension you might be holding.

2. **Step Back from Your Feelings.** Imagine being able to step back from your many thoughts and feelings, and notice there's a part of you able to simply witness yourself having these thoughts and feelings with a deep sense of care, compassion, and curiosity. Notice that this witness within has access to wisdom and maturity and is able to see what's happening in your life from a larger and more well-informed perspective.

3. **Connect with a Deeper, Wider Center Within.** Keep breathing. As you do, become aware that there is a center within you that is deeper and wider than the feelings you're having, where you can know and experience, if only for a brief moment, that you're okay in spite of all you are going through.

4. **Extend Love to the Part of You Suffering.** From this deeper, mature, and wise center within, extend love to the part of you that is feeling overwhelmed with negative emotions. Give this hurting part of you your full attention while staying identified with your mature and wise witness self. Notice where in your body you are holding these difficult emotions, and offer this suffering part of you support and compassion.

5. **Welcome In and Mirror Your Feelings.** With deep kindness and compassion, ask yourself the following question:

"What are you feeling, sweetheart?"

Listen closely for the response and then lovingly mirror it back by saying to yourself:

"I can see that you're feeling _____ [sad, enraged, hopeless, used, etc.]."

Note: Try broadening your emotional vocabulary by stretching to name the specific feeling you're having. For example, rather than just saying "depressed," look to find a word that more accurately names your experience, such as *despondent, desperate,* or *hopeless.* (See the list below to help you with this.)

Continue asking the question "What are you feeling, sweetheart?" until all of your feelings have been named and mirrored.

6. **Breathe Out a Blessing.** For each feeling you identify, on your next in-breath, breathe that feeling straight into the center of your heart, fully welcoming it, and on the out-breath, breathe out a prayer and blessing for yourself and all beings throughout the world who are suffering with this exact same feeling in this very moment. Repeat until all the feelings you are currently experiencing have been tended to.

7. **Name and Mirror Your Needs.** Now, with deep kindness and compassion, ask yourself the following question:

"What do you need, sweetheart?"

Listen closely for the response and then lovingly mirror it back by saying to yourself:

"I can see that you need _____ *[love, closure, an apology, justice, safety, support, comfort, to be seen, to be heard, etc.]."*

Note: While it may be tempting to jump into action to try to fulfill your needs, please recognize that the simple act of attending to yourself is what is most important. Not every need can be met immediately, but all can be counted as valid or worthy of your attention. This is particularly vital if the person you loved was incapable or unwilling to tend to your needs or take them seriously.

Continue asking the question "What do you need, sweetheart?" until all of your needs have been named and mirrored.

For a free audio download of this practice, please go to www.ConsciousUncoupling.com/StepOnePractice.

To help you with more accurate emotional labeling, I offer the following list of feelings you might be experiencing at this time:

Abandoned	Fearful	Paranoid
Afraid	Frustrated	Pitiful
Alienated	Furious	Regretful
Ambivalent	Gloomy	Rejected
Angry	Grieved	Remorseful
Annihilated	Guilty	Resentful
Anxious	Hateful	Resigned
Ashamed	Heavyhearted	Ripped Off
Bitter	Hopeless	Sad
Broken	Horrified	Shattered
Bereft	Humiliated	Sorrowful
Contemptuous	Hysterical	Terrified
Devalued	Insecure	Troubled
Disappointed	Jealous	Unloved
Disgusted	Loathing	Unwanted
Disrespected	Longing	Used
Distressed	Lonely	Violated
Embarrassed	Lost	Vulnerable
Enraged	Lovesick	Weak
Envious	Miserable	Worried

When you're willing to be with your experience, simply naming your feelings and needs without frantically trying to get rid of them, you're practicing what Buddhists call "mindfulness." It is neither passive nor active, but a deep honoring of your own humanity as you come to terms with the vulnerabilities of having a heart that loves.

By resolving to stay present with yourself and refusing to

shut down and dissociate, your breakup becomes an initiation into greater wholeness, rather than the source of brokenness and fragmentation. While we can't spare you the anguish of a hurting heart, by turning toward your inner experience rather than away from it, you can at least put your grief to good use.

Ineffective grieving happens when you allow your pain to calcify your heart closed and fixate your identity as someone who is alone, unwanted, or abused. It threatens to doom you to living a contracted, lessened life for months or years to come. Effective grieving, however, turns the love you've been giving another toward yourself. You can begin tending to the soft spots of your own tender heart, causing a bittersweet breakthrough in your ability to love yourself even when someone else refuses to. When you use the sheer force of your sorrow to crack open your heart, it promises to drop you down into a deeper capacity for compassion and care for all living beings. You become initiated into your own humanity in a way that connects you to all life.

Such is the paradox of grief. It holds the power to either destroy or to save you. Which one is up to you.

> This being human is a guest house.
> Every morning a new arrival.
> A joy, a depression, a meanness,
> some momentary awareness comes
> as an unexpected visitor. . . .
> Be grateful for whatever comes,
> because each has been sent
> as a guide from beyond.
>
> RUMI

> So much that was beautiful and so much that was hard to bear. Yet whenever I showed myself ready to bear it, the hard was directly transformed into the beautiful.
>
> ETTY HILLESUM

What's Right About Rage?

This was never going to be an easy time. Yet, every strong emotion has at its root the seeds of our awakening. By learning to hold our larger-than-life emotions from a deeper center within, we have the opportunity to harvest the potential for growth that is inherent in each. What makes the emotion of rage particularly promising is the huge amount of energy it offers to effect positive change. As you transform the force of fury into a powerful stand to be valued, loved, respected, and honored by both yourself and others, and determinedly declare, "I will no longer tolerate *this* in my life!," you can emancipate yourself from decades of disappointing patterns in love.

> *Bitterness is like cancer. It eats upon the host. But anger is like fire. It burns it all clean.*
>
> MAYA ANGELOU

Much of what can tip us into a frenzy of anger is the way a breakup can re-wound us in ways similar to how we were hurt long ago. This re-wounding is felt as the ultimate betrayal. Your lover was the one person in the world who was supposed to fix your heart of old hurts, not rip the scab off the wound and cause you to bleed all over again. You trusted this person, and opened up your life, bed, psyche, and heart. Yet, rather than save you from past disappointments, he let you down in much the same ways that others have. It is the ultimate bait and switch. Where once he was Jesus, now he's Judas. Where she was the Eve to your Adam, now she's just plain evil.

Nothing inspires rage like a good betrayal—unless, of course, you've been rejected. Few events can ignite wrath in quite the way that rejection can. "Hell hath no fury like a woman *scorned*," astutely observed English playwright William Congreve. Not a woman argued with, one who can't get her own way, or even one who is heartsick over her lover's bad behavior. What inspires outrage in us all, both women and men alike, is to be rejected and abandoned by the one we love. It plunges us into a fight-or-flight response that floods our body with tidal waves of adrenaline and stress hormones, inducing an arousal state of energy surges that are nearly impossible to hold.

Buddhist monk Thich Nhat Hanh likened anger to garbage, yet recognized that it takes garbage to make compost, and compost to make a flower: "I recognize that there is garbage in me and I am going to transform this garbage into nourishing compost that can make love appear." While all feelings on the anger spectrum—from annoyed, to resentful, to pissed off, to enraged—can be hard to contain without reactively generating more toxicity and pain, the benefits of harnessing rage and using it to catapult a breakthrough in your life are unparalleled. For big rage means there's big energy to fuel the determination and drive required to make important life changes. Changes you've probably been trying to make for a really long time.

> *Sorrow fully accepted brings its own gifts. For there is an alchemy in sorrow. It can be transmuted into wisdom, which, if it does not bring joy, can yet bring happiness.*
>
> PEARL S. BUCK

How long have you known that you should have better boundaries? Or wrestled with the awareness that you should speak up for yourself more? Or known you needed to give up being a people pleaser and stop overgiving as a way to try to prove your value? Truthfully, until your ways of selling yourself short in intimate relationships catch up with you, and slap you hard across the face, all your plans for how you might want to improve how you behave when you're in love are kind of just theoretical in nature.

What's healthy about your anger is that it can inspire you to reclaim your rights: your right to be supported; your right to have a voice, to take up space, to be heard; and your right to be treated with dignity, honor, respect, and love. If you've been particularly co-dependent in your relationships, putting other people's feelings and needs before your own, withholding the truth for fear of upsetting others, unwilling to ask questions or set proper boundaries, all for the terror of being abandoned, then your rage is like the life-affirming cry of a newborn who is smacked into its first deep breath. Something in you is waking up, and you want to nourish that life-giving impulse and bring it into the light of day to fully make it your own.

Clearly, uncontained anger gets us into big-time trouble. Yet, rather than act it out, try dancing it, singing it, painting it, or running it around the track instead. Anger is not just an emotional tidal wave; it's also a physical surge, and it needs physical expression to find its way home to a constructive purpose. When you learn to harness and sponsor the impulse that's driving your rage—transforming your ferocity into a stand you take for your value and your right to love and be loved, as well as into a commitment you now make to your own life—all heaven can break loose, as you become free to expand beyond the woman or man you've known yourself to be before this time.

ASK YOURSELF:
"What's waking up in me as a result of my rage? How can I use the intensity of this energy to fuel positive change in my life? What rights am I now willing to stand up for?"

The Up Side of Feeling Down

Few events remind us how fragile we are than the death of intimate love. We human beings live so much in the shelter of one another that the loss of a relationship can be an eviction into exile. We're all vulnerable to our dependence upon each other, yet many believe this reliance to be a sign of weakness or immaturity. We assume psychological health to mean we are self-regulating and self-sustaining, without the pesky need for other people getting in our way. Yet, nature is not aligned with this perspective, suggesting instead that we are interdependent creatures who rely upon each other by organic design.

A number of scientists now purport that our neuro-physiological stability is dependent upon synchronizing with those we're closest to, as we fortify one another's neural rhythms in the collaborative ballet of loving connection. Scientists call this mutually synchronized exchange of energy "limbic regulation," which describes the continual cooperative fine-tuning of biological functions such as heart rate, blood pressure, body temperature, immune function, oxygen saturation, even sugar and hormone levels, among other things. The simple act of sleeping together is a hotbed of exchange. Two different studies compared premature babies who slept with regular teddy bears to those who slept with a "breathing bear"—a stuffed animal that was hooked up to a ventilator and set to inflate and deflate at a rhythmic rate similar to the infants. The babies connected with the breathing bears slept more calmly, and demonstrated better respiration than the infants who slept with the non-breathing bears. Although we grow up to be markedly more self-regulating as we mature, we remain interdependent throughout our lives.

In the 1990s, Dr. Jaak Panksepp, a psychologist, neuroscientist, and emeritus professor at Bowling Green State University, began doing studies on the feeling states of animals, recognizing that our understanding of our own human emotions can be enhanced by studying our furry friends. One area he explored extensively was what happens when an attachment bond is broken. He did this by studying the behaviors of a puppy when she is taken from her mother. First, she will whine, then cry, and then search frantically for Mama before finally collapsing into a passive state of depression and despair, mirroring the behavior of a person in the grip of grieving the loss of an attachment figure. Panksepp's conclusion was that the same neural systems that guarantee connection also plunge us toward depression in response to separation from someone we are closely bonded with. When we lose a relational home it's not pathological to slide into melancholia. It's normal.

Neuropsychologist Mark Solms interprets Dr. Panksepp's findings by suggesting that the lifeless, lethargic apathy of depression is nature's way of slowing us down so we can't move away too quickly from the source of our sustenance. You might think of your feelings of depression as life's way of preventing you from moving away in haste from your loving connection; it's an existentially enforced waiting period that mandates you to take downtime for reflection on the actions you're taking, the choices you're making, the changes needing to be made, and the lessons needing to be learned. Connection is at the very core of what it is to be human, and nature errs on the side of attachment.

If nothing else, the depression you may feel at love's end is a tribute to the value of love, admonishing you to hold your exchange as sacred and not easily toss it aside. While we may live in a disposable society, there is nothing disposable about the relationships we form with one another. Even if you're feeling devalued and dismissed by the one you've loved, your depression is telling you that the bond you shared mattered. Even if your former partner tries to take a shortcut out of grief by shutting down and minimizing your love, your body, laden with the lethargy of depression, knows differently, and vehemently refuses to be rushed to closure too quickly.

These findings mirror the teachings of bestselling author Elisabeth Kübler-Ross, herself uncoupled from the father of her two children with whom she remained friends until he died some twelve years later. Most known for identifying the five stages of grief experienced by those dealing with death (denial, anger, bargaining, depression, and acceptance), Dr. Kübler-Ross recognized that all the losses or rejections that remind us of our existential aloneness and that our stability in life is precarious at best follow a similar path. Yet, what differentiates depression from the earlier stages of grief is that it's about coming to terms with the reality of your losses now, in present time, as opposed to denial, anger, and bargaining, which are all concerned with sorting through, integrating, or holding on to the past. Though we may believe that slipping into a depression is bad, it can actually mean you're heading in the right direction by grappling with life on its own terms, as you crawl your way toward grief's final resting place: acceptance.

As difficult as it may be to tolerate the shadow emotions of love, it's often best to let your heart be. Stop pushing to get rid of sorrow too quickly with a steel will. Rather, make time to cry, pausing to notice how desperately your body needs to sing its sad song without your trying to muscle your way around and beyond it. Something within you

> *Those who do not know how to weep with their whole heart do not know how to laugh either.*
> GOLDA MEIR

is yearning to be born, and it may need the purging of a thousand tears to do so.

If you're like many, all your life you may have been side-stepping solitude, going to remarkable lengths to avoid being left alone—throwing yourself under the bus time and time again to make sure that someone would always be there to help you pick up the pieces. Yet, why not now let that someone be you? Don't abandon yourself; don't numb out in the hundreds of little ways we can that turn us away from ourselves. Be there for yourself in the ways you wished your former partner had been. What were the commitments you wished this person had made to you? Make them conscious, then close your eyes, put your hand over your heart, and fiercely make these commitments to yourself. Do it now when you need to hear those words of solace and support more than anything.

It's time for you to give yourself the love, attention, loyalty, and care you've been trying to get from others your whole life. Grief has you gripped tightly by the ankles, and she may not let you go too soon. There's nowhere to go but home to yourself. This simple gesture of giving yourself your full attention when sorrow is shaking you to the bone promises to carve depth and kindness into the core of who you are—more than anything else I know. It's a wildly painful but exquisitely liberating experience to let yourself surrender to the sheer vulnerability of what it is to be human, and allow yourself to love the defenseless softness of your own underbelly. For your tender need to love and be loved is the most beautiful thing about you.

ASK YOURSELF:

"What commitments do I wish my former partner had made to me that I can now make to myself?"

Note: Breakups can be so unbearably painful that some may feel suicidal or homicidal. If you find yourself wanting to hurt yourself or others, please call the Samaritans at 08457909090 from the UK or Lifeline at 13 11 14 from Australia. Help is close by.

What Are You Making This Mean?

You can't believe everything you think and feel, especially now when your thoughts and feelings are so reactive and extreme and easily based on misunderstandings and misinterpretations about what's happening, or what may happen moving forward. Fear is a breeding ground for mistaken meaning, and many of your big feelings have at their core erroneous assumptions. Let's get something clear: Just because you feel all alone in the world, does not mean that you actually are. Just because you're convinced no one will ever love you again, does not mean that no one ever will. Just because you think yourself to be inferior, damaged, or too flawed to love again, does not mean that it's true.

The wounds of love cut most where we're already weak. The hurt in your heart is likely not new. You've been here before, perhaps many times. Only now you've more evidence for your sad story of how love goes for you. If you close your eyes for a moment, you might even be able to recall the first time it happened. You were young. Maybe so young you didn't yet have language to name your pain, for it may have happened while still in the crib. I call it your *source-fracture wound,* the original break in your heart from long ago. It may have happened in an instant—a little rejection, a shocking abandonment, or a slight misattunement that suddenly made you realize how alone you were in this world. Or perhaps it was a bit-by-bit splintering, as over the years you met with an intermittent meanness, an unpredictable but repetitive abuse, or a neglect that stole your childhood inches at a time. Wherever, however, or whenever it happened, one thing we can assume is that no adult helped you make accurate meaning of your confusing and painful experience. No grown-up sat you down and lovingly said, "No, honey, it's not that you're stupid. It's that your big brother is scared and insecure." "It's not that you don't matter, angel. It's that Daddy has a drinking problem and needs help." "It's not that you're not enough. It's that Mommy has clinical depression, dear, and it's neither your fault nor yours to fix." Without this mature presence to help explain to you what was happening in your little world, you probably came to some pretty strong and wrong conclusions about who you were and what was possible for you to have in life. And those conclusions became a habit of consciousness, a filter through which you interpret and then respond to the events of your life, making your grief all the more complex. It's one thing to be sad about losing someone you love. It's another thing entirely to assume you lost that love because you're fundamentally unlovable.

Much like a pigeon programmed to find her way back to where she began, your source-fracture story is the home base in consciousness you return to again and again, with each re-wounding. Under each of your difficult feelings lies an ancient assumption: that it's dangerous to love, that you can never get what you truly need from others, that everyone leaves no matter how great you are, or that it's your destiny to be alone. Much of your pain and despair is a response to the automatic meaning you revert to when disappointed, compounding the grief you're in and making this whole experience twice as hard.

> *Feel the feelings. Drop the story.*
> PEMA CHODRON

Luckily, however, although you may feel like an abandoned, unwanted, or unloved child, you're actually an accomplished, smart, developed, and very resourceful adult. Though a crowd of lies comes pounding on the door of your consciousness, trying to explain the mess you're in, it's the adult part of you that can sort through the confusion to make more empowered meaning of your experience. Imagine that at the center of you there is a wellspring of wisdom beyond your years, continually whispering words of deep discernment and astute understanding about what's happening in your life. This wise, soulful, and deeply intuitive part of you is able to see your suffering from a larger perspective that is outside of your forever sad source-fracture story. It is the adult part of you that knows that although life is not always fair, it is fundamentally good to be alive. That when one door closes, another will soon open. That you're not missing your former love as much as you're missing the person you thought he or she was. That no matter how much this breakup hurts, it's best for everyone that the relationship ends. Learning to speak to yourself from this adult center, and offering encouraging words of wisdom when negative emotions are threatening to get the best of you, will help you find your way home to wholeness.

....

Creating a Mentoring Mantra

This practice was originally created by my colleague Claire Zammit and has been modified for the Conscious Uncoupling process.*

Once you're able to hold and contain your overwhelming, big

---

* Originally titled "Transformative Self Talk," this practice was first created by Claire Zammit for students of our Feminine Power 9 Month Mastery Program.

feelings, this practice will take you one step further by helping you mentor the part of yourself that's making false meaning of your breakup. (For example: "I'll always be alone," "No one will ever love me as much as she did," or "I can't ever have what I want.") I encourage you to use this practice when you're anxious or distressed and need to be restored to emotional balance.

1. **Name Your Assumptions.** Step back from your emotions, and see if you can identify the underlying assumptions that are driving you to feel the way you do. What are you making this breakup mean about you? Or about your life?

   For example: "There must be something wrong with me"; "Lovers will always disappoint me and leave"; "I can't make it in life without him"; or "Love is for other people, not me."

2. **Challenge Your Assumptions.** Question your assumptions. Push back against their certainty with a compassionate ferocity that will not allow you to be dominated by fear. Speak to yourself as though you were your own loving mentor and guide with great wisdom and insight to offer.

   For example: "You did make some mistakes, honey, it's true. But that doesn't mean that there's anything wrong with you"; "Even though it feels like no one will ever love you like she did, we can't actually know for sure if that's true"; or "Love isn't easy for anyone, sweetie. Everyone I know has been disappointed in love at least once, even those who are happily partnered now."

3. **Offer Yourself Wise Lessons of Life.** From this deeper, wiser, more mature center within, lovingly offer a life lesson that demonstrates a nuanced understanding of what you're going through.

   For example: "I know you're hurting, honey, but hurt is the risk we take when we open our heart to care about someone. Everyone gets his or her heart hurt at one time or another. I promise you, you'll heal."

Reassure yourself, offering encouragement and a perspective that
will enable you to trust life even in the aftermath of profound
disappointment.

4. **Create Your Mentoring Mantra.** Using these wise words of comfort,
encouragement, and support, I invite you to create a self-soothing
mentoring mantra that you can say quietly to yourself over and
over again until you are restored to emotional balance.

For example: "You're okay, sweetheart. This is just what a breakup
feels like. This pain will soon be gone yet the wisdom gained will
long remain. I love you."

....

You've got a hot potato on your hands. The grief that's
weighing on your heart will be nearly impossible to heal without learning to relate to yourself in these kind and nurturing
ways. Your alternative, of course, is to try numbing your discomfort by downing a bottle of wine, eating a dozen donuts,
or chain-smoking your way through the day. It's your choice.
But pain is a demanding taskmaster, and you're going to have to
tame her in order not to be taken out. Imagine you're in what
my friend Lauren Frances calls "romantic rehab." You need to
be organizing your life around self-care in concrete ways. Stick
to a routine, spend time with people who love you, eat fresh
and healthy foods, find a good coach or therapist, take walks
in nature, and read a great novel with characters you love. At
the end of this chapter are some suggestions for self-care. Take
them seriously. This is no time to neglect yourself.

ASK YOURSELF:

"What words of comfort, strength, wisdom, and love can I say to
mentor and soothe myself when I'm feeling overwhelmed?"

"What can I do to demonstrate profound levels of self-care in this time of heartache and hurt?"

Making Something Beautiful of This

In 1995, Dr. Lawrence Calhoun, professor of psychology at the University of North Carolina at Charlotte, coined the term "post-traumatic growth" to describe resilience that not just allows one to come back from a crisis but to come back changed for the better. "It's not about being resilient," he says, "Resilience is when you get punched, stagger, and then jump right back up. Post-traumatic growth is different—when you stand back up, you are transformed."

Well-known Buddhist nun Pema Chodron, who has contributed so much goodness to this world with her bestselling book *When Things Fall Apart*, speaks candidly about how her divorce catalyzed her spiritual awakening and, consequently, her life's work. With humor and humility, she shares about the hatred that consumed her after her husband announced he was having an affair and wanted a divorce. At the time she was a schoolteacher, and raising two children from a previous marriage, which had also ended poorly. In the months that followed, she was filled with a bitter rage that egged her on to act out in mean-spirited ways. Before this time, she'd known herself to be a warmhearted and optimistic person, and she felt ill prepared for this depth of darkness that consumed her with hate-filled fantasies of revenge and retaliation. The incessant and urgent nature of these destructive

> *When you have a great pain in your life, you need a greater purpose.*
> MILLARD FULLER

impulses forced her to actively seek solid ground upon which to safely stand. Dabbling in various spiritual disciplines to try to find relief, she came upon an article written by meditation master Chögyam Trungpa that gave her a way to make sense of her experience. In it he claims that there is nothing wrong with negativity in and of itself, calling our darker emotions "a juicy and creative energy that can wake you up." He asserted it's the spin-off from negativity that poses the actual problem—the endless blaming and the constant raging. The energy-driving negativity, however, is not bad and can actually be helpful. This realization enticed her to begin a path of Buddhism. Within a year she'd become a nun, and she has since gone on to help hundreds of thousands of people around the world to find peace and deeper contentment in life.

Only when it is dark enough can you see the stars.

MARTIN LUTHER KING JR.

Breakups change us. They hold the potential of helping us make great leaps forward in ways we'd not otherwise have done. You will never return to being the person you were before. Yet, whether you change for better or for worse is your choice to make. Your biggest clue as to whether or not this ending will expand you toward the realization of your highest potentials and calling in life, or narrow it down for years to come, will be the conclusions you're coming to in response to your suffering. In the face of great pain, some will determine to never love like this again, or will conclude that they just aren't good at having intimate relationships, or that romantic love is for others, not them. The end of love is a crossroads, and there will be those who go on to live lesser lives in the aftermath of heartbreak. My hope is that you are not one of them.

There's no better time to take a stand for your life than this very moment. You want to let the agony you're in wash you squeaky clean of every unconscious, fear-driven, and habitual way you've shown in life as a dimmed-down, inauthentic version of yourself. You want to take your hurt and transform it into a huge commitment to realize your potential for liberation, health, happiness, contribution, and the fulfillment of love in your life.

> *The world breaks everyone and afterward many are strong at the broken places.*
> ERNEST HEMINGWAY

You may not care all that much about becoming who you have the potential to be in this moment, because all you want to do is to go back to being the person you *were.* But life has seen to it that you can't, and there is nowhere to go but forward. You're in that nasty in-between place. But don't you dare get stuck and die in that birth canal. Like a mama on the day of delivery, you've got to push yourself out the other side of this. As Winston Churchill once said, "If you're going through hell, *keep going.*" When struggling through the dark and snaking tunnel of lost love, you want to fiercely determine you're going to make it to the light, and then do everything in your power to make sure you do.

Whenever life hands us a big disappointment, we have a choice to make. With all my heart, I implore you to choose life, goodness, truth, beauty, and love. I promise, while you may be filled with regrets right now, this is one choice that you will never be sorry you made.

ASK YOURSELF:

"What intention can I set that will support me to use the pain I'm in to transform my life in positive ways?"

STEP 1 SELF-CARE SUGGESTIONS
(Take at least 2 each day)

1. **Keep a journal that is for your eyes only.** Write out your rage, disappointment, indignation, embarrassment, sorrow, guilt, and horror. Let yourself express the entire spectrum of your emotions, censoring nothing, judging nothing, and turning away from nothing.
2. **Move your body, even if it's just for a few moments.** Walk, stretch, run, swim, ride your bike, do yoga, jump on a trampoline, skate, lift weights, bounce a ball, dance, etc.
3. **Listen to music** that mirrors your emotions and sing along at the top of your lungs.
4. **Look for opportunities to offer kindness to others,** particularly to those who may be suffering even more than you are.
5. **Visit great art** to remember that so many of the things you are feeling right now have been felt throughout the ages by those who created something beautiful of their suffering. Go to the symphony, opera, theater, or a museum.
6. **Sit under the stars and turn your face upward** to remember how vast the universe is and how many possibilities it holds for love.

NOTE TO COUPLES DOING THE PROGRAM TOGETHER

In this first step of the Conscious Uncoupling process, take a more formal stance with one another, stepping back from your normal level of engagement in a way that allows each of you to come to terms with the changes you are going through on your own. Do not look to be loved, validated, or comforted by your former partner before loving, validating, and comforting yourself and/or seeking outside support to help you do so. Be exceptionally polite, thoughtful, and respectful, yet do not "care-take" each other's difficult feelings. Give one another the time and space to independently deal with what's happening. Be supportive, generous, and kind while at the same time moving into greater levels of autonomy.

reclaim your power and your life

Out with the old, in with the true.

JEFF BROWN

In Step 2 of your Conscious Uncoupling program, you'll let go of being a wounded victim of love and shift your perspective to begin taking personal responsibility for your part in what happened. By doing so, you'll start to see how you have been a source of your own suffering in a way that liberates you from ever repeating this dynamic again, and empowers you to evolve beyond disappointing patterns in love.

In Step 2, Reclaim Your Power and Your Life, you will:

- Let go of being a victim and craft a holistic and accurate breakup narrative that starts you on a path of peace and true completion.
- Reflect on yourself as the source of your experience in a way

that feeds you power and supports you to grow beyond your painful patterns in love.

· Release unconscious and habitual patterns of people pleasing, self-abandoning, overgiving, or tolerating less than you deserve, and begin showing up in ways that are reflective of your true value.

· Learn how to make amends to yourself in a way that frees you from the residue of resentment and regret.

· Evolve beyond the person you were when you created your relationship and discover how you can truly trust yourself to love and be loved again.

You'll need to tell the story: going over it again and again and again in your mind, laboriously trying to piece together a narrative that weaves the fragmented, jagged, and ill-fitting bits of memory and information into one cohesive whole. All the signs you should have seen, all the things you should have known, come sharply into focus as the nebulous details of your intimate life come crashing into conscious awareness. Ruminating upon the subtle clues missed, conversations ill timed, and fatal mistakes only now clear in hindsight, you will try to craft a story you can live with and that will go on to become the legacy of this love affair.

Most likely your tale will be centered on the multiple ways you were misunderstood, mistreated, devalued, and wronged. It may feature the deplorable ways you brought this heartache upon yourself, as you gather rounds of ammunition with which to torture yourself for years to come. The victimized, blaming, and shaming story of your love will go round and round in your mind, building momentum and gaining traction as you struggle to figure out what went wrong, who is to blame, and why. All this ruminating is to try to protect yourself from its ever happening again, for how can you live in a world where all you hold sacred and dear can betray you in an instant? Where your very identity can be stolen out from under you, and where all you have counted on for your future can disappear in a flash?

If you're the one who left, your story may take a different tack. Less shocked and doubled over in pain, you may actually feel euphoric to have finally found the courage and strength to break free of the bonds that constrained you. Yet paving the way for this grand emancipation are the count-

> *When you complain,*
> *you make yourself*
> *into a victim . . .*
> *So change the*
> *situation . . . leave the*
> *situation or accept it.*
> *All else is madness.*
> ECKHART TOLLE

less and covertly logged slights, flaws, failures, and imperfections of your former partner, as for weeks, months, or even years you patiently gathered evidence against him and solidly built your case for why he gave you no choice but to leave. Feeling guilty, but with enough self-righteous indignation to fuel your way forward, your breakup narrative will tell the tale of the many ways you've been underfed, underseen, unappreciated, and alone in this relationship, again from a one-sided and decidedly victimized perspective.

Either way, in an attempt to integrate this breakup into your overwhelmed and fragmented psyche, the majority of your attention will likely be drawn toward pinning blame, as you carefully craft a grievance story that justifies your indignation. And for good reason, too. Your former partner probably did behave like a beast. He let you down. She didn't keep her word. He was deceptive. She was a cheat. What happened *was* most likely crappy, unfair, immoral, or self-serving. She probably does deserve to be run out of town, forced to wear donkey ears and a dunce cap, and branded on her buttocks as a warning to any potential lover she may ever hope to have in her future.

Yet, here's what's *more* true: as long as your attention stays fixated on what he did or didn't do that was shameful, wrong, bad, and immoral, you're not looking to discover all of the covert and toxic ways that you are responsible for the mess you're in. Even if the monster was 97 percent at fault, unless you take ownership of your 3 percent, and figure out how to change your ways of being in a relationship that make you vulnerable to being disempowered, disappointed, or abused in love, you will never be able to trust yourself to fully open up your heart again to another human being.

How's that for inspiring you to take responsibility for yourself as the source of your suffering? So, this question, *Where is my attention?* needs to be your mantra as you continually turn away from the finger pointing that your mind will automatically gravitate toward, and look deeply into the mirror to try to see clearly your part in things, so that you might be liberated to begin doing it differently from now on.

ASK YOURSELF:
"Where is my attention?"

Understanding Yourself as the Source of Your Experience

When we first try to understand ourselves as the source of our suffering, we often begin by asking self-reflective questions that will slide us straight toward shame, self-hatred, and self-blame. I always have to remind people that "What the f—— is wrong with me?" is not a question that will ever lead to positive growth and change. Shame-based questions like "Why can't I ever do anything right?" "Why does everyone always leave me?" "Who's going to love me when I'm this messed up?" "When is life going to cut me a break?" or "How could I be so stupid?" can only serve as further evidence for your faulty source-fracture story and validate the false conclusion that you're somehow cursed when it comes to romantic love.

> *Always the beautiful answer who asks a more beautiful question.*
>
> E.E. CUMMINGS

To break free of relational patterns that left you vulnerable to being hurt and disappointed in love *yet again*—patterns of co-dependency, love addiction, abuse, and/or neglect—you must learn to ask yourself questions that can harvest the growth necessary to ensure you can trust yourself to never, ever do this again. Because for every self-centered, narcissistic man, there's a woman who chronically self-abandons and disappears herself to try to win his favor; and for every judgmental and critical woman, there is an insecure man desperately giving himself away to try to gain her approval. And if you're gay, well . . . you get the point, right? Yes, the other person may be messed up. But your primary focus needs to be on you, so you can discover all the ways you set yourself up to repeat these heart-wrenching, painful patterns.

Your mission right now is to reclaim your power and your life. That can only happen when you start asking yourself questions that inspire you to be ruthlessly honest about all the ways you've been giving your power away, self-sabotaging, turning away from truth, and/or showing up as less than who you are. I

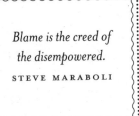

Blame is the creed of the disempowered.
STEVE MARABOLI

know. You suddenly want to put down this book and go for the pint of Häagen-Dazs. Please don't. Stay with me here. For once you allow yourself to clearly see the unconscious ways you've been covertly setting yourself and others up to repeat your sad source-fracture story ad nauseam, you finally gain the ability to make a different choice; because responsible self-reflection is the beginning of reclaiming your power. Yet, if you choose instead to root your story of victimization and build a shrine around it, you'll never access the power you'll need to change your love life in any meaningful way.

Questions that will support you to grow and evolve are going to be ones like:

"How did I give my power away in this relationship, and what can I do to reclaim it?"

"How do I let myself down in ways that are similar to how I feel let down by my former partner?"

"Where was I pulling on my former partner to take care of me in ways I was refusing to take care of myself? What has this cost us both?"

"What were the lies I was telling myself in order to stay in the relationship?"

"How does it work for me to have chosen someone so clearly unavailable?"

"What disappointing story from my past is being repeated here, and how have I behaved in way(s) that covertly re-created it?"

The moment you can tolerate seeing things as they really are, and can hold the complexities of your own inconsistencies and flawed humanity with a tender, humble heart, your life can begin to radically change for the better.

There is always a victim story to be told, and most are exceedingly convincing. When my client Monique's husband of five years, Larry, left her and their three-year old son, Zachary, a child with Down syndrome, not one of their friends or family members understood why. And once he started missing his child-support payments, he gained a reputation as a heartless and selfish man. Even his mother stopped speaking with him during this time. Yet to Monique's credit, she did not take the easy way out for what was obviously bad behavior. While she was understandably upset, before running back to court she paused and deliberately turned her attention toward trying to discover herself as the source of her experience of being undersupported and abandoned by Larry. By doing so, she unleashed a tremendous amount of clarity that has since changed her life.

Monique had a rough ride early in life. Her father was a drug addict and her mother a prostitute, and she was left to fend for herself at a shockingly young age. She has memories of standing in front of an open refrigerator when she was a mere two years old, scouring the shelves for something to eat. Her source-fracture story was that she was all alone in life and that no one ever took care of her, leaving a cavernous hole in her heart that was reopened in numerous ways and with various partners over the years.

Many of us make these kinds of connections where we can see how the painful wounds from our childhoods are played out with our lovers, again and again. Yet, this is as far as most of us get, and we become victims not just of our parents and the partners we choose but also of our own consciousness, which seems to somehow find a way to repeat painful disappointments in

> *Freedom is the willingness to be responsible for ourselves.*
>
> FRIEDRICH NIETZSCHE

spite of all the efforts we make to evolve. Monique, of course, had a sinking moment of despair in seeing how she'd duplicated this dynamic in her former husband's refusal to take care of her and their son.

Yet, I encouraged her to look below the surface beyond any sense of victimization by taking responsibility for the choices she had made that had led to her current state of affairs. And this is when she saw it. There was a part of her that was forever a two-year-old child sitting in the center of the room, holding her breath till she was blue in the face, until someone else came along to take care of her. She admitted that throughout her marriage, she had let this part of herself run the show by refusing to earn money even though her husband had begged her time and time again to go back to work. She insisted he take care of her in ways she really could easily have done herself, particularly before their child was born. Yet once their son came along, she had an excuse to not bother earning money. She was all set to ride on his financial coattails for years to come, when he rebelled and gave her the message loud and clear that he was not about to be the sole support for the two of them for the rest of his life.

> *The most common way people give up their power is by thinking they don't have any.*
>
> ALICE WALKER

It was humbling for Monique to admit how infantile and selfish her behavior had been. Yet it was the first time she'd ever made this toddler part of her conscious. In doing so, she was finally given a choice. Did she want to stay in the middle of the floor (metaphorically speaking), kicking and screaming, and playing out that sad story of deprivation and neglect? Or did she want to cut her childhood losses, take responsibility for her life, and learn to stand in the world as the powerful, resourceful woman she actually was? When we put it this way, it was kind of a no-brainer.

Today, Larry and Monique have a great co-parenting partnership in which they amicably share custody of their son. She financially takes care of herself, and they both contribute to the economic care of their son. She is excelling in her dream career as an entrepreneur and life coach, and she is becoming more and more known for her unique wisdom, bright wit, and sharp intelligence. It's all because, in spite of his obvious guilt, she refused to be a victim, choosing instead to take responsibility for herself.

I encourage you to look below the surface. To stretch beyond the obvious guilt of your former partner, and become deeply curious about all the ways you've covertly re-created a situation that could wound you in ways similar to how you've been wounded in the past. If you're the one who was

> *When we are no longer able to change a situation, we are challenged to change ourselves.*
>
> VIKTOR FRANKL

clearly in the wrong and you're consumed with guilt, then you want to ruthlessly turn toward examining your behavior with a decidedly objective eye, looking to uncover the truth about the choices you made and what was motivating you. It's important we learn to look at our mistakes straight on, and let the consequences of those mistakes touch our hearts. It's called *an awakening of conscience,* and it's a good thing because it means that you're becoming a more wholehearted and mature human being.

By looking to discover yourself as the source of your experience, you're essentially becoming a seeker of truth. Not just your own personal truth, which is important, of course, but also truth from an objective, rather than a subjective, perspective even if that means seeing things about *yourself* that are less than flattering. The rule of thumb: you want to be more interested in developing yourself than you are in defending yourself, more interested in being rigorously honest than being right. Seeing ourselves clearly can be a humbling experience, for sure. Yet, as they say in Alcoholics Anonymous, "You can't save your face and your ass at the same time."

ASK YOURSELF:

"When I stop pointing the finger and look below the surface to examine the actions I took and the choices I made, what can I see about how I am responsible for this situation?"

....

Your Breakup Story: A Creative Exercise

Eventually, you'll want to make sense of what happened by creating a breakup narrative that honors your life together and values all that was learned and gained through your union.

Yet, in this moment, the horror of your breakup may be living in your body as a tension, an ache, a shortness of breath, a heaviness, or a repressed scream. Norwegian painter Edvard Munch created his masterpiece *The Scream* after a two-year love affair with his married cousin ended unhappily, capturing the existential angst of what it can feel like to lose a relationship with someone you love.

As a way to help move the story through you, I invite you to draw, paint, sculpt, or write the horrifying parts of it to rid it from your body. This is where you get to be a victim and capture the dark underbelly of emotions of what it is to be rejected, humiliated, oppressed, abandoned, or abused. See if you can catch the powerlessness, rage, shame, and despair in color, form, or language. Love the pure humanity of your emotions, and do not be concerned with whether or not you are depicting the story accurately. Exaggerate. Embellish. Amplify and inflate. Unleash the hot rage, the dark despair, and the frozen helplessness into a swirl of colors, shadows, shapes, and designs.

By allowing yourself to create uncensored, you are documenting your journey into the depths of your own vulnerable humanity, and helping to move yourself along toward the light of acceptance and integration. When done, place this work on your altar, if you have one, as a symbol of your intention to work this through to a place of conscious completion; or simply in a private, safe place where no one else will see it.

Making Amends to Yourself

By now you may be starting to suspect that the amends you've been hoping to get from your former partner may actually be yours to make to yourself. When Kate, an intelligent and accomplished woman nearing forty, met Jack, she was so swept off her feet that she ended her engagement to a good-hearted man who loved her to pursue the connection. Charming, elegant, wealthy, and irresistibly handsome, Jack dangled the carrot of commitment for five years as Kate gave more and more of herself to the relationship. Leaving her career behind to tend more to his needs, and moving away from her family to be closer to him, she made countless sacrifices, relentlessly trying everything she could to convince him to marry her and give her the family she desired. Yet, when her doctor told her at age forty-four that it was too late for her to bear a child, Jack suddenly decided he was ready to start a family. He soon left Kate for another woman ten years younger, marrying her, and getting his new bride pregnant within the year.

When she first heard the news, she took to her bed for a week. Yet as time went on, her bitterness did not abate. Feeling victimized, resentful, and despondent, she was challenged by the suggestion that she examine her own choices and take responsibility for what had happened, for clearly there was a strong case to be made for what a monster of a man Jack was. Yet, once willing to look for the ways she'd colluded in her own demise, she was flooded with new understanding. To start, she admitted Jack's abandonment of her was a perfect reflection of her own abandonment of herself throughout their entire relationship. Without his giving up much of anything to her as a prerequisite for the many sacrifices she'd made, she'd given up everything—her fiancé, her career, close ties with her family and friends, and even her dream of being a mother. Looking back, she saw countless examples of how she'd overgiven to try to prove her value and convince him to choose her, minimizing her own feelings, needs, and desires; withholding opinions that differed from his and rarely making waves, she desperately tried to be the woman she thought he wanted, essentially disappearing herself. So much that, in the end, there was really no Kate to love. To rub salt in the wound, rumor had it that the woman Jack married had a huge life and career that demanded Jack organize his life around hers for their relationship to work. Jack seemed proud of his new wife, and apparently couldn't do enough to demonstrate his willingness to accommodate the demands of partnering her. While humbled to admit it, Kate saw that it wasn't Jack who needed to make amends to her. It was she who needed to make amends to herself, as she was confronted by the myriad of ways she gave herself and her power away to be in that relationship.

That insight changed her life. Kate set about making amends by setting an intention to outgrow the self-abandoning woman she'd been with Jack. Recognizing that part of her still believed Jack to be the man for her, she took on becoming a wiser, more mature, happier, and healthier version of herself in order to evolve into a woman who would not at all be interested in a man who treated her as poorly as Jack had. Though a high bar to set, Kate let go of overgiving and people pleasing as a way to convince people to like her, and focused on becoming a woman who knew her own mind, lived true to herself, and was organized around the realization of her own potentials, before martyring herself to support those of others. She started setting healthy boundaries with her friends and family, and began sharing her feelings, needs, opinions, and desires with those close to her, with the healthy expectation that they care enough to respond appropriately.

Today Kate is happily married to a kindhearted, successful, and intelligent man. Having adopted twin girls, Kate is now deeply grateful that Jack broke her heart. She's convinced that her resolve to use heartbreak as a wake-up call, running toward her own growth and development like her life depended upon it (for surely it did), is the reason her life is so happy and fulfilling today. She admits that the passive, people-pleasing woman she was with Jack is not a woman she even recognizes anymore. Nor would that version of her have been the right partner for

> *For everything you have missed, you have gained something else; and for everything you gain, you lose something else.*
> RALPH WALDO EMERSON

Jack, who she now believes chose wisely for himself, doing them both a great service in the process.

....

Making Amends to Yourself

To help you evolve beyond being a victim, and start making amends to yourself, I invite you to take your journal and reflect upon the following questions:

1. **Who Do You Resent and for What?** Notice the resentments you're holding toward your former partner (and anyone else involved in your breakup) and write them down. Don't censor yourself, or try to talk yourself out of your suffering, anguish, and rage. Write it down as it lives in your body.

   For example: "The bastard ruined my life," "The witch destroyed my capacity to ever trust anyone again," "That thief stole my final childbearing years from me." "I hate myself for sabotaging my chance for happiness."

2. **What Can You Take Responsibility for in Each Situation?** Step back and shift your perspective. Recognizing that taking responsibility is not an admission that something is your fault, nor the condoning of bad behavior, look to see how you may have contributed to things happening the way they did.

   ASK YOURSELF:

   "In what ways did I give my power away to this person?"

   · *"Where might I have skipped over my own knowing, dismissed my feelings, or avoided telling the truth and/or asking for clarification?"*

   "How was I trying to get someone to love, want, or approve of me more than I was attempting to make an authentic connection?"

"Why didn't I do what I knew I should have done that may have averted a bad experience, and what made me hesitate to do it?"

"In what ways was I selfish, unkind, or even abusive that may have caused my former partner to respond in defensive and destructive ways?"

"What choices did I make that contributed to how things went down, and what motivated me to make them?"

3. **What Else Has It Cost You in Your Life to Give Your Power Away Like This?** Become present to the cost of showing up in ways that belie your true worth, power, intelligence, goodness, and values.

   For example: "Being unwilling to set appropriate boundaries has trained everyone in my life to take advantage of me," "By withholding my truth and staying silent when I should have spoken up, I have modeled being a doormat for my kids," "By giving myself away to men who don't value me, I've deprived myself of being loved," "By only going after men I believe I can control, I leave myself unfulfilled time and time again."

4. **What Amends Do You Need to Make to Yourself in Moving Forward?** Commit yourself to the positive growth and development that would allow you to evolve beyond these destructive and self-defeating behaviors.

   For example: "I commit to honoring my own feelings and needs as much as I honor the feelings and needs of others," "I will wait until I know someone well before becoming sexually involved," "From now on, I am going to negotiate on my own behalf rather than silently suffer being taken advantage of," "I promise to listen more closely to my own inner knowing and have the courage to act upon my intuition."

   Note: The first thing that comes up for many of us when identifying new ways of relating that would liberate us from old patterns is that we don't know how to interact this way with others. Perhaps healthy ways of relating were never modeled in the home you grew up in, or you were discouraged from learning basic skills that would allow you to assert boundaries, resolve conflicts, or communicate your needs. Until now, you may have felt powerless in the face of these limitations, as though held hostage by your own missing development. Luckily, we human beings are ever-evolving creatures, and have been given the re-markable gift of being able to learn new things at birth. With this in mind, I invite you to answer the following question.

5. **What New Skills and Capacities Will You Now Need to Develop to Live This Way Consistently?** To make these amends, you'll need to develop new skills and capacities. See if you can identify exactly what they are and take on the challenge of learning them.

For example: "I will learn to identify what my feelings and needs are in order to share them with others," "I will learn to negotiate on my own behalf to stand up for what's mine," "I will learn how to set appropriate boundaries to ensure I am not taken advantage of again," and/or "I will grow my capacity to tolerate disapproval from others in order to stay true to myself."

For a free audio download of this practice, please go to www .ConsciousUncoupling.com/StepTwoPractice.

....

At this point, you may be seeing so much about yourself as the source of the breakdown in your relationship that you want to pick up the phone, write an e-mail, or drive over to your former partner's house to try to make things right. I won't dampen your enthusiasm if you feel compelled to take such an action. However, if you stay with the process a bit longer, there are more pieces to the puzzle of conscious completion that I'd like to offer before you reengage. Unless you're doing this program together, I suggest you wait until you've completed Step 4 before extending yourself to make things right, particularly if you're still a bit lovesick. The impulse to make amends is often accompanied by a secret desire for reconciliation, and you may hope that by taking responsibility for what happened, your former partner will change his or her mind about leaving. It's understandable. Yet it taints the amends with an agenda that covertly pulls on the other person to give you something in return. Ideally, your amends should be a clean offering to right a wrong, lessen suffering, initiate healing, or give your blessing as you release this person from your life. Check in with yourself to discover your motives before moving too quickly into action.

A Conscious Uncoupling will not always mean a neat and tidy ending. Sometimes it will mean you wake up out of your habitual unconscious behaviors, understand the hurtful impact of your conduct and choices on yourself and others, and use the discomfort of seeing yourself clearly to inspire you to change in the future.

When Lily, an interior decorator in her midthirties, shifted her focus away from blame and toward understanding herself as the source of her very bad breakup, she was overwhelmed with remorse for how badly she'd

> *I wanted a perfect ending. Now I've learned, the hard way, that some poems don't rhyme, and some stories don't have a clear beginning, middle, and end. Life is about not knowing, having to change, taking the moment and making the best of it, without knowing what's going to happen next.*
>
> GILDA RADNER

treated her former boyfriend, Jason, the forty-three-year-old manager of her local bank. For the first six months of their relationship, things went well as Jason, a soft-spoken and serious man, asked her out regularly and seemed to genuinely care about her. Yet, at some point he began calling less often. Sometimes she would not hear from him for three or four days at a time. When Lily asked why, her words were more like an accusation than an inquiry. He tried reassuring her by saying this was a time of year he generally had to work longer hours, suggesting that in a month or two, things would go back to normal. Yet, Lily felt overwhelmed with anxiety. She started pulling on him to pay more attention to her, and used her sexuality to try to get him to affirm her value. She'd compulsively call and leave sexy messages, hoping he'd call her back immediately. When he didn't, she'd feel hurt and rejected. She asked him during lovemaking if this was the best sex he'd ever had, a question he seemed uncomfortable with and ill equipped to answer. When she didn't get the reassurance she was looking for, she became critical and started accusing him of being an uncaring, duplicitous, and selfish man. Things devolved quickly. When Jason broke up with her, he did so by cutting her off entirely, calling her abusive and forbidding her to contact him again.

> *Love is unconditional.*
> *Relationships are not.*
> GRANT GUDMUNDSON

As the post-breakup weeks passed and the phone refused to ring, Lily had time to reflect on her behavior. With great embarrassment, she saw how immature, manipulative, and destructive her conduct had been, how motivated she'd been by the ancient, unhealed rejections from her alcoholic father from long, long ago that had nothing to do with Jason. She yearned to apologize directly, yet he'd have nothing to do with her and refused to acknowledge her communications. Realizing she'd hurt him, yet without the ability to make direct amends, she vowed to never again behave like this with another man, making the commitment to evolve and pay forward the lessons learned as a way to make things right.

Not everything can be taken back. The following is a recent share from a Facebook friend:

Grab a plate and throw it on the ground.
Okay done.
Did it break?
Yes.
Now say sorry to it.
Sorry.
Did it go back to the way it was before?
No.
Do you understand?

We can't always undo the damage we've done, and feeling bad about that is appropriate. The rules of common decency are spot on, and when you violate them it's good to feel a little sick to your stomach—it means you're not a sociopath. Over the years, I've learned it's best to give the pangs of conscience our full attention, with deep respect for the ways in which we're being challenged to become more mature, more wholesomely motivated, and yes, even more moral people. Such are the relentless lessons of life, as we're continually offered maturations, insights, and awakenings that only seem to come to us through myriad mishaps and mistakes.

Our impatient desire to be free from these messy, muddled stages of grief—the resentments, sorrows, depressions, and regrets—may compel us to move in haste and rush to

> *The antidote to tragedy is learning.*
> ISABEL GILLIES

133

forgive. Yet one of the world's foremost experts on forgiveness, Dr. Frederic Luskin from Stanford University, tells us that forgiveness is the end of our journey, not the start. He calls forgiveness "the last stop of our suffering" after many rounds of wrestling with the pain we've caused ourselves and others by the foolish, short-sighted, and/or immature choices we've made. It's only after we have felt the sting of remorse and become present to the costs of our confusion that we're given the chance to redeem ourselves with a pledge to do things differently. After suffering has realized its purpose by pushing us to rectify, repent, grow, and evolve, it is then free to find relief through the deep letting go that forgiveness allows.

The great Austrian psychiatrist Viktor Frankl, himself well acquainted with suffering, having survived a German concentration camp in World War II, once said, "In some ways suffering ceases to be suffering at the moment it finds a meaning." By working with heartbreak, and allowing it to peel away years of unhealthy habits and immature, self-defeating ways of relating, you can transform your anguish into something deeply meaningful that promises to bless you and those you love for many years to come.

ASK YOURSELF:

"What amends can I make to myself that promise to give purpose and meaning to the mistakes I have made, as well as help me to reclaim my power?"

STEP 2 SELF-CARE ACTIONS
(Take at least 2 each day)

1. **Carefully gather all reminders of your relationship** from your home, such as pictures, gifts, and love letters, and store them somewhere safe, out of sight, and far away from your bedroom.

2. **Throughout the day take a deep slow breath,** inhaling and exhaling deeply, as though you could breathe all the way down to your hips.

3. **Find a confidant to support you** through this difficult time, whether that's a wise and caring friend, a paid coach or therapist, or both. Make sure you trust and respect this person and feel safe telling him or her the truth without the need to keep up appearances, or the fear of being criticized or judged unfairly. Allow yourself to be witnessed and supported as you move through this by someone who cares about you and who has your back.

4. **Look in the mirror**, gazing deeply into your own eyes, and share with yourself all the ways moving forward that you're going to improve your behavior to reflect more self-love, self-respect, dignity, and honor.

5. **Sit outside and turn your face upward** to soak up the warmth of the sun and remember how much life loves you.

6. **Practice what the Buddhists call mindfulness** by giving your attention to whatever is happening within you throughout your day. Be deeply present and self-aware, noticing all of the feelings and sensations in your body, and witnessing your feelings, needs, and desires with kindness, as though you were able to hold yourself as you walk through this experience with great tenderness and love.

Note to Couples Doing the Program Together

In this second step of the Conscious Uncoupling program, I suggest you continue to engage in a formal manner and give each other plenty of room to self-reflect outside of the need to be right or save face. If you are secretly hoping to reconcile, make sure the amends you offer are wholesomely motivated and given simply to right a wrong, rather than as a covert attempt to renew the relationship. Do not push on your former partner to make any amends to you, or share insights about how they might be responsible for what happened between you. Be respectful of each other's right to do the program at your own pace, and grant each other privacy to do the work without needing to make amends before feeling fully ready to do so.

STEP 3

break the pattern,
heal your heart

If you don't like being a doormat, then get off the floor.
AL-ANON

I n Step 3 of your Conscious Uncoupling program, you'll begin to identify your source-fracture story, and start to understand how it's been the underlying cause of your disappointing patterns in love. You'll awaken from the trance that your painful patterns in love have simply been happening *to* you over and over again, and begin to distinguish exactly how they've been happening *through* you instead, giving you access to the power you'll need to evolve beyond them.

The opportunity at hand is to be liberated from your habitual story of heartache and empowered to generate more fulfilling and gratifying relationships moving forward.

In Step 3, Break the Pattern, Heal Your Heart, you will:

- Identify those core beliefs that have been sabotaging your love life, and awaken to the power you hold to create a new narrative of happy, healthy love moving forward.
- Discover precisely how you've been unconsciously generating your disempowering patterns in love, as well as how you can move beyond them.
- Be restored to a positive self-sense as someone who is safe, loved, valued, and honored.
- Learn the new skills and capacities that will ensure successful relationships in your future.

As a young woman in the early 1970s, Veronica Shoffstall wrote the poem "After a While."

> After a while, you learn the subtle difference
>   between holding a hand and chaining a soul,
> And you learn that love doesn't mean leaning
>   and company doesn't mean security.
> And you begin to learn that kisses aren't contracts
>   and presents aren't promises.
> And you begin to accept your defeats
>   with your head up and your eyes open
>   with the grace of a woman, not the grief of a child
> And you learn to build all your roads on today
>   because tomorrow's ground is too uncertain for plans
>   and futures have a way of falling down in mid-flight.
> After a while you learn that even sunshine burns
>   if you get too much.
> So you plant your own garden and decorate your own soul
>   Instead of waiting for someone to bring you flowers.

And you learn that you really can endure

that you really are strong

and you really do have worth

And you learn and you learn

with every goodbye you learn . . .

Your mission right now is to learn to love yourself, even when the one you love is unable to love you in the ways you need to be loved, standing strong in the truth of your own value and worthiness to be loved, no matter what. The worst part of a breakup is not the mountain of sorrow that comes with the loss of a treasured connection, as much as it's the sheer insult it can be to one's core sense of self. As you make the dreaded shift from being one who is wanted to being one who is unwanted, from one who is loved to one who is not loved, from being special to now being ordinary and decidedly not special. This shift in identity can easily be internalized as proof that your worst fears about yourself and your life may well be true: that you will never be loved, that you will always be alone, or that true love is for other people but not for you. Particularly since the one person who knew you best in the world is now validating negative beliefs you've struggled with for years.

It seems so unfair that after all you've done to outgrow the disappointments of your youth, you again find yourself here. Alone, undersupported, devalued, unloved, abused, or left behind for what might be the umpteenth time in your life. It's like those zombie movies in which the ghosts from the past refuse to die, tenaciously coming back to torture and taunt you. It's enough to inspire a vow of celibacy. Or better yet, how about a vow to finally outgrow your painful patterns in love?

You may find yourself feeling disheartened and resigned by what appears to be a repeat of old childhood wounds, as though

> *What the caterpillar
> calls the end of the
> world, the master calls
> a butterfly.*
>
> RICHARD BACH

you are somehow just cursed when it comes to finding true love. Yet no matter how much you may feel you're at the mercy of the many things outside your control at the moment, the sooner you can see clearly how your life has been happening *through* you, rather than just *to* you, the sooner you can graduate from your discouraging patterns in love and go on to create a much happier, healthier experience of love in your future.

So, snap on your red cape, grab your black boots and Spandex, and follow me. We're going on a journey of emancipation.

Discovering Your Source-Fracture Story

This has happened before, hasn't it? Different faces, names, and circumstances, yet similar painful dynamics come back to bite you in the butt. You again are left feeling disappointed, abandoned, mistreated, or unloved. Sigmund Freud named our tendencies to duplicate the deepest hurts of our childhood the "repetition compulsion." And common wisdom has it that when we unconsciously re-create our worst-case scenarios over and over again, we're trying to heal the hurts from our past. Unfortunately, you and I know that this doesn't tend to work out too well.

One woman I counseled described her childhood as hell; she had a dominating father who terrorized her and her mother with

> *Most of the shadows of
> this life are caused by
> standing in one's own
> sunshine.*
>
> RALPH WALDO EMERSON

his unpredictable rages, which frequently had her cowering underneath her bed for hours at a time. She came to see me after getting entangled with an ex-con who carried a gun wherever he went, which initially made her feel safe because she felt he could protect her from all of the dangerous people out there. I assure you this did not wind up being a "healing experience."

While we human beings seem ever optimistic when it comes to believing that *this time* we'll be loved, nourished, and protected in the ways we've always needed to be, our tendencies to duplicate past disappointments are largely a function of the beliefs we formed long, long ago. I call these beliefs your *source-fracture story*. It's the meaning you gave to the original hurt in your heart that became your underlying narrative about yourself and the possibilities you hold for happy, healthy love. In the case of my client, her source-fracture story was: *I'm not safe, men are out to get me, and love is dangerous.* Through the lens of these beliefs, she unconsciously responded to the uncertainties of life in a way that couldn't help but re-create that narrative: she grabbed on to a guy

> We are disturbed not by what happened to us, but by our thoughts about what happened.
> EPICTETUS

with a gun who wasn't afraid to use it; who else could protect her from a world filled with potentially predatory men? While it may sound extreme, and something no smart woman would ever do, I'll add that this woman was a highly educated college professor. We're all a little remedial when it comes to our core beliefs, and even the wisest, most advanced of us can have huge blind spots.

Author Anaïs Nin once said, "We see life not as it is, but as we are." Through the worldview of beliefs formed long ago, we respond to what's happening in our lives in ways that end up validating these ancient, skewed perspectives. Making choices and taking actions that lead us to manifest more of the same, as though following some distorted inner compass set to lead us home to the same misery we grew up with. All of this happens outside of conscious awareness, and occurs to us simply as our fate to wind up here again, in yet another abusive relationship, with yet another philandering man or with yet another critical, nagging woman. It appears as though Heaven and Earth are conspiring against us to ever find true happiness in love, as we remain oblivious to the actual ways in which we are the authors of our own experience.

My client Sarah was a stay-at-home mother of two small children under the age of five. She grew up with a single, high-powered executive mom. An only child with virtually no extended family, Sarah was raised by a series of nannies. She remembers feeling isolated and alone through most of her childhood. In her lonely little world, relationships were tentative, fragile things. Conflict of any kind was seen as dangerous, for when a nanny disagreed with her mother, they often disappeared the next day. Sarah's heart broke bit by bit, as over the years she formed this solid source-fracture story: *I am alone. Other people always leave. I can never get what I really need from others.*

While in graduate school, Sarah met Andrew and was immediately drawn to his warm and outgoing personality. She remembers deciding on their very first date that they would one day marry. To realize this goal, she set out to be everything she thought Andrew wanted in a wife. She agreed with everything he said. She let him make all of their decisions. She laughed at all his jokes and learned about all his interests. And above all, she avoided conflict, certain that a disagreement would be the beginning of the end. Andrew thought he'd met the perfect woman. Within two years they married, bought a lovely little house back in Andrew's hometown, and started their family.

Sarah aspired to always be sweet, agreeable, and pleasant, and she set about to create the happy home she'd not had while growing up. Yet, as the years passed, she found herself growing more and more depressed. Her feelings confused her, as she seemed to be living the ideal life. Yet, as Andrew's hours at work grew longer, and Sarah found herself alone each night after the children had gone to bed, she started drinking wine to soothe the puzzling ache in her heart. As she'd waited for her mother to come home from work each evening when she was small, she now waited for her husband. And as her mother had arrived home tired and preoccupied by life outside their little family, so too was Andrew distracted by a world that Sarah was not a part of. The marriage drifted along, lifeless and flat, as they ignored the ever-widening gap between them and filled the emptiness with small talk centered on their children. They might have gone on this way for many years had Andrew not fallen in love with a co-worker. He left with few words spoken, for they were not in the habit of speaking from their hearts about those things that mattered most.

> *The life of the psyche . . . is an eternal return, a river which seeks its own source . . . thereby producing a circular movement which brings back whatever has been.*
>
> CARL JUNG

Shattered, Sarah came to see me to help sort out what had happened. We began piecing together the subtle and pervasive ways she'd behaved in her marriage that had covertly re-created the worst of her childhood. She admitted that her unwillingness to risk upsetting Andrew caused her to avoid conflict like the plague, and was stunned to learn that by so doing, she'd failed to ensure their relationship would go through the normal stages of building an authentic union. When I shared the

results of Drs. John and Julie Gottman's studies at the Relationship Research Institute, demonstrating that long-term
unions are forged and stabilized through the reconciliation of
conflicts and differences, she gasped. Having only been willing
to present a carefully crafted image of an idealized wife who
never disagreed with anything her husband said or did, she'd
not allowed emotional intimacy to take root between them in
any meaningful way. She was also horrified to see that in subju-
gating her true feelings and needs, she'd essentially left herself
as emotionally neglected and alone as she had been when she
was a child, ignoring herself in ways similar to how she was ignored as a child. She was equally as disturbed to note that she'd
also left Andrew alone in the relationship, without any viable
partner to go through life with. It was a shock when she realized, sitting across from me in my office, her face contorted
with the unwanted truth of it, how much he must have actually
wanted a partner as he'd left her for a woman whom he frequently collaborated with at work.

You may be wondering why I would ask Sarah to be responsible for Andrew's questionable behavior. Wasn't I blaming
the victim? Yet, I didn't ask Sarah to
be accountable for Andrew's hurtful
choices. I did, however, invite her to
see herself as the source of her lifelong
pattern of alienation and aloneness so
that she might begin to finally evolve
beyond it. I was helping her to see the
indirect and ubiquitous ways she'd set
both herself and Andrew up to play
out her worst-case scenario over again
to ensure that this shocking abandonment would be the last one she'd

> Trauma has the
> quality of converting
> that one sharp stab
> into an enduring state
> of mind. . . . The
> moment becomes a
> season; the event
> becomes a condition.
>
> KAI ERIKSON

ever unconsciously re-create. It was a stunning and sobering realization.

While initially painful to see herself as the source of her experience
so clearly, in recognizing the specific
ways she'd duplicated the pain of her
past, she had the wonderful realization that her lifelong experience of
isolation was not the dreaded fate she
was destined to live, but simply the fic-
titious story she'd made up as a confused and hurting child. As a little girl,
she couldn't possibly have understood

> *It's often said that a traumatic experience early in life marks a person forever, pulls her out of line, saying, "Stay there. Don't move."*
>
> JEFFREY EUGENIDES

that her mother had an avoidant attachment style and was not bonding properly with her daughter. The only meaning Sarah could make of the big hurt in her little heart was that everyone she loved would eventually leave her. God made the mountains, God made the sun, and God made little Sarah to be alone in this lonesome world.

This shift from relating to her beliefs as though they were the awful *truth* about her life, to suddenly understanding them as the invented construct of a sad and lonely little girl, changed everything. Sarah finally understood that she wasn't actually handicapped, as much as she was just habituated: prone to rou-tinely relating in ways that couldn't help but re-create the un-resolved traumas of her past. In facing herself as the creator of this nightmare, she also saw that she possessed the power to wake herself up from it.

With encouragement from me, she began challenging the validity of her childhood story, and she found the courage to profess a more truthful narrative. Tears streaming down her face, she declared, "I was not born to be alone! I have a deep capacity to love and be loved. And I have the power to learn how to have happy, healthy relationships with people I love who love me back in the ways I need to be loved!" Thus began her highly transformative journey of evolving beyond her source-fracture story.

ASK YOURSELF:

"How has my former partner disappointed me in ways similar to how I was disappointed in my youth?" (For example: "He abandoned our family in the same way my father had when I was five.")

"How might I have disappointed my former partner in ways similar to how I was disappointed in my youth?" (For example: "I was hyper-critical in the same way my mother was hypercritical of me.")

Identifying Your Source-Fracture Story

Liberation from your painful patterns in love begins with seeing your source-fracture story clearly. For once you make conscious the underlying beliefs that have been driving you to duplicate your sad story in love, you become free to create happier, healthier dynamics moving forward.

The following exercise will support you to identify your source-fracture story by helping you name the beliefs you formed in childhood about yourself and the possibilities you hold for happy, healthy love. It was co-developed with my colleague Claire Zammit.[*]

---

[*] Originally called "Transformation of Identity," this exercise was created as part of the curriculum for the online Feminine Power Transformative Courses for Women (see www.FemininePower.com). It has been taught in both the Calling in "The One" (see www.CallingInTheOne.com) and the Feminine Power online courses to tens of thousands of participants over the years to help them break free of repetitive and painful patterns and realize their higher potentials in life and in love.

1. **Become Still.** Find a quiet space to sit for a few minutes uninterrupted. Close your eyes, take a deep breath as though you could breathe all the way down to your hips, and relax your body to the best of your ability.

2. **Become Aware of Your Feelings Regarding Your Breakup.** Become aware of all the feelings you're holding about this breakup. Notice where these emotions are in your body.

   For example: "The emotions are like a burning in my solar plexus," "They are a heaviness on my heart," "They are a hole between my shoulder blades as though someone stabbed me in the back," or "They are a lump in my throat making it hard for me to swallow."

3. **Welcome In Your Feelings.** Breathe deeply and notice the part of you able to witness these feelings with deep compassion. Extend love to the part of you experiencing these painful feelings, welcoming each one with a sense of kindness and care. Repeat your Step 1 practice by asking yourself what you are feeling and tenderly reflecting back each of your feelings one at a time. Notice that, in doing so, your ability to step back and lovingly observe your feelings, rather than be swallowed up by them, grows stronger.

4. **Notice the Meaning You Are Making of Your Breakup.** Let go of trying to figure anything out from your mind, and drop your awareness down into your body, becoming aware of the emotional center of all your difficult and dark feelings. As though you could let the emotional center of your feelings speak for themselves (not your mind), I invite you to answer the following questions:

   "What am I making this breakup mean about me?"
   For example, "I'm not loved," "I'm not wanted," "I'm alone," "I'm disposable," "I'm not good enough," "I'm inferior," or "I'm a failure."

   "What am I making this breakup mean about my relationship with men/women [whichever gender you're attracted to]?"
   For example: "Men always choose other women, not me," "Women

don't like me," "No one really cares about my true feelings and needs," "People only love me because of what I can do for them," or "Men only want me for one thing."

"What am I making this breakup mean about the possibilities I hold for happiness in love?"

For example: "Life doesn't support me to have love," "I can never have what I want," "My love life is cursed," or "It is dangerous to let anyone get too close."

5. **Identify Your Source-Fracture Story.** I now invite you to weave these beliefs together to name your source-fracture story.

For example: "I'm not enough. Men like other women more than they like me. There's never enough love to go around."

"I am not valuable. Women just use me for what they can get and then dispose of me. I have to work really hard all the time to try to prove my value."

"I'm not worthy. Men leave me if I don't constantly try to please them. My life is empty and void of love."

6. **How Old Is This Part of You/How Big Is the Energy Held in Its Center?** See if you can now identify the chronological age of the part of you that is stuck in this story. This answer need not be literal, but more like a felt sense in your body of the age you were when you first came up with this perspective.

ASK YOURSELF:

"How old is this part of me that's stuck in this story?"

For example: "I'm just a baby," "I'm about five or six," or "I'm twelve."

Notice also how big the energy is that is being held in this center.

ASK YOURSELF:

"How big is the energy that I'm holding here?"

For example: "It's huge, taking up an entire city block," "It's extending about 6 inches out from my body," "It's a dense, black knot that is wrapped around my entire heart."

7. **Open Your Eyes and Shake It Out!** To help you return to your strong, adult self, open your eyes and shake your body.

ASK YOURSELF:

"What's the best thing about being my current age as opposed to being me when I was _____ [the age you discovered you are at the core of that story]?"

For example: "I have a lot more choices than I had back then," "I can set healthy boundaries to protect myself," or "I have a lot more resources than I did back then and can get the help I need."

For a free audio download of this practice, please go to www .ConsciousUncoupling.com/StepThreePractice.

....

Perpetuating Your Source-Fracture Story

When Emily, a twenty-six-year-old law student, met Rick, the lead singer in a rock band, she fell head over heels in love. He was taken with her as well, and they began seeing a lot of each other, each date more exciting than the last. Yet about four weeks in, Rick stopped calling. Whereas earlier he'd at least texted every day to check in, suddenly Emily heard nothing for one day, two days, three days, then four. By the fifth day, she was beside herself. Having had a father who walked out on the family when she was five years old, her abandonment fears got the best of her and, to break the tension, she texted Rick with what she thought was a brilliant preemptive strike against being rejected. She told him she'd met someone else and was no longer interested in pursuing the connection. It wasn't until three years later when they ran into each other at a club that they discovered what had happened. Rick hadn't gone silent because he was no longer interested in seeing her. Instead, he was actually taking some time to contemplate making a deeper commitment to Emily, and to bring closure to a few other casual relationships he'd begun in order to make himself available to ask her to be in an exclusive relationship with him. When Emily found out, she was stunned. Inside of her core belief that men always leave, she was certain that Rick's silence was an indication he was choosing out of the relationship, and she was heartbroken to discover how she'd been the source of her own experience of abandonment by being the one who bailed on him.

> *While you can't keep your heart from getting broken, you can stop breaking your own heart.*
> LEIGH NEWMAN

Our relational patterns don't just happen to us. They happen through the lens of our own assumptions, which influences how we then respond to our circumstances. In order to graduate from your painful patterns in love, I invite you to take stock of how you may have unconsciously shown up in your relationship in ways that literally caused your source-fracture story to happen again.

To begin, reflect upon the following questions:

1. **How Did You Relate to Yourself in Ways That Validated Your Source-Fracture Story?** As your relationships with others can never be better than your relationship with yourself, I invite you to identify the specific way(s) you treated yourself that was reflected back to you in the treatment you received. Look for the ways you may have

trained your former partner to treat you by how you tend to treat yourself.

For example, if your former partner abandoned you, look for the ways you self-abandoned throughout the relationship. If he or she was self-absorbed and self-serving, look for the ways you may have treated your own feelings and needs as if they didn't matter. If he or she was critical, look for the ways you might be inappropriately hard on yourself.

2. **How Did You Set Your Former Partner Up to Validate Your Source-Fracture Story?** How did you covertly set your former partner up to disappoint you in ways similar to how you've been hurt in the past?

For example: "I failed to share my feelings and needs, and so my former partner couldn't possibly have known what I needed from him and couldn't help but disappoint me."

"I didn't want my former partner to be mad at me, so I failed to set healthy boundaries until it seemed the only way out of my chronic self-abandonment was to leave."

"I was so desperate for love that I settled for less than I deserved; constantly tolerated bad behavior, hoping that he would change. Yet by not standing up for myself, I actually gave him permission to treat me poorly."

Note: Beware of the tendency to be victimized by your own weaknesses and old wounds. Rather than say, "I can never stand up for myself because my father abused me when I was a child," try being responsible for your choices by saying, "I have continually chosen to abuse myself in ways similar to how my father abused me. By doing so, I trained my boyfriend to treat me just as badly." As long as you stay victimized and helpless, you will not grow beyond your old patterns. Look to own the volitional component of the choices you've made, as those are your leverage points for change.

3. **How Have You Related to Life in Ways That Have Validated Your Source-Fracture Story?** We tend to project onto the universe the worst of our childhood, imagining life to be punishing, withholding, uncaring, or cruel in much the same way we experienced our primary attachment figures (such as our parents or older siblings) to be when we were young. Inside of this worldview, we relate in ways that covertly create evidence that our beliefs are valid.

ASK YOURSELF:

"Because of the beliefs I have about life, how did I contribute to how things went down in my relationship?"

For example: "Because I believed that I couldn't have what I wanted, I chronically compromised and settled for less than I deserve until I couldn't take it anymore and left."

"Because I believed it's dangerous to be seen, I was not authentic about my true feelings and needs until I felt so invisible I had to end things."

"Because I believed that life is a battle, I was constantly combative and on the defensive until he got tired of fighting and left."

Note: Understanding your contribution to the breakup can be an eye-opening and humbling experience, and you may be tempted to move into self-hatred and shame in response. Remember, however, that if you allow yourself to be swallowed by shame, you risk becoming stuck in it, unable to use what you're discovering as a catalyst for positive evolution and change. I encourage you, therefore, to hold your imperfections tenderly. Value the learning of life lessons as an important part of becoming a wise and mature human being. You've already had one person not love you the way you need to be loved. Please don't repeat that letdown with yourself.

What's Really True?

Just as a near-death experience can wake us up to the true meaning of life, so too can the death of love awaken us out of the trance of false beliefs and to the magnificence of our own being. In an instant, our old story is revealed to be just that— a *story*. One constructed when we were far too young to have understood things any other way. In awakening to this truth, we can begin to question the conclusions we came to and start to see a more nuanced picture of what may have been happening between ourselves and others at the time we formed these worldviews.

Beliefs are relational—meaning, we created them in relationship with those we loved and depended upon the most. We didn't just pluck these stories out of the ether. Something was going on between you and your mom, or you and your dad, grandma, or weird Uncle Jim that was wildly painful and confusing, and beyond your capacity to comprehend. Given that, as a kid, your main developmental task was to form a sense of who you are and where you fit into this world, it's understandable that you would make whatever was happening mean something about you. It's only when you revisit the conclusions you came to with the rationality of an adult who has an enhanced capacity to hold complexity and nuance that a more sophisticated and accurate picture can emerge.

You must go back to rescue the younger you from that wacky and distorted hall of mirrors. Because the meaning you made about yourself and your life—that you are bad, not wanted, not loved, too much, not enough, powerless, and/or destined to be alone in life—is simply *not true*.

Until we identify and challenge these core beliefs, they will return to haunt us. Yet, once we do, we are finally free to graduate from that old, painful story once and for all. Author of *The Courage to Love,* psychologist Stephen Gilligan, tells us that "It may take years, even generations, but a negative experience returns until human presence is brought to touch it with love and acceptance and integrate it. . . . On this point, nature seems eternally patient and forever cruel." The part of you stuck in that old story has been waiting for you to love it. I invite you right now to put one hand over wherever that story has resided in your body (for example, your solar plexus, your heart, or your throat), and just say to yourself, "Sweetheart, that story is not even true. What's more true is ____" and fill in the blank. For example:

 . . . you are deeply loved by all of life.

 . . . you have the power to keep yourself safe.

 . . . no one knows more than you what's right for your life.

> *Of all the nostalgias that haunt the human heart, the greatest of them is an everlasting longing to bring what is youngest home to what is oldest, in us all.*
>
> LAURENS VAN DER POST

As my client Sarah did when she caught a glimpse of how much power she was holding to create deep and rich relationships with others, I encourage you to fight to wake yourself from the trance of your source-fracture story in a way you wished others had fought for you. Be the hero or heroine of your own journey and kiss yourself awake from your slumber. Do it now. Don't waste one more precious day of your beautiful life sleepwalking through the nightmare of those erroneous assumptions.

Belief or Truth?

ASK YOURSELF:

"Regarding my source-fracture belief(s), what's really true?"

Belief: I'm not enough.

Truth: My very existence is more than enough to be worthy of great love. I am inherently worthy of receiving respect, honor, and love.

> *I wish I could show you when you are lonely or in darkness the astonishing light of your own being.*
>
> HAFIZ

Belief: I don't matter.

Truth: My feelings and needs matter. They matter to me. And it is appropriate for me to have a healthy expectation that they also matter to those who are closest to me.

Belief: I am not lovable.

Truth: Even when the man I love closes his heart to me, I am still deeply lovable and worthy of being loved.

Belief: I'm bad.

Truth: Just because I'm feeling shame, that does not mean I actually have anything to be ashamed of.

Or

Truth: The mistakes I've made are lessons learned and I commit myself to cleaning up my messes. It is the mark of a good person to humbly learn from his or her mistakes and make amends moving forward.

Belief: I'm alone.

Truth: I was not born to be alone. I came here to love and be loved, and I have the power to learn how to have happier and healthier relationships moving forward.

Belief: I'm not valuable.

Truth: I am a treasure unto all of Life. I need never do a thing to try to prove my inherent value.

Belief: I'm not safe.

Truth: I have the power to learn how to keep myself safe by learning new, healthier ways of relating.

It's so easy to provide wisdom and counsel for a friend in need—reminding her in moments of weakness of the truth of her own value and power—yet that's so much harder to do for ourselves. Caught up in our big emotions, we can easily mistake our feelings for facts, and slip into seeing our situation from a child's perspective. When you find yourself in the downward spiral of your source-fracture story, look for the part of you that is a wise, intelligent, educated, and developed adult who can see what's happening with clarity, perspective, and compassion. From this adult center, lean in and lovingly tend to the younger part of you that is confused and hurting, as though you were caring for a treasured friend whom you loved with all your heart. Offer yourself your pearls of wisdom, your nuggets of truth, your common sense, and the profound insights and understanding you have access to when you dig deep into the recesses of your heart and soul.

Soul-to-Soul Communication

The temptation of a breakup is to see yourself through the eyes of your former partner as somehow less than who you are. Maybe he or she has a negative, judgmental story about you that played a part in your breakup. Maybe this person is now devaluing you as a way to lessen the pain of losing you. While you cannot know for sure what he feels or thinks of you, your imagination can run wild with the piercing experience of no longer being wanted, loved, adored, or chosen. Under such an assault, can you hold steady the truth of your own power and goodness? Can you take back the permission you've given another to determine your worth, and hold strong to the truth of your value in the face of being devalued by the one who just yesterday was everything to you?

Because beliefs are relational, when a lover leaves, we are often left struggling with the residue of what that means about us. We forget the thousands of ways that the relationship reflected back our value to us, and remember instead the few horrible moments when we felt dishonored, discarded, and/or devalued, leaving us to struggle with a wounded sense of self from having endured this experience. Because it might not be possible to restore a sense of balance in the actual relationship itself at this time, I offer the following practice to help free you from this residue and shift you back into a deep sense of your own worthiness, value, and power in a way that you can feel in your body.

Note: If you are doing the program with your former partner, I suggest you do this exercise as a personal practice rather than try to engage it directly with one another. You may wish to share the experience afterwards in your debrief of this step of the program.

1. **Become Still.** Find a quiet space to sit uninterrupted for a few minutes. Close your eyes, take a deep breath as though you could breathe all the way down to your hips, and relax your body to the best of your ability.
2. **Anchor into Your Adult Self.** Connect with the part of you that is a strong, resourceful, intelligent, developed, wise, and loving adult and, as though you could anchor the energy of this adult self all through your body and beyond, breathe deeply as though you could breathe all the way down to your hips, your legs, and your feet, extending your energy down into the earth and out to the edges of the room.

3. **Invite Your Younger Self to Leave the Room.** Lovingly instruct the younger part of you to go someplace safe, much as you might ask a child to leave the room when the grown-ups are about to have a serious conversation.

4. **Invite Your Former Partner to Sit Before You for a Soul-to-Soul Communication.** (**Note:** If your former partner was physically threatening or violent, I suggest you imagine putting up a firewall of protection around you that prevents him or her from being able to touch you.) As if you could invite the soul of your former partner in for a meaningful conversation, ask this person to come sit before you. Keeping the tone between you cordial and respectful, imagine looking into his or her eyes, and say the following (feel free to use your own words and embellish, but do your best to keep the overall meaning of the communication intact):

"I give you the benefit of the doubt by taking responsibility for training you to treat me in the ways you did. I recognize your behavior toward me in many ways mirrored my own."

Imagine this person listening to all you are saying with rapt attention and authentic interest. Continue on by saying:

"Your poor treatment of me helped wake me up to the truth of my value, my power, my goodness, my intelligence, and my worthiness to love and be loved. For that, I thank you."

"Yet, I now wish to right things between us by sharing with you who I truly am so as to correct any misperceptions you may have been left with."

Speak what's really true about who you are and what is possible for you.

For example: "I am a powerful, loving man who is deeply worthy of being seen, supported, honored, and respected," "I am a sexy, sensual, voluptuous woman who is worthy of being sexually ravished by a partner who is turned on by my body," "I am an amazing, smart, and intriguing woman who is worthy of being treated like a queen," "I know I showed up as less than who I have the potential to be in our relationship, but there is so much more to me than that and I will take all I've learned with you and apply it to my next relationship so that I can create a much happier future in love."

Let this person see the full truth of who you are, especially if you showed up as a dimmed-down version of yourself while in the relationship. Imagine your former partner seeing you as if for the very first time. See the respect, admiration, and appreciation in his eyes and feel him extending a sense of goodwill and love toward you.

Now, repeat the following, as though you had a direct line of communication to the soul of your former partner:

"I ask that you treat me with honor and respect from now on. Whether or not we see each other in person, I ask that in your thoughts, words, actions, and deeds you relate to me in ways that are reflective of my true value, power, intelligence, goodness, and worthiness to love and be loved. And I give you my word to do the same for you."

Ask this person: "Do I have your agreement?" and wait for the "Yes" before moving on. Visualize looking directly into his eyes, fully present and available to restore dignity and honor between you.

Now, imagine all moments of humiliation, shame, embarrassment, dishonor, or disrespect dissolving between you, and feel yourself restored to a place of honor, dignity, esteem, and love in your former partner's eyes.

5. **Imagine You and Your Former Partner Offering a Deep Bow to One Another.** Picture your former partner and you offering a deep bow

to one another to complete your conversation, recognizing that these new agreements have now been set in motion.

Note: If and when you find yourself slipping into a feeling of low self-worth prompted by how things were left at the end of your relationship, stop yourself from dwelling on the moments when you felt devalued, dishonored, disrespected, and unloved. Instead, turn your attention toward remembering your experience here. You may also wish to consider the moments of delight, admiration, desire, tenderness, and authentic love that passed between you while in the relationship, and make a decision that these were the times when your former partner was seeing you most clearly.

Graduating from Painful Love Patterns

Happy, healthy relationships aren't just about meeting and falling in love with the right person. Nor are they about being born under a lucky star or having your astrological chart line up a certain way. Good relationships are about having the necessary development—both inner and outer—to sustain healthy intimacy and goodwill over time between yourself and another person. And while most of us assume we've been repeating old patterns in an attempt to heal the past, it's just as likely we've been duplicating these dynamics because we simply haven't known how to do it any differently.

> We have to stop asking why this is happening to me and start asking why it is happening for me.
>
> AUGUST GOLD

By becoming aware of the ways you've been setting yourself up to lose in love, you now have the opportunity to set yourself up to win. You can begin learning how to show up in ways that are congruent with the truth of your value, rather than behave in ways consistent with your false beliefs. You can learn to stand up for yourself, speak your truth, set healthy boundaries, ask questions that would create safety for yourself, identify your own deeper knowing, or even extend care to others in ways that build trust and connection. By identifying these specific new ways of relating, you'll begin to feel relief from the hopelessness of your heartache, recognizing the opportunity at hand to graduate from old, dysfunctional ways of showing up in life.

For most of us, emancipating ourselves from these old, disappointing habits will require us to learn some basic skills and capacities that we somehow never acquired. Imprisoned by our source-fracture stories, our development was stunted. If you really don't believe that others care about your feelings and needs, why bother learning how to communicate what they are? If you know beyond a shadow of a doubt that others always leave, why learn to navigate conflict in ways that deepen understanding? Wouldn't that only hurt more in the long run? If you assume that love is dangerous, why take down your guard and drop your aggressive defensiveness? In doing so, you'd surely leave yourself at risk for harm. Yet, without healthy relational skills and capacities, you won't be able to graduate from your old patterns in love, because you'll be ill-equipped to create anything else.

Out of difficulties grow miracles.
JEAN DE LA BRUYÈRE

No matter how psychologically savvy you've become over the years—able to recite your issues backwards and forwards, stating with great accuracy exactly what happened to you, when it happened, who it happened with and why—until you learn those specific skills and capacities that will allow you to create a more satisfying experience of love, you'll stay stuck repeating the past. When my client Sarah took a stand to evolve beyond her source-fracture story of chronic alone-ness in life, she was immediately confronted with how little she knew about creating emotional intimacy with another human being. Recognizing how ill-equipped she was to have an au-thentic relationship, she felt overwhelmed and confused about how to proceed. She didn't even have much of a relationship with herself. After years of pushing aside her emotions, dis-missing them as unimportant, she realized that much of her inability to share her feelings and needs with others was due to how clueless she was about what they actually were.

In our work, Sarah learned that emotional intimacy occurs when people take the risk of sharing what's happening in their inner world. To prepare for this, we began by helping Sarah learn to distinguish her own feelings and needs. Rather than simply say she was feeling down, we worked to help her discern the many shades of blue that one can feel: despairing, discour-aged, disappointed, dazed, numb, despondent, hopeless, or bereaved. Rather than simply report that she was having a better day, she learned to label her inner experience more accurately by saying she was feeling hopeful, engaged, optimistic, serene, revived, excited, or restored. She then learned how to use her feelings as important information to assist her in discerning her needs, learning to name these needs in a way that gave her the chance to address them. She needed to be recognized as valuable, treated with respect, listened to, and loved for who she is.

Ideally, Sarah would have discovered how to distinguish her own feelings and needs between the ages of four and eight, when it would have been developmentally appropriate for her to learn the skills of emotional literacy. Yet in the home she grew up in, no one was helping her to decipher her own, inner experience. And because her source-fracture story included the assumption that she could never get what she needed from anyone, it never occurred to her to even try to develop herself in these ways.

Once we identified the missing skills and capacities that were sabotaging Sarah's ability to form a healthy relationship and got to work developing them, she was free to evolve beyond her painful patterns of isolation and aloneness that had permeated her whole life. Within a relatively short period of time, Sarah became a good communicator. I'm happy to say that her efforts paid off. As of this writing, Sarah is now in a markedly more satisfying relationship than the one she had with her husband. She and her boyfriend sometimes argue, yet they're apt to do so in ways that bring them closer, and leave them more capable of tending to each other's well-being and happiness. While wistful about what might have been in her marriage had she been the woman then that she is now, she would tell you she'd not trade what happened for the world. The shattering of her marriage was the opening she needed to wake her up to a whole new possibility of what life, and love, could be.

You may be confronted with the fact that you don't yet know how to evolve beyond your old patterns. Perhaps you're confused about what healthy boundaries even are, let alone how you might set them with others. Or maybe you feel remedial when it comes to negotiating the fulfillment of your needs, clueless about which ones are even appropriate to ask another person to fulfill. You may feel totally baffled when it comes to knowing how to self-soothe so you don't fly off the handle and go into a rage every time you don't get your way. We all have

blind spots that prevent us from realizing the potential each relationship holds for love and happiness. Yet, this is where most
of us get stopped, for we are intimidated by what we don't yet
know, and we are quick to step back into our habitual, limited

> *What makes you*
> *vulnerable makes you*
> *beautiful.*
> BRENÉ BROWN

ways of doing things simply because,
well, that's just what we know to do.

So that you might outgrow your repetitive patterns in love, I invite you to
take on what the Buddhists call "Beginner's Mind." It's softening into an
inquiry toward all you don't yet know,
valuing uncertainty over certainty and
vulnerability over the protection of
looking good. You look to identify the specific skills and capacities that would set you free, and commit to learning them as if
your life depended upon that, because in many ways it does.
None of us who've suffered a shattered heart, or who have broken the heart of another, wishes to do so again. Which leaves
you two choices. One is to shut down, and never let yourself
love and be loved ever again; the other is to take on your own
development so that you can trust yourself to create a happier,
healthier experience the next time around.

Fortunately, we are ever-evolving creatures who are capable
of learning new things throughout our entire lives. Also fortunate is the fact that there are a slew of amazing teachers who
teach what you missed in your youth. In the Online Resources
section of this book, I provide a partial list of some gifted teachers whose life mission is to empower you to have happy, healthy
love in your life, in all of its many forms. I hope you make the
choice to allow some of them into your life so you can have the
relationships you'd hope to have.

Let this be an amazing beginning, and not just an end. Most

of us need wake-up calls such as the one you've just received to be inspired to become all we have the potential to be. And many go on to call their biggest lessons their biggest blessings, because they choose to relate to their losses as opportunities to live and love more deeply than ever before.

ASK YOURSELF:

"How can I relate to myself in way(s) that would demonstrate the truth of my value, power, and worthiness to love and be loved? What new skills and/or capacities might I need to develop to show up this way?"

For example: "I can begin paying attention to my own feelings and needs before automatically tending to the feelings and needs of others. The skill I would need to learn is to better gauge what my feelings and needs are."

"How can I relate to others in way(s) that demonstrate the truth of my value, power, and worthiness to love and be loved? What new skills and/or capacities might I need to develop to show up this way?"

For example: "I can take the risk to share my authentic feelings and needs with others so that I can discover who cares about me, and who doesn't, and to know which relationships to continue to invest myself in. The capacities I'd need to grow are (1) the ability to tolerate being more vulnerable and (2) expanding my willingness to receive."

"How can I relate to life in way(s) that demonstrate the truth of my value, power, and worthiness? What new skills and/or capacities might I need to develop to show up this way?"

For example: "I can raise my expectations and begin asking for what I truly want and need in life. The capacity I'd need to cultivate is the ability to hold a bigger vision for my life, stretching my picture of what might be possible for me beyond what was possible for the women in my family."

....

STEP 3 SELF-CARE SUGGESTIONS
(Take at least 2 each day)

1. **Drink lots of pure, clean water** as a symbolic gesture of flushing toxic habits from your life.

2. **Eat healthy, hearty, and nurturing foods** that are packed with nutrients and love.

3. **Fill your home with fresh air,** lots of light, beautiful flowers, and things that smell good.

4. **Stretch to try out at least one new way** of relating each day that demonstrates the deeper truth of your own value, power, intelligence, goodness, and worthiness to love and be loved.

5. **Put on some music that you love and dance,** allowing your body to fully express the emotions you've been holding.

6. **Write three lists.** The first is a list of 20 things you are losing that you are happy to be losing (e.g., listening to his snoring all night long!). The second is a list of 20 things you are actually gaining by losing this relationship (e.g., I finally have time to tend to my own creative projects). And the third is a list of 20 ways you could turn this disappointment into the best thing that ever happened to you (e.g., I could finally start being an adult woman and fully in my power with men).

Note to Couples Doing the Program Together

In this third step of your Conscious Uncoupling program, you'll want to share with one another those insights and breakthroughs that will begin to create a sense of closure and cohesion so that you continue moving forward toward greater levels of autonomy. The motivation for sharing should not be to feel closer to your former partner, although that could, paradoxically, be a by-product of doing this exercise together. Your incentive for the conversation should simply be to liberate yourself from ever again repeating your source-fracture story with anyone new.

Notice that I said "liberate *yourself*." You are each responsible only for your own growth in this regard; neither of you should bear the burden of trying to fix the other, nor should either of you feel compelled to hold up a mirror to point out the missing development of one another. To this aim, you want to be rigorously honest and transparent about your own flaws, blind spots, and false motivations, and be willing to lose face in service to saving your soul. Remind yourself that your former partner doesn't actually need to "get it" as much as *you* need to get it, in order to be free.

I suggest you refrain from giving advice or feedback unless specifically asked by your former partner to do so, keeping the focus entirely on yourself and cleaning up your own side of the street. After each of you has shared, make sure to thank your former partner for being honest and having the courage to tell the truth. It is important that you allow for diverse perspectives, recognizing that not all things need be resolved between you. Do your best to simply tolerate the tensions of those chasms that cannot be crossed, and honor them as the wisdom of life that is now leading you in different directions. Remember that the opportunity of this conversation is to help you mature beyond these patterns, as well as to restore a wholesome sense of goodwill between the two of you as you bless each other to do better in future relationships.

STEP 4

become a love alchemist

Freedom is what you do with what's been done to you.
JEAN-PAUL SARTRE

In Step 4 of your Conscious Uncoupling program, you'll awaken to yourself as an indomitable force of nature, capable of generating a positive future for yourself and others no matter how hurtful or hard things have been until now. For at this point, you can begin to make choices and take actions that promise to graduate you from the painful patterns of your past and radically transform the dynamic between you and your former partner to reflect the truth of your value and power. By doing so, you'll allow for the emergence of a healthy new form the relationship has the potential to take, and ensure that the new life you're embracing will be greater than the one you're letting go.

In Step 4, Become a Love Alchemist, you will:

- Protect the love that brought you together by learning to value both what you're releasing and what you're now creating, recognizing all stages of your relationship as worthy of honor, respect, and appreciation.
- Set a conscious intention for a positive future that will serve as your North Star and support you to navigate this separation with integrity, vision, and strength.
- Discover how to dissolve any residual anger or hurt still present between you so that you can begin this next life chapter with a clean slate.
- Learn to communicate in ways that will empower you to create and sustain a healthier dynamic moving forward.

Dismantling a relational home can be every bit as distressing as if you were to start removing the walls, floors, and ceilings of the house you live in, leaving you feeling exposed and undefended against the harsh, abrasive elements of life. At the same time this deconstruction is happening, you're required to make weighty decisions that could define your life and the lives of those you love for decades to come. It's not hard to understand why, given this difficult combination of tasks, a breakup can quickly become a hostile and violent process filled with power struggles and escalating molehills that can easily morph into high and mighty mountains to scale.

The most terrifying of all endings is the wrecking-ball breakup that aggressively sweeps through your house, taking all of the love, goodwill, and hope that went into building that home and turning it loose, to be lost forever. Damage done in such explosive expressions of hatred and rage is difficult, if not downright impossible, to repair. In a Conscious Uncoupling, we don't allow this to happen. Rather, you're invited to purposefully protect the love that brought you and your former partner together and honor all you've co-created as you safely midwife the relationship to its healthier new form. The tendency to lash out, degrade, and destructively dismiss the connection as a way to cope with its loss comes at too great a cost. Devaluing love once shared is like snubbing the sun at sunset, pretending the garden that grew in the warmth of those rays is now just a basket of plastic flowers. The danger of such a perspective is that one might be tempted to never open the blinds again, lest you be "tricked" into believing that the light being offered is real. Unless you're the victim of an impostor who scammed you out of your fortune, what you and your former partner shared *was* real. One or both of you may have made mistakes that exposed fatal flaws you failed to notice or minimized before now, but that doesn't mean what you had was untrue or held no value. Longevity is not the only measure of love.

> *I miss my heart when it's closed.*
> JEFF BROWN

Holding this complexity is not easy for most of us. We tend to see things in black and white terms, and honoring the good times while suffering through the bad is a stretch for the best of us. Learning to value both what you've had and what you now have the possibility of creating takes determination and discipline. Yet, this kind of diligence is required to lay the foundation for a healthy, happy future for yourself and others in the aftermath of heartache. Even if your former partner is taking the seemingly easy way out by devaluing you and the love you once shared in order to create distance, that does not mean you need to follow suit. Sometimes you have to be the leader of love by refusing to go down a lesser path, and simply hold space for the other person to follow.

Future? What Future?

When I was thirty and an aspiring singer-songwriter, I moved from New York to Los Angeles with my girlfriend, Price, driving a truck with all of our belongings across 3,000 miles and stopping at truck stops for biscuits and gravy with the rest of the truckers. Yet, frequently, I'd return east and stay with my happily partnered friends, Ralph and Richard, drawn back by promising music projects left undone in the bedlam of my move—lyrics that still needed music or songs that still needed recording. For weeks at a time, I'd move into Ralph and Richard's second bedroom and get back into my New York groove of writing during the day while rehearsing and recording at night. The uninterrupted, silent afternoons of songwriting in their Brooklyn apartment were luxurious. Having stepped out of the swirl of the life I'd created in L.A., I finally had the psychic space to drop down into my own creative process. The songs I wrote in those precious weeks live on as the soundtrack of my life to this day.

How interesting, then, when more than twenty years later and pregnant with this unborn book, that I would once again find myself in the same apartment, sitting at the same dining table, overlooking the same lush green park, listening to the same gritty sounds of traffic moving up and down the avenue,

> *Every evening I turn my worries over to God. He's going to be up all night anyway.*
> MARY C. CROWLEY

and drawn once more into a deeply creative process. That of birthing the manuscript you now read. The irony, however, is that this time Ralph and Richard no longer live here together. Two years earlier, they dissolved their union and, unfortunately, neither consciously nor kindly. Theirs was a severing of the worst kind. Having lived in partnership for over thirty years, the only way they could find to untangle the gnarly knots of their connection was for Richard to cut and run with his new beau, leaving everything behind with little more than suitcase in hand. And while Ralph's home remains identical to the home that I remember, for the same art hangs steadfastly on the walls, the same antique furnishings fill the somewhat cluttered rooms, and the same photographs stare out from the bookshelves, that which was once a home filled with light and laughter is now a tomb, a fading tribute to his life with Richard. Even pictures of the two of them in happier times remain framed and fixed upon the shelves. I may as well be staying with Miss Havisham. I half expect Ralph to walk through the front door in a frayed and graying wedding gown any moment now.

> *Have you ever been hurt and the place tries to heal a bit, and you just pull the scab off of it over and over again.*
>
> ROSA PARKS

That's not to say that Ralph is not working through his grief. He is. He's grieving not just the loss of his relationship but also all the years he looked the other way, pretending not to know what deep down inside he knew. He's grieving for the weeks, months, and years that he refused to speak up, ask the right questions, or raise his expectations. Years spent hoping, waiting, and praying that things between them would change . . . the *wrong* use of positive thinking. Those are decades of his life that he'll never get back, and he can't help but be confronted by them every time he looks at his wrinkles in the morning mirror.

In Ralph's mind, there is no vibrant future. There is only a vibrant past. His sorrow cannot help but be compounded by an environment that is a shrine to all that no longer exists, perpetually pulling his attention backwards with little room for new life to emerge. It was all that I could do to not start hurling the many reminders of their relationship into jumbo trash bags and drag them all down to Goodwill while Ralph was at work. Sure, I would have left a trinket or two to honor those years spent together, some meaningful mementos lovingly tucked away in a special place. But I'd also empty out a few drawers where a handsome new man could place a T-shirt or two. I'd purchase a couple of beautiful picture frames that lay waiting for images of new, happy love. And I'd carve out spaces in the closet where the suits of a serious suitor might rest.

Sometimes it's hard to know what a good friend should do.

Since Richard left, Ralph has not wanted for dates. Yet, no one has come close to touching his heart in any meaningful way. For a time he had a new man in his life, a dog groomer who was himself grieving the loss of a forty-year relationship with a partner who'd passed away two years before. Ralph and he spent several months together that were, frankly, in my opinion, a little more like sitting shiva than starting a new life. The relationship fizzled out undramatically, having never really bonded very deeply, leaving Ralph to return home alone to his monument to past love.

> Bereavement is the deepest initiation into the mysteries of human life, an initiation more searching and profound than even happy love.
>
> DEAN INGE

I share this story as a cautionary tale of what can and *will* go wrong when we indulge in the hypnotic pull of the past. Letting go of love is rarely an organic, go-with-the-flow kind of process. You can't just wait until you're in the mood. Releasing a relationship in a way that leaves your heart happy and light, open and free to love again, is a conscious choice you must make a thousand times a day, as you deliberately turn your attention away from the past and make a concerted effort to align your energies with the creation of a bright and positive future. To do this you must become more interested in what's possible from here on than you are in rectifying the past, and more invested in how you might midwife this transition harmoniously than in getting what you want in the short term. You must be more devoted to creating safety, cohesion, and well-being for all involved than in being right or exacting revenge. You have to consciously create the possibility of an affirmative future while coming to terms with the painful loss of the future you'd envisioned. It's a little like building a plane while flying it, and it's not for the faint of heart.

Yet what will provide momentum for this is an intention for what you want to create in its place. Like a bridge between worlds, a strong intention can help generate a positive future for all involved and will provide safe passage to the other side of this transition. It will help you avoid the potentially lethal mistakes that can easily destroy what's left of the goodwill between you, as you find your way through a minefield of potentially charged issues that now need negotiating.

When my friends, authors Janet Bray Attwood and Chris Attwood, decided to divorce, it was amid a sea of confusion. On the one hand, they were the best of friends and loved each other dearly. On the other, they were, in Janet's words, "sexually incompatible." To have gotten it so right, and yet have it also be so wrong, was deeply disappointing to them both. One night over dinner they decided to celebrate this new phase of their relationship instead of making it a terrible experience. Together, they set an intention for a future they had never seen any other divorced couple create. They would remain in each other's lives as the best of friends, and support each other's success in the world in an ongoing way. They pledged that when one or the other fell in love with someone new, that they would each strive to navigate that transition in a way that kept their friendship intact.

That intention turned out to be more significant than either of them could have imagined at that time as, several years later, Janet was given the opportunity to partner with two hugely successful *New York Times* bestselling authors. Because she and Chris were such good friends, he was the first person she called to share the good news. As a result, Chris was also invited to participate, and Janet and Chris went from being best friends to business partners. Thus beginning a journey that led to their becoming *New York Times* bestselling authors themselves and creating a global movement around their book *The Passion Test*.

Not long after, their intention was tested when Chris met Doris, the woman who is now his wife. When Doris found out that her new suitor was knee-deep in business with his former wife, she wasn't pleased. Tensions ran high as Chris courted Doris, while also refusing to abandon his work with Janet. It took a lot for Janet to convince Doris she was no threat to their budding relationship. Yet those efforts paid off, for a decade later, not only do Janet and Chris remain business and teaching partners, but Janet and Doris are the best of friends and Janet is also the beloved godmother to Chris and Doris's three beautiful children. The intention that Janet and Chris agreed upon provided them with a North Star that helped them find their way home to an unpredictable and decidedly positive future, informing the actions they took and the choices they made that allowed them to create their happily-*even*-after life.

....

Setting an Intention for a Positive Future for All

Whether or not the two of you choose to remain friends as Janet and Chris did, setting an intention where fairness reigns, goodwill flows, generosity prevails, and your children flourish and thrive promises to pull you toward that future with an energy equal to the vitality used to create it. Rather than being haphazardly hurled into the frightening unknown, by deliberately intending what shall be, you own your power to generate the best of all possible futures from this point on. You may not know exactly what it will look like, or how it could happen, but by grabbing hold of a vision worth realizing and pledging your fidelity to that possibility with all you've got, you initiate momentum in the direction of the fulfillment of that future. As my friend Reverend Dr. Michael Beckwith says, "Pain pushes until the vision pulls." By aligning with that possibility, you now have a North Star to help guide you through the darkest nights, as your intention coaxes you to take the high road whenever possible to bring that future to fruition.

> *You can live your life out of circumstance or you can live your life out of a vision.*
>
> WERNER ERHARD

There are three components to creating a strong intention for a Conscious Uncoupling.

1. **It Must Be About the Future.** You don't want to set an intention to try to go back to being friends the way you were before you were lovers, or to finally get to the bottom of all your unresolved and

unsolvable problems. Rather, you want to generate a new possibility for how your relationship might unfold from here.

For example: "Our intention is to foster an atmosphere of honor, respect, and generosity between us so that our daughter can have a great relationship with us both."

2. **It Must Be Created in the Affirmative.** For example, you don't want to set an intention to stop fighting so much, or to quit being so petty with each other. Rather, you want to create an affirmative declaration.

For example: "My intention is to create a tremendous amount of goodwill and generosity between myself and my former husband so that we are comfortable in the same room with each other, and our grown children and friends feel safe and supported in remaining close to us both."

3. **It Is Infused with a Sense of Noble Purpose That Inspires You to Rise to Meet It.** An uninspired intention, such as the goal of trying to get along a bit better, or a pledge to try to be nicer to each other, will inevitably fall flat and soon be forgotten. Yet one that calls you out to truly strive to be your best self has the power to inspire miracles.

For example: "Our intention is to create one extended, expanded, and evolving family that honors our new roles with one another and provides each of us and our children with comfort, support, and happiness for years to come."

Take a few moments now to craft an intention for a positive new future for yourself and your former partner, as well as those who may be impacted by your separation. Keep it short and simple so that you can easily remember and recite it back to yourself in a moment of emotional upheaval. The more you can hold on to your intention in such times, the saner you'll behave throughout this journey. And the saner you behave, the more likely you will be to fulfill your vision.

If you're doing this program with your former partner, feel free to share your intention with this person, and invite him or her to do it with you. However, even if he or she agrees to do so, I caution you against falling into the trap of trying to police each other to act in integrity. Instead, keep your primary focus on yourself and relate to this vision as yours to fulfill. Not because you're letting the other person off the hook. But because you want to fully own your power, regardless of who someone else is choosing to be, refusing to give anyone the authority to determine how you are going to behave. Remember, kindness is contagious. It's hard for someone to stay mean and petty when you're behaving in ways that are consistently thoughtful, respectful, and generous.

Should your former partner decline your invitation to stand with you in this intention, I encourage you to proceed anyway, staying faithful to the possibility of a miracle between you, and choosing to model good behavior that could lead the way to safer shores for all involved.

Note: If your former partner is behaving in seriously dangerous and/or sociopathic ways, it may not be possible to allow him or her to remain in your life. If this is the case, I suggest you consult with law enforcement professionals who can help protect you and your children, if you have any. A more appropriate future to create in this situation will be one where you (and all impacted) are safe, healthy, well, and thriving in the aftermath of this breakup.

ASK YOURSELF:

"What gifts has this relationship given me that I can acknowledge, appreciate, and be grateful for?"

For example: "I received a greater appreciation for music, a love for being outdoors in nature, an awakening to my attractiveness, and the opportunity to know my own value."

"As I release the future I'd once hoped for, what bright new future can I create in its place?"

For example: "My intention is for us to leave one another enhanced and enriched by the experience of having been together, whole-heartedly more capable of loving and being loved."

"What's my next step in generating this future? What action could I take or choice could I make that would begin to bring it to fruition?"

For example: "I can invite my former husband and his new live-in girlfriend to join the kids and me for Thanksgiving dinner," "I can pray for the happiness of my former partner and send blessings her way," or "I can be flexible with our custody agreement and tell the children that they can see their dad more often if they want to."

Toward a Transformed Future

The ancient art of alchemy is the quest to turn lead into gold, and the alchemist is the artist who inspires such radical change. For the most part, alchemy and its assumption that base metals are simply less developed forms of gold has long since been discarded in favor of our more modern and sophisticated scientific understanding of the basics of chemistry. Yet in 1980, Nobel laureate and chemist Dr. Glenn Seaborg stunned the world by taking a minuscule amount of the base metal bismuth and transmuting it into gold, surprising even the most open-minded and progressive of

> Cry. Forgive. Learn. Move on. Let your tears water the seeds of your future happiness.
> STEVE MARABOLI

scientists. The key to this transformation was not in adding something to the mix, as early alchemists assumed would be required, but by the brilliant act of taking something away. Forcing the release of three of bismuth's eighty-two protons, Seaborg discovered that he could, indeed, transform lead into gold.

It's an apt metaphor for those of us who wish to transform the searing sorrow of a breakup into a positive and life-affirming turning point. Transformation often begins with what we're willing to subtract from our lives, rather than what we're trying to add. Setting an intention to midwife a radical change of heart will immediately reveal everything you need to let go of in order to realize that goal. The bitter grudge that burns a hole in your stomach each time you hear his name. The primal, unhealed injuries of not being seen, valued, or cared for in the ways you've needed to be. The horror that grips you when contemplating the choices you made that led you to this. Or the residue of unkind words that can never be unspoken, left lingering unresolved between you.

Forgiveness (or the F-word, for those who prefer to be left festering in peace, thank you very much) is not so much a feeling as it is a decision you make from the strongest, soundest part of yourself. It is a perspective to adopt, a practice to engage, and a proclamation of life declared in the midst of death. Now, in this moment, you may be wondering if it might not be *easier* for you to turn lead into gold than to try to forgive the unforgivable and create goodwill from the ashes of your broken love affair. Yet my guess is that there's also a part of you curious to discover what it's like to live from the wisest, most advanced parts of yourself in the aftermath of having been wronged. Or what it feels like to respond to disappointment from vision rather than react from victimization. We all have an inner, noble Nelson Mandela deep down inside. And anyone who's

> *Keep in mind that the true measure of an individual is how he or she treats a person who can do them absolutely no good.*
> ANN LANDERS

ever sported a peace symbol or sung along with John Lennon in a traffic jam, "All we are saying is give peace a chance," believes at least in the ideal of finding another way.

At first glance, it appears too hard to do, as though nature herself has designed us for war. The experience of being victimized takes over and begs us to start victimizing those we feel most wounded by. The Japanese even have a saying, "You never know your wife until you divorce her," pointing to the radical change of personality that can overcome the best of us when our emotional home has been decimated by a breakup. It's ridiculously easy to behave badly at the end of love. Suddenly, the decent person you've always known yourself to be disappears, as you're confronted with the latent crazy person you have the potential to become. Irrationally consumed with morally questionable fantasies of nasty, blood-hungry, and retaliatory acts of revenge, you're faced with the ultimate litmus test of your character. Who will you choose to be in the face of this? Which part of your self will you align with and respond to your hurt from? These are the questions you're now confronted with, and you will forever live with the consequences of how you choose to answer them.

If you've been betrayed, abandoned, or deceived, you can expect to feel enraged. That's your biology in action. Yet, you can also choose to respond with decency, self-respect, and integrity. For that's your consciousness in action. What will allow you to behave in this dignified way in the aftermath of being wounded by Cupid's slings and arrows is the simple, yet good-hearted decision to take the hit, learn the lessons, and release the pain you're in, rather than to lay hurt down as your foundation and build a home there by acting out your wrath.

To step into this deep release, you're going to have to be willing to hold your righteous narrative a little less rigidly about how you were wronged. We all have our stories to tell, most of them so steeped in biased interpretations about what happened that it's hard to discern "my truth" from "The Truth." The story you've been telling yourself and others about your breakup is filled with assumptions that may or may not actually be true. Ask any detective whose task it is to get eyewitness reports of a crime scene, and he will tell you that he rarely hears the same story twice. Same crime, yet very different stories emerge from even the most reliable of witnesses all trying hard to just recite the facts of what occurred.

Human understanding can't help but be highly subjective, and memory even more so. Recent studies show that we're prone to recount events not the way they happened but through the interpretive lens of our own preexisting worldview. So, wear your conclusions lightly. If you insist on telling your breakup story from a victimized perspective, making your former partner the villain while setting a halo upon your own head (or vice versa), then you're probably not capturing the complexities it holds, and the subtle ways your experience was likely co-created. To be free, you'll want to let go of ruminating on who did what to whom, and turn your attention to the ongoing practice of forgiving yourself and your former partner for the many mistakes made during the course of the relationship.

Forgiveness Practice

On forgiveness, my dear friend, and bestselling author of *Enchanted Love,* Marianne Williamson writes:

> *The question becomes this: Where do I put my faith? Do I put my faith in something loveless that someone did to me, or in the eternal love that lies beyond and corrects all things? To the extent that I withdraw my attachment to what you did, I will no longer be affected by what you did. I have decided to put my faith elsewhere. That is the miracle of forgiveness.*

To the extent you cling to a grudge, you'll bind your soul to its perpetrator and leave yourself at his or her mercy to find freedom from what's happened—or *not.* You may as well wrap your personal power up in a box, stick a bow on top, and hand-deliver it to one who's already demonstrated his unworthiness of your trust and devotion.

When Jesus admonished us to pray for our enemies, he did not do so because it was the nice Christian thing to do. He was teaching us to be spiritual masters. Demonstrating how we might trump the temptation to react from the lowest, most base parts of ourselves, and thereby risk locking ourselves into a lesser life. He was challenging us to be a force for goodness and love in the world regardless of what was coming at us. That's personal power. And that's what it is to be a Love Alchemist.

If you are angry, it's likely for good reason. It's not wrong to slide into a story of victimization and blame. It's human. You may wake up into that narrative each morning, or find it running like a soundtrack in the background of your days. The work is to continually shepherd yourself to higher ground. And this is where spiritual practice comes in. Certainly you will want to return again and again to the practice included in Step 2 for all resentments that crop up and threaten to consume you, as it will help you to keep the focus where it belongs right now—on *yourself and your own transformation.*

One of the world's foremost happiness experts, a dear friend of mine, bestselling author of *Happy for No Reason,* Marci Shimoff, shared with me the practice that supported her to stay centered and strong during her own divorce. She learned it from the late Reverend Roberta Herzog, who'd created it based upon the passage in the Lord's Prayer, which asks God to "forgive us our trespasses as we forgive those who trespass against us." It was Reverend Herzog's belief that when we forgive and ask for forgiveness in return, we neutralize and defuse the negative momentum of the situation we're in, and return our destiny to our own hands.

This practice requires you to repeat the following visualization twice a day, once when you rise and right before you go to bed, every day for two weeks in a row. In doing so, you'll find your heart becoming lighter through an almost magical release. As you determine to let someone else off the hook, so too are you released from suffering.

....

Sit and close your eyes. Imagine the person you need to forgive happy and smiling. Then say the following out loud:

[Your former partner's name], I forgive you for everything you've ever said or done to me in thought, word, or deed that has caused me pain. You are free and I am free!

And, [your former partner's name], I ask that you forgive me for anything that I have ever said or done to you in thought, word, or deed that has caused you pain. You are free and I am free!

Thank you, God [Universe, Spirit, or Life], for this opportunity to forgive [your former partner's name] and to forgive myself.

....

When you are angry, rather than ruminate, try turning your attention in a constructive direction by looking to discover what's waking up in you. Try relating to your anger as the ferocious energy of change, and ask yourself what stand you can take that will quell the urgency of your rage. Anger begs us to make a powerful commitment to what we will or will not tolerate in our lives any longer, making it our best friend if we can turn it in the right direction.

Another potent practice you can do when you find yourself on a resentment rant, particularly against yourself, is the ancient Hawaiian prayer *Ho'oponopono,* which means "to make right." Based upon the assumption that anger causes illness, both physical and mental, this elegant exercise promises to clear your mind, soothe jagged emotions, and help you rise above any impulse to retaliate for perceived wrongdoings so that you can break the cycle of escalating attacks.

> *When you forgive . . . it's like spring cleaning for your heart.*
> MARCI SHIMOFF

If the one who needs your mercy most is you, you may do the *Ho'oponopono* practice on yourself. Begin by placing your hand over your heart; then tenderly say your name and speak the prayer silently to yourself, as though you were able to breathe each statement straight into the core of you.

Ho'oponopono Practice

1. **Identify What's Disturbing You.** Bring into awareness a memory that is disturbing to you and causing you to resent your former partner and/or yourself.

2. **Suspend Your Certainty About What Happened.** Become willing to suspend your certainty about what actually happened, seeing your current understanding of events as valid, yet incomplete. Recognize that other valid interpretations of this experience coexist with yours; expand your awareness to include all perspectives as worthy of consideration.

3. **Repeat the *Ho'oponopono* Prayer.** With humility and a desire to make right all wrongs, repeat the following as often as you like:

   I love you.
   I'm sorry.
   Please forgive me.
   Thank you.

Self-forgiveness will usually require an act of contrition to help right a wrong, and you may find yourself heavy with the awareness that an action must be taken in order to bring restitution to a situation: an apology offered, amends made, or a promise given to behave with more self-respect and self-love from this moment forward in life. When you see what needs to happen clearly, you'll want to take action to rectify the wrongs you've perpetrated against yourself or others, as it will be nearly impossible to truly forgive yourself without some act of contrition.

Choosing to forgive is not about condoning bad behavior. Nor does it require you to let someone back into your life. In fact, forgiveness is not about anyone else at all. It's about *you*—and your choice to not be defined by this painful experience moving forward. It's about your decision to not live a compromised life because of this disappointment, and your resolve to be liberated from all toxic emotions that could seriously diminish your chances for happiness and love in your future.

Note: If your rage is not about the past, but about an abuse that is happening in the present, then you'll want to use the sheer force of your emotions to facilitate positive change. Rather than react to the boundary violation, look to discover what needs to change, and have the courage to take empowering steps in that direction. Find your voice, locate your power, and ferociously act in the best interests of all involved.

ASK YOURSELF:

"What victimized story am I willing to let go of and what can I take responsibility for in how I co-created this situation?"

For example: "I can let go of blaming her for leaving and take responsibility for the ways I was shutting her out that pushed her to do so," "I can give up ruminating on all the ways my former partner mistreated me and look instead at how I mistreated myself by staying in an abusive situation for so long," or "I can let go of my conclusion that my former partner was using me for sex and take responsibility for how much I was using my sexuality to manipulate him to try to get what I wanted."

"What is my anger demanding I change? What wants to wake up in me right now?"

For example: "Anger is demanding I stop being so tolerant of being treated poorly. What's waking up in me is the right to say *no* to being abused," "My anger is insisting that I stop settling for less than I deserve in life. What is waking up in me is my right to have the best that life and love have to offer," or "Rage is bringing me to my knees and requiring me to give up trying to get blood from a stone. The commitment I am making to myself from now on is to only give my heart to someone who has demonstrated that he has the capacity to love me back."

"What amends to myself or others can I now make to bring completion to this situation?"

For example: "I can apologize to my former partner for setting him up to fail me by rarely telling him what I felt or what I needed," "I can make amends to all men from now on by vowing to build them up as opposed to tear them down every chance I get," or "I can make a promise to myself to never, ever again overgive as a way to try to prove my value."

> *To navigate safe passage through a dark night of the soul you must have faith in yourself and the goodness of life. Even if you can't feel it, and especially if you have no evidence for it, make choices and take actions as though you believe that all of life is supporting your healing, evolution, and ultimate success.*
>
> CLAIRE ZAMMIT

Resolving the Past

Remorse. Regret. Guilt. Shame. These big emotions beg for resolution. Yet in a poorly navigated breakup they instead become fixed within us, and the imprint of the relationship is frozen in its most destructive state. We all know those couples who broke up years before yet still go rigid and cold when their former partner walks in the room. Time doesn't make things right. We must. And if we don't make an effort for a clean and peaceful parting, we will pay a very high price.

One of my more soul-crushing breakups occurred when I was far too young to appreciate the long-term impact of a bad ending. I was eighteen, and my boyfriend of nearly four years, Frank, sat across from me in a cushy red leather booth at a local steakhouse. His face red and twisted in frustration, he was vehemently insisting I *not* go to college. Rather than pursue higher education, he'd chosen to go into his family's business, and he wasn't about to let his future bride run off to a swanky school where she'd surely be swept off her feet by some full-of-himself college man. Choking back tears, I was overcome with the shocking realization that we'd come to the end of the road. The chasm between us too wide to cross, I made a spontaneous decision to cut and run without further explanation. I may have loved him, but the idea that he would try to *control* me was deplorable, and I had to get out of there fast. Yet, unable to bear the thought of never seeing him again, I made a desperate, impassioned plea. We would go our separate ways now, yet make a pact to find each other again and marry when in our sixties, after all our major life decisions had been made.

Whether or not he ever agreed to such a foolish scheme I can't recall. I believe he just sat there in shock as I told him we were through. Yet for me, the promise stuck. And though Frank married another woman the following year, severing contact between us completely and throwing me into an almost unbearable grief, I lived with the vague notion that one day in the faraway future, we would again be reunited. The ill-fated hope of that reckless pledge plagued me for the next two decades, as I frequently woke in the middle of the night, sweating, heart pounding, and with a piercing longing for my long-lost, phantom love.

Fast-forward many years later to when, still single at the age of forty-one with no prospects for a husband in view, I made yet another outrageous pledge. A firm believer in the power of intention, I called a friend to boldly declare my resolve to be engaged by my forty-second birthday. To her credit, she did not laugh, or tell me that a woman over forty has a better chance of being the target of terrorists than she has of finding a great husband. Instead, she quietly replied she'd be happy to support my efforts to pull a rabbit out of a hat if I gave her permission to hold me accountable for being the woman I'd need to be for that to happen. And thus, the now globally recognized Calling in "The One" process for manifesting love was born, as I shifted my attention away from running out to try to find love, to going within to seek and release all the barriers I'd built against it.

No stone was left unturned in my inner excavation as I fiercely began examining and releasing my beliefs, assumptions, habits, and ways of relating that had covertly been keeping me single, in spite of my best efforts to the contrary. It was not long before I stumbled upon the memory of my rash and hasty pact with Frank, and I quickly set out to undo the decision I'd made when I was too young to know any better. I now understood that this agreement had been clandestinely influencing me to stay single. Just in case he returned, you see, so I'd be there to meet him. It was all very romantic in an overly dramatic, pathetic Romeo-and-Juliet sort of way.

To align my life with my intention to find a life partner, I decided to resolve the unfinished business between us by completing the pact. Unwilling to disrupt his family life—for by this time, Frank had been married for over twenty years and had three children—I decided against trying to call him, and instead brought him into a Soul-to-Soul Communication (see Step 3).

Closing my eyes and taking a deep breath, I imagined Frank sitting before me. I thanked him for the love he'd given me, and apologized for the ways in which I'd hurt him. I reminded him of the promise I'd made, letting him know that I could no longer keep it. I needed to be free to find a mate and was therefore letting him go. I shed a few tears, filled a few tissues, and by the end of the practice, felt free to move forward unencumbered. My dreams about Frank stopped and, in fact, I met my husband, Mark, just a few short weeks later.

Eight years down the road, after not speaking with Frank for nearly thirty years by this time, a mutual friend facilitated a telephone reunion between us. I was nervous and flooded with things I'd been yearning to tell him for many years. I knew I'd hurt him deeply and more than anything I wanted to apologize. It was an emotional conversation, with both of us pouring our hearts out and confessing our deep regret for the traumatic way we'd ended our relationship. Frank shocked me by admitting that I'd not been the only one disturbed by torrid dreams. He, too, had dreamt about me for years after our breakup, stunning me by sharing when his troubling night visions had finally stopped—right at the time I did the Soul-to-Soul Communication some eight years before. It was too bizarre to consider anything other than chance, and I quickly put it out of my mind.

Frank and I did not plan another time to speak. Our conversation was too intense for two people who were married to others. It was enough to have this sweet closure after all this time. Without a word, we both simply knew to not call the other. Yet one night, about a year later, as I sat laboring at my computer late at night, a wave of warm feelings melted my resolve and I dashed off a simple e-mail letting Frank know that I thought of him often and should he ever need a friend to please reach out. As I pushed the send button it hit me like a ton of bricks. "Frank is getting a divorce," I gasped. And sure enough, an hour later he wrote back. "I can't believe you are writing me. Tonight over dinner, my wife told me she wants a divorce." It was my second confirmation of the nonlocal, nonlinear nature of a love bond, and a startling wake-up call to the profound levels of interconnectedness we're all living with continually.

One of the discoverers of quantum mechanics, physicist Niels Bohr, also a Nobel Prize winner, introduced the world to the idea of non-locality, also called "entanglement" back in the 1920s. My friend Lynne McTaggart, journalist turned thought leader and author of *The Bond,* explains entanglement to be the "strange, poetic phenomenon of doomed indivisibility, like a pair of star-crossed lovers who may be forced to separate but remain mentally and emotionally intertwined forever." Ugh. How's that for validating your worst nightmare? Albert Einstein, a colleague of Bohr's, called it "spooky action at a distance," which seemed an accurate description to me. I was definitely spooked. Yet I was also motivated to finally bring healthy closure to a relationship that had haunted me for most of my adult life.

So while I was shocked and disoriented to hear that Frank's marriage was ending, I was also incredibly grateful for the opportunity to make things right between us by being a true friend. Over the next several months, we spoke frequently as I first tried to help him repair his marriage and, when that proved futile, to support him to end it well. Not only was it a chance to make amends by extending my love to him, but it also provided the opportunity to see how right we'd been to part ways some thirty years before. We had more than one good belly laugh over the vast disparity of our worldviews and core values. And Frank's frequent and humorous observations that I'd made a good decision to leave him comforted me, and assuaged any anxieties I may have had to the contrary.

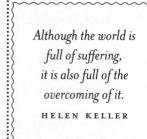

Although the world is full of suffering, it is also full of the overcoming of it.
HELEN KELLER

Evolving our relationship to this place of true completion was like removing deeply embedded splinters from our psyches. No more do Frank and I yearn for one another in the wee hours of the morning, or wrestle with what might have been. No longer are we tormented and diminished by the loss of love. Rather, we both feel expanded and enriched by the experience we shared. Enhanced by the awareness that we've been deeply loved by someone who glimpsed the beauty of our soul, and found their way into the inner chambers of our heart. This is ideally how we want to leave each other at the end of love. Not consumed with bitterness and hostility, but enlarged by the depth and breadth of the care both given and received.

The Art of Conscious Completion

Clean completions consist of three parts. First, acknowledging what this person has meant to you. Second, appreciating the gifts he or she brought into your life. And third, making a sincere attempt to restore wholeness to the situation by offering amends, either to the people you've hurt directly, or by declaring your commitment to never again repeat the same mistakes with someone new. As you can see, this list does not include reconciling your irreconcilable differences, being vindicated once and for all, or finally getting your emotional needs met.

There are reasons you and your former partner are parting ways. Your values are too diverse, your perspectives too polarized, or your core needs too much at odds. In a Conscious

Uncoupling, this is not a problem, as we make room for differences and discordant perspectives assuming, as philosopher Ken Wilber suggests, "everyone's right about something." This isn't about winning a war. It's about giving up the idea of war altogether, and going the extra mile to make sure everyone wins moving forward. The truth is, at this point, it doesn't really matter who's right and who's wrong. It doesn't matter who hurt who more. It doesn't even matter if you can't agree on the reasons your relationship is ending. What matters is that you seek to bring closure in ways that help all involved to thrive when they get to the other side of this disappointment.

When Robin and her husband, Gary, decided to end their marriage of nineteen years, they wanted to do so in a way that did minimal damage to their twelve-year-old twin boys, Zach and Miles, and their ten-year-old daughter, Emma. Yet, in the weeks that followed Gary's move out of their home, all three children started showing signs of distress. Emma began writing morbid poetry, Zach's grades took a plunge, and Miles got into a fight with another kid at school, causing their parents to schedule an appointment with me. I explained that while their resolve to not fight in front of their children was admirable, it was insufficient to create the well-being and cohesion they were hoping for. On some level, kids know everything. A hint of eye rolling, slightly pursed lips, unconscious arm crossing, or deep, revealing sighs all have a way of letting everyone know how you really feel, in spite of what you say. Because Robin and Gary were caring parents, they agreed to do a practice to help them clear the air between them in the hope they might free their children from the unspoken yet palpable tensions between them.

Robin had initiated the divorce because she couldn't get what she needed emotionally from Gary. She'd been dragging him into therapy for years trying to get him to talk about his

Never cut what can be untied.
JACLYN SMITH

feelings, heartfully listen to hers and extend empathy. But this was all pretty unnatural for Gary. He was more mind oriented than heart, and the chronic unhappiness of his wife wore on him. No matter how hard he tried to please her, he was always failing. So, after nearly two decades of marriage, they chose to part ways. They did not raise their voices or overtly fight in front of the children, yet there was resentment below the surface. He felt chronically criticized, as though nothing he did was ever enough. And she felt deeply unloved, as he should have tried harder to give her what she needed so their marriage could survive.

In the spirit of conscious completion, they were willing to hear each other out, and discuss the hurtful impact they'd had. Robin listened first as Gary haltingly spoke of the intense demoralization of constantly being asked for something he was ill equipped to provide. She let it touch her heart when he shared about how inadequate it made him feel. Rather than coming back at him with trying to get him to understand how painful it was for *her*, or trying to get him to see *why* she needed more emotional support, she instead just listened, taking in what he was trying to tell her about his experience. No longer needing to work this out with him, she had the luxury of focusing instead on how she might make amends to him. She offered a heartfelt apology for the suffering she'd caused, and promised to adjust her expectations moving forward. She pledged to genuinely relate to him from a place of appreciation from this moment forward, and give up her demand that he be anyone other than who he was. The relief Gary felt was palpable, clearing away the residue of hurt and resentment he'd been carrying for years.

He was then able to turn his attention to Robin and listen as she poured her heart out about how disappointed she was that after all she'd invested in their marriage, he never came through for her emotionally. She spoke of how alone she'd felt in their marriage, and Gary, relieved that he no longer needed to do anything to fix her feelings as much as just hear and acknowledge them, was able to have compassion for his wife. He began wanting for her what she wanted for herself, and understood for the first time why their divorce could actually be the right thing for everyone. His amends was to let her go so she might find a more suitable partner who could meet her emotional needs, releasing Robin from the guilt she'd been feeling.

The energy between them transformed from a festering hotbed of hurt to an almost warm and mutually supportive friendliness. Their children felt this shift and, as if by magic, began doing better almost immediately. Their divorce became a kind of family adventure rather than a failure, as the children took an interest in helping Dad find a new apartment and then assisting him in decorating it. Robin is now in a new relationship with a heart-centered, emotionally generous man who is in many ways her dream partner. The children love their mom's new partner, and, in seeing his former wife so happy, Gary has come to accept and appreciate him as well, understanding even more why the decision to end their marriage was the best choice they could have made.

The latest studies in neurobiology show that a negative conversation will stay with us far longer than a positive one. When we are left feeling cursed, condemned, shamed, and blamed by the one we loved, our bodies produce

> *In the course of my life, I have often had to eat my words, and I must confess that I have always found it a wholesome diet.*
> WINSTON CHURCHILL

higher levels of cortisol, the stress hormone that stimulates us to behave in combative, self-protective ways. So hurtful are the rejections of an intimate partner that we'll perceive the final actions and words of insult as far worse than they are, affecting our memories of the relationship and creating toxic tensions in the relational field that can feel like crossfire to any children involved.

Few of us consciously try to hurt others and ourselves at the end of love, and most will at least attempt an amicable separation. Yet when attempting a completion conversation to try to reconcile the damage done, we'll often spend an inordinate amount of time explaining why we behaved as we did. *My father treated my mother that way. I never learned how to do it any differently. It's in my astrological chart to be like this. I only behaved this way because you behaved that way.* More than anything, we're trying to be understood. And we'll pull on our former partner to exonerate our behavior long before we've become sufficiently present to the cost it's had on him. As if his pain was not nearly as important as our distress at being misunderstood.

....

Clearing the Air

In order to dissolve the tensions still churning between you, you'll need to be a lot less interested in being understood, and a lot more interested in understanding the impact of your choices and actions. A lot less invested in being right, and a lot more invested in how you might actually *make things right.*

To this end, I offer the following, a modification of a similar practice created by my colleague Claire Zammit.*

---

* This practice is a modification of an exercise called "Clearing the Field," created by Claire Zammit for participants of the Feminine Power 9 Month Mastery Program (see www.FemininePower.com). It is also taught in my 9 Month Calling in "The One" Love Mastery Training (see www.CallingintheOne.com).

You may want to invite your former partner to do this exercise with you. However, if it's not possible or safe to do so, you can also engage it as a Soul-to-Soul Communication (see Step 3), using your imagination to envision an evolution toward a more wholesome closure between you.

Relationships that do not end peacefully, do not end at all.

MERRIT MALLOY

1. **Understand the Sole Purpose of This Exercise Is to Clear the Air.** Recognize that the purpose of this exercise is simply to clear the air of any festering hurts and resentments between you and your former partner. As such, I invite you to set aside the goals of getting your needs met, changing your former partner's mind, winning an argument, or resolving your irreconcilable differences.

2. **Identify the Active Hurts and Disappointments You're Each Still Struggling With.** I invite you each to list the hurts and festering resentments still incomplete for you, even if apologies have already been offered.

3. **Become Willing to Take Responsibility for the Impact Your Behavior Has Had on Your Former Partner.** Decide who will speak, and who will listen, first.

   For the Speaker: You're invited to share the hurts you're still struggling with and the impact your former partner's behavior has had on you. (For example: "I'm devastated you lied to me, and I'm not sure I'll ever trust anyone again," "My self-esteem is at an all-time low because of your constant put-downs and complaints," "I've not been able to sleep or eat for weeks because of how traumatized I am by how suddenly you left.")

   For the Listener: You're invited to put aside your defenses, and strive to be present and available to hear what your former partner is saying. Regardless of whether you think he or she is telling the story accurately, try seeing the situation from his or her perspective. Recognize that many of the ways we hurt each other are unintended; we unconsciously repeat old patterns, we're distracted, self-absorbed, or simply assuming that others are like us. Whether you meant to hurt your former partner is not the point. That he or she was hurt is all that matters. Set aside who's right or wrong (unless you can now see how *you* may have been wrong), and become willing to take responsibility for the impact of your behavior. Don't negate, minimize, or dismiss what he or she is saying. Instead, be interested in discovering how you may have contributed to and co-created the pain with which your former partner is currently struggling.

4. **Let Your Former Partner Know What You Now See About the Impact Your Behavior Has Had on Him or Her.**

    For the Listener: Do your best to not interrupt the speaker, unless you are requesting more clarification about what he or she is saying. Allow your heart to genuinely be touched by what your former partner is sharing about their experience. Without explaining *why* you did what you did, or how the situation may have impacted *you,* place your attention fully on him or her and extend a sense of authentic care and concern for the impact your choices and actions had upon him or her.

    With deep humility and a willingness to tell the truth, mirror back to your former partner what you can see about how your choices and actions impacted him or her or others.

    For the Speaker: Do not move on until you feel that your former partner truly understands the impact his or her actions and choices have had upon you, and on others that you love.

5. **Offer to Make Amends by Taking Wholesome Right Action.** Past hurts don't go away just because we feel badly about what we've done. Nor does saying "I'm sorry" always restore well-being to the

relational field. What genuinely clears the air of toxic emotional residue is an amends taken with the clear intention of restoring wholeness to the situation.

For the Listener: Consider the amends you can now make to your former partner. While you can't go back and undo the choices you've made, you can take wholesome right action to try to repair the damage that's been done. For example, offer to pay for what your mistakes cost your former partner, take steps to clean up a mess you helped make, or make a promise to never do this again to anyone else in the future.

For the Speaker: Think on what would actually help repair the damage done by your former partner and allow yourself to receive the restitution being offered. While nothing can undo what has happened, an act of genuine contrition and retribution can set you and everyone involved up to heal from this experience and move forward unchained to the mistakes of the past.

Once the speaker feels complete, switch roles so that you each have an opportunity to clear the air of hostility, hurt, and resentment.

For a free audio download of this practice, please go to www.ConsciousUncoupling.com/StepFourPractice.

Note: Communication exercises are ordinarily used to bring people closer, not help them move apart. You may find at this point, though, that engaging the Conscious Uncoupling process has opened up the potential for reconciliation. If you and your former partner wish to explore the possibility of reconciling, please go to www.ConsciousRecoupling.com for information on how best to support an attempted reunion.

··

Evolving Your Relationship

Kintsugi is the centuries-old Japanese art of repairing broken pottery with silver, gold, or platinum, turning a seemingly ruined object into one of unique beauty and elegance. The philosophy behind Kintsugi is to honor the history of a damaged object by validating its value in how it's repaired. Often the process creates something even more beautiful than the original object. So, too, can we repair a fractured relationship in a way that dignifies its history and validates its worth by how we behave when it's over.

When my former husband, Mark, and I first separated, we worked out the financial details on our own, without the help of attorneys or a judge. For several months, all went well as we were both able to honor our agreements. Yet a few months in, as I sat eating lunch one weekday afternoon, I received a call from Mark to say he'd lost his job. My first thought was to worry he wouldn't be able to pay his rent. My second was the dreaded realization that he wouldn't be able to pay *me,* either, to help support our daughter. Nothing like the bottom dropping out to tempt one to throw all good intentions for a conscious breakup out the window. Assuming he was more upset than he was letting on, I offered words of encouragement, suggesting he'd be back on his feet in no time. Secretly, however, I was panicking. It was hard enough to go from one household to two, without one of us losing a steady paycheck. Knowing Mark would soon face some tough choices about how to spend his

> *Grief does not change you. It reveals you.*
>
> JOHN GREEN

suddenly finite funds, I immediately began reciting in my mind a litany of reasons as to why he needed to put the care of his daughter above all else, making good on his financial promises during this upcoming period of unemployment.

All afternoon I struggled to understand what right action was in this situation. Certainly, I depended upon Mark's contribution to pay the bills. Yet, I was also pretty creative and resourceful, having pulled a financial rabbit out of the hat more times than I could count. By the end of the day, I'd made an important decision. I figured there had to be hundreds of ways I could increase our family income other than to strain my relationship with the only father my daughter would ever have. And so, with our child's psychological well-being at stake, I chose this as the perfect moment to build some goodwill into our newly evolving family. I called Mark and told him to not worry about giving me money while he was unemployed, gifting him with some seriously needed financial relief while he struggled to secure employment as quickly as he could. I spent the next few weeks figuring out how to expand my office hours to include more time to see private clients and, by the end of two months, had managed to cover the loss of Mark's monthly contribution.

That act of teamwork and generosity was an investment in the new future we were building. A golden repair of the broken family we were in danger of becoming. One that set the tone for many such moments of generosity and thoughtfulness that have since come to characterize our connection. Because I had the foresight to recognize that moment for the opportunity it was to generate benevolence between us, our transition from a traditional to an expanded family has continued to blossom. We may be an unusual little clan, but we are far from a failed one. It may not be what I'd hoped for when I stood at the altar promising lifelong love and devotion, but it's beautiful in its own creative and quirky way.

Odd as it may sound, it's possible to feel even more loved at the end of a relationship than at the beginning. For in the first blush of romance, we often project we're going to get all we want and need from our partner, making it easy to give of ourselves. It's at the end of love, when we know better, when we're wrestling with the disappointments and very real limitations of the relationship, that we have the opportunity to give and receive authentic care—care that has no motivation other than to do the right thing for the right reasons. These generous gestures of fairness and goodwill go a long way toward building new bridges at a time when the old ones are being torn down.

We want to get into the habit of asking ourselves: What am I generating by how I'm responding to the challenges we're now facing? Hostility? Division? More stress? Or cohesion? Repair? Well-being? We all know that good relationships take time and care to build. Yet so, too, do newly forming expanded families. We want to continually extend ourselves to make amends, bring restitution, learn from and correct our mistakes, grow more tolerant, reach beyond our comfort zones in order to see another's perspective, re-earn trust, restore honor to the family, and repair any damage that's been done. It may take time to turn things around. Yet, we'll want to seize those moments when we have the opportunity to evolve the relationship in wholesome, healthy ways. Every gesture of generosity you can authentically offer has the potential to create ripples of goodness that can be felt for many years to come. When children grow up in such a family, they

> *The only people you should get even with are those who have helped you.*
> JOHN E. SOUTHARD

grow up whole, whether or not their parents are married or unmarried.

ASK YOURSELF:

"What generous gesture(s) could I extend to my former partner that has the potential to mend any damage that's been done, build peace, and/or generate greater levels of goodwill between us?"

A Word to the Wise

At this point, I suggest you adopt a more formal way of relating to one another, offering some much needed space to adjust to your new life circumstances. No longer responsible for your partner's happiness in life, I encourage you to give up being overly involved and grant your former partner the right to his or her own privacy and process. Yet, if and when you do communicate, you'll want to do it in ways that build peace, so you can avoid petty arguments and do all you can to create an ever-escalating sense of goodwill between you.

> *Always seek less turbulent skies. Hurt. Fly above it. Betrayal. Fly above it. Anger. Fly above it. You are the one who is flying the plane.*
>
> MARIANNE WILLIAMSON

To help those who must continue communicating cooperatively throughout your separation and beyond, whether because you share children, business connections, or a common community, I offer the following: Please remember that these are ideals to aspire to. If you make a mistake, simply clean up any messes you've made and start again.

POST-BREAKUP COMMUNICATION GUIDELINES

*1. Do your best to communicate from your wise, strong, and re-
sourceful adult self, and not from the powerless, wounded parts
of you.*

When we lash out in needy, destructive, or hurtful ways, it's
usually because we're centered in a younger part of ourselves
that's unable to access the wisdom, strength, and resourceful-
ness we now possess as high-functioning adults. Rather than
repress these tender, younger parts of yourself, you'll want to
turn toward them and self-soothe *before* speaking to your former partner, so that you can behave as the powerful, mature
adult you actually are (see Step 1 practice: Creating a Mentoring
Mantra). Remember, it's the adult you, and not your younger
self, who's holding the keys to an empowered future.

*2. Speak in ways that are generative of the future you're commit-
ted to creating.*

The word *abracadabra,* used throughout the world to represent
the creation of magic, is thought to derive from the Aramaic
phrase meaning "I create what I speak." Don't assume that just
because you've set an intention for a positive future for all that
your goal will fulfill itself. Rather, you'll want to start relating
to your speaking as an act of creation.

Rather than simply report on what's happening, which often
has a decidedly negative slant, try seeing your words as having
the ability to build a new world. Speak your intended future
into existence by making positive, life-affirming statements
such as "We may have hit a few snags along the way, but our
ability to problem-solve together seems to be improving," "I'm

learning so much from all your feedback that I know is going to help me to have better relationships with everyone from now on," or "This is a golden opportunity for us to discover how to better cooperate with one another."

3. Strive to respond rather than react.

Don't give your power away to someone who's communicating from an infantile and unconscious part of himself or herself by reacting in kind. Rather, see if you can elevate the conversation by responding with maturity, intelligence, and wisdom. Begin by redirecting the conversation, reminding your former partner of the intention you're committed to causing, and modeling the civility and thoughtfulness that will help get you there.

While you may be required to adjust your expectations, set new boundaries, make a clear request, or even draw a line in the sand, do it in a way that's true to the healthy new future you're committed to creating. Say things that de-escalate a potential spiraling situation such as "I hear you and it makes so much sense why you're upset. This is challenging for us all. Yet, my intention remains to make sure this a win-win situation for everyone, so let's see if we can't figure this out together."

By making the choice to become a Love Alchemist, you have taken the lead in your heavy heart and transformed it into the gold of your new bright future. This choice is not a forced, naïve, or superficial optimism but, rather, an intelligent, inspired, and informed one. It is an optimism that knows the worst of what can happen

When all else fails, love.

ELIZABETH LESSER

and yet chooses to affirm the overall goodness of life in the face of it. And not just affirm the goodness of life but willingly become an agent of it. Truly, one can search the whole world over and find no greater love than this.

....

STEP 4 SELF-CARE SUGGESTIONS
(Take at least 2 each day)

1. **Be social.** Call a friend just to catch up, go to dinner with an old buddy, or simply take the time to chat with a neighbor. Reach out and make an effort to authentically connect with those around you.

2. **Go outside.** Spend at least five minutes in the sun, take a walk on the beach, do some gardening, or take your shoes off to walk on the grass barefoot.

3. **Learn something new just for fun.** Pick up a book on a subject that has nothing to do with what you do for a living, learn the basics of a new language, or sign up for a cooking or painting class.

4. **Re-create your living environment.** Open wide all the windows to let a breeze run through your home, rearrange the furniture, or give away those things you've been accumulating that you no longer want, need, or love.

5. **Look to create happiness for others.** Be generous with your time, attention, money, and heart. Give $5 to a person who needs it more than you. Surprise someone by offering a random act of kindness just to lighten his or her load. Listen with depth and presence to someone who may be feeling more isolated and alone than you.

6. **Make a list of the top 100 things you can be grateful for** and keep it somewhere near so you can access it when needed.

NOTE TO COUPLES DOING THE PROGRAM TOGETHER

In this fourth step of your Conscious Uncoupling program, I encourage you to speak directly with one another in order to align upon a shared intention for the new future you're committing yourselves to co-create, as long as you both feel safe to do so. Each of you should offer ideas about the intention that could be set, working together to choose goals that feel authentic and achievable to you both.

Do your best to make the intention memorable, as you will need to refer to it to help you respond to the challenges facing you in ways that support its fulfillment. Should one of you forget and behave in a way that is misaligned and even destructive of your shared intention, the other should gently steer you both back to your mutual goals, by using reassuring and respectful words and by taking fair and honorable actions.

Remember, each of you must be willing to be the leader, concerning yourself more with how you might powerfully respond to setbacks and delays than you are with whether or not your former partner is behaving himself or herself and adhering to the rules. Assume you'll both make mistakes. Be gracious in the face of them, and recognize that it's impossible to do this perfectly. Leave lots of room for errors, both yours and your former partner's. What matters most is not how often you fall off the wagon, but how many times you're willing to get back on.

create your happily-*even*-after life

It's understandable to fight for a bigger slice of the pie,
but it's admirable to fight for a bigger pie.
GLENNON DOYLE MELTON

I n this fifth and final step of your Conscious Uncoupling program, you will be supported to make wise, healthy, and life-affirming decisions as you take on the essential tasks of reinventing your life and setting up vital new structures that will allow you and all involved to thrive after this transition.

Having been consumed with the many crises brought about by the loss of love, you may not yet be fully aware of the beautiful life that is waiting for you on the other side of grief. And while your new life may look little like the one you left behind, your goal is not to try to create a better version of what you once had, but to expand what's now possible to include fresh new horizons, friends, and interests—and the exploration of forgotten, yet promising possibilities.

All leading you, and those you love, safely home to your happily-*even*-after life.

In Step 5, Create Your Happily-*Even*-After Life, you will:

- Complete the old agreements your relationship was founded upon and generate new ones more appropriate to the form it's now taking.
- Create cohesion and alignment with your community at large to ensure a supportive and nourishing environment in which to reinvent your life.
- Learn how you can engage a heartwarming and meaningful Conscious Uncoupling ceremony that liberates and empowers you, your former partner, and all involved to move on with loving and conscious completion.
- Discover wholesome, healthy, and cooperative ways to care for the kids, divide your property, and navigate the legal process that will ensure all involved are set up to win moving forward.

In his dialogue the *Symposium,* the great philosopher Plato referred to love as the child of fullness and of emptiness. While we'd all love to spend the majority of our days reveling in the fullness of love, we will each have our time of entering emptiness as well, for none of us can escape the cyclical nature of life and of love. Though this breakup is not what you had hoped for, it is what you've been given. And if you are wise, at some point you'll know to cease your battle against the inevitable, lay down the sword of your discontent, and soften your heart into a state of simple surrender and accept life on its own terms.

As resistant as we are to move into emptiness, once there we

> *How do these geese*
> *know when to fly to*
> *the sun? Who tells*
> *them the seasons?*
> *How do we, humans,*
> *know when it is time*
> *to move on? As with*
> *the migrant birds, so*
> *surely with us, there*
> *is a voice within . . .*
> *that tells us when*
> *to go forth into the*
> *unknown.*
>
> ELISABETH
> KÜBLER-ROSS

may find it a rather peaceful place to be. In letting go, you become not only empty of the life you once lived and the person you once were in your relationship, but also empty of petty, mean thoughts, reactive and hurtful impulses, the torturous chatter of disempowering and only-partially-true stories, and festering toxic emotions such as shame, destructive guilt, or self-hatred. While many fear entering the abyss of this hollowed (or perhaps hallowed?) terrain, this particular emptiness is, of course, a pregnant void, one that is filled with creative potential. As the Sufi poet Rumi once said, "It looks like the end, it seems like a sunset, but in reality it is a dawn."

The best part of the worst thing in the world actually happening is that it liberates you to reimagine. Though you may have fought against this moment with all of your might, you could find that surrendering into the sheer spaciousness of it offers surprising relief. Who you are, what you love, and how you spend your time are suddenly up for reinvention. You might even wake up to the delightful fact that you're now free to re-create your life in ways that are true to your deeper longings, core values, authentic interests, and higher callings. Bettering your life significantly by assimilating all you've gained and learned in your former relationship, as you stretch to find a future that's worthy of all you've endured.

Agreements 2.0

At the heart of each bond lies a series of agreements, some consciously consented to and some simply assumed. In fact, it could be said that the very definition of a relationship is to enter into a complex set of pacts and promises that inform how much of our hearts and souls we will invest in one another, and the level of expectations we should have of ourselves and each other. Promises of devotion such as "You will be my one and only love in this lifetime," "I will always be there for you," or "I will be faithful to you all the days of my life" serve as intentions that take on a life of their own, setting in motion habits and relational dynamics that make it easier to live day-in, day-out inside of the confines of that partnership. Yet, these agreements, often made in earnest and with great emotion, can pull on us long after the relationship has ended, leaving us ambivalent, divided, and somewhat handicapped moving forward.

> *Your present circumstances don't determine where you can go; they merely determine where you start.*
> NIDO QUBEIN

Emily, an attractive and intelligent forty-eight-year-old entrepreneur, had been divorced from her husband for over ten years. Though he had long ago remarried and started a new family, she had not dated in all that time. She came to me to try to figure out why. As we sat and spoke about her life—her hopes, dreams, history, and hardships—it occurred to me to explore the vows she'd made to her former husband on their wedding day. Midway through sharing memories of their ceremony, she suddenly gasped. "Oh, no," she exclaimed, eyes wide. "I've been keeping my vow of fidelity to him! All these years, I've been loyal to the promises I made to him at the altar." Having been raised Catholic, she'd been taught that marriage was for life. While on a conscious level she had different ideals, deep down she was steadfastly faithful to the vow she took before God, her husband, and their family and friends. Though they'd not spoken for nearly a decade, she decided to call him later that day. Surprised to hear from her, he was fortunately gracious and kind as she shared that she would no longer keep her vow of fidelity to him. Though obvious, the opportunity to say it directly and receive his blessing in return liberated her to finally start dating again.

To truly be free, you'll want to carefully consider the agreements upon which your old relationship was founded, and adjust the expectations you have of yourself and your former partner to be more appropriate to the decision you've made to go your separate ways. Expectations that he will always be your rock, that she will never love anyone like she loves you, that he is your source for financial well-being, that she is the one who takes care of you when you're sick, that he is your safe space, that she will always put your needs before everyone else's— these must be brought to light and consciously evolved to fit the new future you are now each required to create.

In his book *Your Brain at Work,* Dr. David Rock asserts that maintaining the right expectations is central to living a happy, healthy life. It feels good when our expectations are met. In

> There's a trick to the graceful exit. . . . It means leaving what's over without denying its validity or its past importance to our lives. It involves a sense of the future, a belief that every exit is an entry, that we are moving up, rather than out.
>
> ELLEN GOODMAN

fact, when what we anticipate should happen does, the dopamine in our brains lights up circuitry just as surely as if we'd injected a dose of morphine into our veins. We feel as though we are on track in life and that all is well in our world. On the other hand, unmet expectations generate a large drop in dopamine levels, instigating a threat response in our brains. This accounts for some of the torment of a bad breakup, where the shock of failed expectations can expose us to painful and perpetual little losses as we hope in vain for the restoration of the solid ground of the old agreements, and we are met with disappointment again and again.

In light of this (and this is likely to be one of the few times you'll ever hear me say as much), it's important you lower your expectations, adjusting them to be much more appropriate to your current circumstances. Let yourself off the hook for the agreements your relationship was once based upon, so that you might consciously create new, more suitable ones. Generating new contracts that can safely passage you both to your new lives, whether you're transitioning to a new form of the relationship such as cooperative co-parents, lifelong friends, or thriving business partners, or simply moving toward a kind goodbye.

> *When you get stranded, the way to start moving again is not to search for an answer, but to find a new question to which your life can be the answer.*
>
> JENNIFER KRAUSE

ASK YOURSELF:

"What agreements did I make to my former partner that are no longer appropriate for me to keep?"

For example: "I will wait for you for as long as it takes," "I will never love anyone like I love you," "You are my one and only soul mate."

"What agreements did my former partner make to me that are no longer appropriate for me to expect him or her to fulfill?"

For example: "I will be responsible for your happiness in life," "I will always take care of you emotionally," "I will bail you out whenever you get into trouble."

"What new agreements can I make instead that are aligned with the new future I am committed to creating?"

For example: "I will always honor you as the father of my children and support your relationship with them," "I will always treasure our precious time spent together as intimate partners," "You will always be a part of my extended family, and I will encourage all of my family to continue having a good and loving relationship with you."

Note: In cases where you are doing the Conscious Uncoupling process alone and are unable to share directly with your former partner, you can communicate these changes with him or her in a Soul-to-Soul Communication (see Step 3), imagining yourself having a heart-to-heart conversation where you complete your old agreements and create new ones that match the future you are now committed to creating.

Creating Community Cohesion

Sophie and her partner, Mary, had been together for nearly a decade when it became apparent to them both that it was time to go their separate ways. Like many couples, their social networks were intricately tied to one another, and they found themselves reticent to cause a cold war by pulling on their friends to take sides. One Sunday, when Mary was out of town visiting a family member, Sophie found herself having brunch with a handful of their mutual friends. None of them knew that the couple was breaking up, largely because Sophie and Mary had kept their process private up to this point. Yet, Sophie felt it was time to "come out of the closet," so to speak, and took the opportunity to confide in them what was going on. Shocked and upset by the startling news, several of her friends began to take barbs at the absent Mary, covertly criticizing her to demonstrate their support and loyalty to Sophie. Yet, Sophie wisely stopped and redirected them, reminding them that there are two sides to every story, and that Mary was hurting as much as she. Rather than take sides, she admonished them to pray for both of them, reiterating that they'd both need their friends to be there for them each step of the way.

In their fervent desire to help minimize your pain, your family and friends may quickly turn against your former partner, revealing all sorts of negative opinions and feelings you had no idea they harbored. Their impulse to do so is usually well meaning, motivated solely by the instinct to offer emotional support. You may have even trained them to disparage your former partner in the months leading up to your separation, pulling on people to collude with your victimized perspective. While at first this display of social solidarity may cushion you from the blow of the breakup, ostracizing your former partner by fanning the flames of blame, such condemnation can easily have the far-reaching and negative consequence of making it virtually impossible to transition the union successfully to a healthy new form. While your primitive nature might want to boot someone out of your shared social circle as punishment for the crime of not loving you in the ways you've needed to be loved, doing damage to someone's overall sense of belonging in the world by getting others to reject that person is just as harmful as if you broke her arm or bashed her head with a frying pan. Truly, it's a form of violence.

Dr. Naomi Eisenberger from UCLA studied the effects of social rejection on our brains. To do this, she designed an experiment where participants' brains were hooked up to a scanning machine while they played a computer game called Cyberball. Cyberball is a simple ball-tossing game supposedly played by three people on the Internet—the virtual equivalent of an elementary school playground game. Participants can see their own avatar as well as two others for the "people" they believed they were playing with. At some point, the two playmates begin tossing the ball only to each other, completely ignoring the subject. "This experiment generates intense emotions for most people," Dr. Eisenberger reports. "What we found is that when people [are] excluded, you see activity in . . . the neural regions [of the brain] that are also involved in the distressing component of pain, or what sometimes people call the 'suffering component' of pain." Social rejection—or the feeling of not belonging, of being less than others, unwanted, and an outcast—activates the same brain regions as physical pain. In fact, not just one but five different brain regions that signal physical pain light up as a result of being left out of a simple ball-tossing game, indicating that social pain can be truly agonizing.

Many of your friends and family members will just assume they'll need to now turn against your former partner to demonstrate their loyalty to you, and you may need to train them in much the same way Sophie did. When I first told my mother that Mark and I had decided to divorce, she did what any loving mother would do—she began to covertly devalue him and our relationship as a way of showing her faithful support of me. Yet, the moment she slipped into that hole, I pulled her out of it. I thanked her for her love and support. But I explained that I wanted to do this differently from most folks. I wanted us to remember that Mark was the only father her granddaughter would ever have, and as such, I wanted us to always speak well of him and support him in his life. While he was not a perfect man, I confessed that I myself was a pretty imperfect woman. I explained that we were more interested in creating a healthy future for our changing family than we were in laying blame. I let her know that the division of our assets was not going to be a fight, and that we would both come into the conversation wanting to do the right thing for the right reasons, looking out for the well-being of everyone involved, and not just ourselves. Then I asked her to join me in this conscious, kind way of ending our marriage. While she may have been a bit confused at what seemed to her a radically new way to conclude a marriage, I believe she was also relieved. She didn't have to lose her son-in-law. She just had to get used to the fact that he was no longer going to be married to her daughter.

Relationships have two distinct faces. One is obviously the very private connection that two people share—the secret language of love that most reveals itself between the lines and between the sheets. Yet the other face is the public aspect of love: who a couple is for those who have grown with them over the years, those who stood for them when they took their vows, those who've broken bread with them on Thanksgiving, or those who've come to rely on them as pillars of the community. Relationships don't just belong to the two people who are in them. They belong to an entire network of others who may now have a lot of feelings about the dismantling of that partnership. Part of the wreckage of a "broken home" are the investments others have made in that union, who may feel bereft, betrayed, or unglued by its loss.

Conscious Uncoupling is about mindfully generating well-being for all who may be impacted by your breakup, carefully creating cohesion and alignment in your extended network of family and friends, and helping everyone to adjust to the new status of your relationship. One couple who had been together for three years, Dr. Sheri Meyers and Jonathon Aslay, both highly regarded relationship experts, announced their breakup on Facebook with the following post:

Dear Friends and Beloved Community,

It is with deep sadness that we announce a change in our relationship status. While we are soulmates and still love each other dearly, we both recognize that walking down the romantic path together is not our lifelong destiny. Sometimes, even with great love, getting all the relationship pieces to fall into place doesn't always work out. Thus, with deep sorrow, we have decided to end the romantic leg of our journey.

We are parting with gentleness and respect . . . celebrating the profound and rich lessons learned, and with gratitude for the amazing love and blessings shared too numerous to count. We're dedicated to learning how to uncouple with dignity and grace that honors our time together and the love we've shared.

Currently, we are each navigating how much space we need to fully return to our "I" after being so strongly identified with our "we." We're also aware there are some potentially uncomfortable emotional hurdles to navigate ahead as we both enter single life. But we are in communication and committed to parting with love. While we are both sad, we are also hopeful that we can and will continue to consciously uncouple with great love and re-create our relationship in a form that will last a lifetime.

We ask our dear friends and community to respect our privacy and allow us the time and space to heal and process this big change in our lives.

With great love,

Sheri & Jonathon

In the weeks following, both of them made sure to respond to one another's posts with encouraging words, demonstrating their high regard, respect, and mutual support of one another publicly. Today, they are both in new relationships, recently posting a picture of them both joined by their respective new partners. While not everyone is going to be able to transition their union so graciously, Sheri and Jonathon's modeling of this possibility is admirable.

To help create well-being and cohesion in your social circles when telling people about your breakup, I offer the following suggestions:

1. MAINTAIN YOUR DIGNITY

Remember that inside the happily-ever-after myth that was created roughly three hundred years ago, most people simply assume that relationships are supposed to last "till death do us part." When a couple ends their relationship for any reason other than one or both of you die, many will automatically relate to it as a "failure of love."

When you bump into the brick wall of this bias, both in yourself and others, try not to take it personally. Instead, see it as a programmed collective ideal of love that made sense in its time, but that is not necessarily appropriate to your lives now. Hold your head high, and recognize that breakups are hard enough without holding others and ourselves accountable to a standard that may no longer be aligned with your true values and callings in life. Recognize yourself as part of a growing movement of like-minded individuals who also are midwifing this new, more enlightened way of ending a romantic union, and stand strong in your resolve to relate to your changing relationship as valuable and worthy of respect.

2. SHOW RESTRAINT IN HOW YOU RELAY YOUR STORY

In the aftermath of a traumatic event such as a breakup, most of us will have the need to tell our stories to help us integrate and come to terms with what just happened. Yet in sharing your story with others, you may be tempted to tell it from a victimized perspective by pointing your finger at everything your former partner did wrong. It's easy to fall into this trap, because most likely he or she did some hurtful, irritating, and destructive things. Yet, please remember that it's in taking personal responsibility for the many ways you unconsciously conspired with your partner and co-created what happened that you'll access the power you will need to create a different experience in the future.

> *The way to make a mountain out of a mole hill is to add dirt.*
>
> ANONYMOUS

When you speak disrespectfully of your former partner, you not only diminish that person but you diminish yourself as well. Whenever you share from a victimized and reactive place, you risk losing the respect of others. They will likely begin feeling sorry for you rather than admire you for the gracious and deeply wise human being that you are. In a subtle way, you may actually cause others to be less invested in supporting you because you are using them as a dumping ground, and they feel that. They may be sympathetic at first, but eventually they may not be able to help and will just watch the clock, wondering how much "supportive friend time" they're on the hook for.

On the other hand, if you can speak from a nonreactive and responsible place, without pulling on them to have to suddenly begin disliking your for-

> *If you can't say anything nice, at least have the decency to be vague.*
> SUSAN ANDERSEN

mer partner to prove their loyalty to you, you will not only gain the respect of others but may also inspire them to have better endings themselves by the good modeling you provide.

My mother, who'd had a pretty nasty divorce from my step-father some twenty-five years before witnessing the kind and conscious way that Mark and I uncoupled, was so moved by the experience that she was inspired to offer an olive branch to her former husband in spite of the cold war that had festered for decades. Out of the blue, she called him up one cold and frosty morning and invited him, along with my brother Scott, to visit her in her Florida home during a particularly harsh winter. Shocked by her kindness, he accepted the invitation and he and Scott joined her for a fun family holiday together, melting away years of animosity between them. Proving that it's never too late to have a Conscious Uncoupling.

3. OFFER CLEAR GUIDANCE TO OTHERS ON HOW THEY SHOULD BEHAVE

To defuse a potential division in your community, make sure to take the lead in letting others know that they need not take sides. Give people permission to maintain their relationships with both of you regardless of how tempted you may be to split your friends and family down the middle. Because once that happens, it could take years, even decades, to repair the damage, if at all.

My mother and father divorced when I was only two years old, and like most divorcing couples of their day, they disliked each other with a vengeance. Their enmity didn't end until forty years later when I was visiting my mother and my father stopped by to take me to lunch. I suddenly found myself in the rare position of having them both in the same room at the same time. So excited was I to finally be in this unusual position that I forced them to stand on either side of me and smile for the camera, producing the one and only photograph I have to this day of the three of us together.

For me, the worst part of this story was not just the loss of cohesion I felt as a child, but also the loss of my extended family that was caught in the crossfire. I spent the better part of my early adult life trying to rekindle lost connections with grandparents, uncles, and cousins. Relationships that, frankly, would have been a great asset to me while growing up. Today, while my parents have never become friends, I'm glad to say that there is more civility between them. Yet the years when war raged between them are forever lost between us.

Given the history of antagonistic separations in my family, it was no surprise that when Mark and I chose to end our marriage, some assumed he was now moving into enemy territory. It took time to make it clear this was not the case and to train people on how they needed to behave. In the first couple of years, some were deeply confused by the holidays that Mark and I continued to spend together with our daughter, Alexandria. And when I invited Mark to join us on a weekend trip to visit Grandma and Grandpa so our daughter could enjoy a day when all of her family was together, people were downright dismayed.

Yet the kindness and civility of this new approach intrigued them, and as a result, they all eventually opened up and allowed Mark back into their hearts. Today we are one happy, healthy "expanded family," and Mark gets invited to family gatherings and Christmas Eve dinners along with everyone else. And his family, too, has taken his lead by inviting me to join them in their family activities.

Let's Just Be Friends

Melissa, a thirty-four-year-old soft-spoken, thoughtful, and intelligent woman from New York, was struggling to come to terms with the fact that her boyfriend of three years had recently told her he wanted to demote their relationship to a mere friendship, rather than take things to the next level, as she'd hoped. The vision board that hung fading on the wall of her walk-in closet, with its images of laughing flower girls, a silhouette of a bride and her adoring groom, and a bright, brilliant diamond ring seemed to mock her each time she changed clothes. Deflated, and with only the hope that he would change his mind to keep her company at night, she desperately tried to figure out how to accommodate his desire. Yet being relegated to the status of friend felt like being asked to move into the small basement apartment of a beautiful house she once lived in and loved. Caught between the choice of losing him completely or "just being friends," she was paralyzed to do much beyond reluctantly agreeing to the latter. When I asked her, however, what authentic gestures of friendship he'd extended her way, she admitted that he basically wanted the same sexual privileges he'd always had, yet without the responsibilities of fidelity or offering any hope for a shared future. "And how is that being

> Let us forget, with generosity, those who cannot love us.
>
> PABLO NERUDA

your friend?" I asked—a question to which she had no good answer.

True friendship is earned, one kind and selfless gesture at a time, until trust builds a home in one another's hearts. While Conscious Uncoupling promotes a friendly parting of the ways, it is not to be confused with advocating for a transition to true friendship, which some might consider a promotion, rather than demotion, from erotic love. Aristotle believed friendship to be the purest form of love, far elevated beyond sexual love, and he described it as wishing and doing well to another for his own sake, relating to someone as though he were a second self. He called this kind of love *philia:* where one loves another for the person that he is, and not because he is useful to him in some way. As a breakup is often the emotional equivalent of being banished, accompanied by the desperate, frantic need to hold on at all costs, the impulse then toward "friendship" may not necessarily be the desire to extend authentic care to another, as much as the impetus to avoid the existential annihilation that comes with the death of intimate love. One's motives for this sudden large-hearted gesture of lifelong devotion are often questionable, as they are easily mingled with the self-serving agenda of self-preservation, making the desire to remain "friends" the antithesis of true friendship. Authentic friendship is the willingness to sacrifice oneself in meaningful ways for the benefit of another, and not simply a flippant alternative to being lovers. Clearly, Melissa's former love was not seeking to extend himself in any real way to care for her true needs, as much as he was cushioning himself against the blow of having to bear the consequences of the choice he was making to end the relationship.

Consistent, small, and considerate gestures of thoughtfulness are required to truly transition to friendship. Recently, I was fortunate to share a meal with Chris Attwood and his former wife, Janet Attwood, at a local restaurant. As we waited for the valet to retrieve our cars, someone offered to take our picture. In that moment, we all stopped talking, looked at the camera, and smiled. Yet, just before the shot was taken, Janet suddenly stepped away from Chris and ran over to stand on my left, putting me between the two of them. She leaned in and whispered in my ear, "I never stand next to Chris when our picture is taken, as I wouldn't want his wife to be uncomfortable. I always want her to feel respected by me." The friendship these two have maintained after their divorce did not happen just by chance. Theirs is a bond built one thoughtful gesture at a time over the many years they've remained friends. I was deeply moved when a former partner of mine, someone whom I'd disappointed quite a bit by ending our relationship, came to my aid upon hearing that I'd taken ill some months after our separation. Putting aside his own feelings, he showed up consistently to care for me over the months that I was sick, demonstrating true friendship in a time of need. Because of this, he remains a good and cherished friend to this day. In the wise and immortal words of Julia Roberts, "You know it's love when all you want is that person to be happy, even if you're not part of their happiness."

While you might hope with all your heart to transition your sexual relationship to a platonic one, I will warn you that biology will work against you. For nature has designed it that, for weeks or months to come, the scent of his cologne, the touch of her hand, the sound of his laugh, or the sight of her smile can change your body's chemistry in a heartbeat, flooding you with chemicals that instigate that state of euphoria that comes with falling in love. Because of this, most experts advise a clean break of at least a few months, and possibly more whenever possible, in order to detox from the chemically addictive aspects of love.

Be prepared to give the relationship some much-needed breathing room by taking time apart to reorient yourself to the changes between you. Granted, this may be easier said than done, particularly if you share children. Yet, if you must see one another, please remember that touch of any kind can be confusing. For this reason, I usually recommend no kissing or handholding. Even the running of flirtatious energy can keep the hormones flowing, so do your best to keep your emotional and sexual boundaries clean. Rather than run to your former partner for comfort when you're down, find new confidants. Don't confide in him or her about the troubles you're now having in your love life. Make sure your communication is clear of any mixed messages or motives. Keep your conversations simple and focused on the tasks at hand, remembering to cultivate a more formal position with one another until such time as you both feel ready to dip your toes in the waters of potential platonic friendship.

For the Sake of the Kids

Many of us grew up during the seventies and eighties when the divorce rate more than doubled in America, and we ourselves lived through the nasty and contentious breakup of our parents. In the late 1960s, no-fault divorce opened the floodgates for the dissolution of marriages without having to prove abuse, abandonment, or infidelity. All hell broke loose as angry couples began raising their kids in a courtroom, rather than a community. Study after study showed the negative effects that divorce had upon children from broken homes, reporting on those who were sandwiched between the constant animosity and enmity of their warring parents, who often used them as weapons against each other. Those studies were accurate. I can personally attest to it. I was one of those kids, and we were plenty messed up. We were partying into the wee hours of the morning long before we even knew what wisdom teeth were, and we were having sex before we knew what a condom looked like. We were sneaking out at night, running away from home, clipping our classes, stealing money from our parents' wallets, and smoking Marlboro cigarettes in dark, dank basements. Many of us were depressed, anxious, aggressive, and failing at school. We developed eating disorders. And we later went on to have unstable, troubled relationships. It's assumed, of course, that it was the divorce that did us in. Yet, truthfully, any time kids find themselves in the middle of two highly contentious parents who pull on them to take sides and model morally questionable behaviors, they're going to wind up in deep doo-doo.

Well-known author of *The Seven Principles of Making Marriage Work*, Dr. John Gottman, most known for his pioneering work in creating healthy marriages, did an interesting study with sixty-three preschool children who were living in intact homes with high levels of conflict and strife. He found that these children had chronically elevated levels of stress hormones not found in other kids. Following them through the age of fifteen, he also discovered they had the kinds of problems I describe above, such as chronic truancy, peer rejection, flunking out of school, and lower achievement than those kids whose home life was harmonious and peaceful. In other words, whenever children live in a war zone, they suffer, whether their parents are married or not.

I wish the days of parents' acting like kindergarteners fighting in a sandbox were long gone, but unfortunately they are not. Recently, a survey was done in England by Resolution, an organization that supports a nonconfrontational approach to divorce; it showed that roughly one-third of the teens and young adults questioned had experienced one parent's trying to turn them against the other. Over a quarter said their parents directly involved them in their divorce dispute, and almost as many discovered that their mom or dad had a new partner from social media. Perhaps most heartbreaking of all was the discovery that nearly one in five said they'd completely lost contact with one or more of their grandparents. If this is how we're behaving at the end of love, then the term "broken family" certainly applies.

I'd like to impress you by telling you that I never behaved as poorly as these other parents did. Yet, I must confess that creating my happily-*even*-after family has been more of a process than an event. When Mark and I first married, I embraced his daughter, Sarah, who was just entering her teen years and lived several hours away with her mom, Mark's former wife, Anne. One Thanksgiving, when our daughter, Alex, was just a toddler, we invited Sarah to join us for dinner, as we knew that she and her mother were coming to town. At first she agreed, but as the day grew closer and she saw that her mom would be alone on Thanksgiving, she called her father and asked if we could invite her, too. While Mark liked the idea, I did not and I said a firm and not-to-be-argued-with "no." That Thanksgiving we did not see Sarah. She'd chosen instead to go for pizza with her mom rather than dine with us.

In many ways, this episode was the start of the ideas I share in this book. I was rightly ashamed of my behavior, and I reflected deeply upon my stinginess. Because of it, Sarah and Alex had missed an important holiday together. And why? Because I felt threatened? Competitive? Anne wasn't trying to get my husband back. While I wasn't a big enough person at the time to pick up the phone and apologize to Anne directly, I changed my tune. From then on, Anne was always invited to our home for holiday celebrations along with Sarah.

> *Life always waits for some crisis to occur before revealing itself at its most brilliant.*
> PAULO COELHO

For the past several years, it's become traditional that we all spend Christmas together. Sarah's now grown and lives in another state, but each year she flies home and she and Anne make the five-hour road trip to our home. It's something we all look forward to, and our girls have had the opportunity to build a sweet relationship over the years. Anne and I have become friends as well. Several years ago, as we all sat around the living room on Christmas Eve, enjoying the soft glow of the decorated tree, my daughter curled up next to me and whispered in my ear. "Mommy," she said, "can I ask Anne to be my godmother? I want to have the same mommy that my sister has," to which I replied a heartfelt and wholehearted "yes," solidifying Anne's place further in our eccentric and ever-expanding happily-*even*-after family.

While we may be able to undo a marriage, we can never undo a family without leaving the children in that family emotionally homeless. With all we're now learning about attachment theory and our critical need for secure and stable bonds throughout our lives in order to be happy, healthy people, we have to seriously rethink how we behave at the end of long-term love.

Two decades ago, Dr. Constance Ahrons, author of the pioneering bestseller *The Good Divorce,* demonstrated that it's not so much the divorce itself, but the profoundly barbaric and decidedly uncreative ways that we've been going about it that have been hurting our kids. Even so-called amicable divorces may be getting it wrong. While they're certainly an improvement over un-amicable divorces, any time we create two separate families where once there was one, we're setting our children up to suffer. Expecting them to go from family to family is essentially asking them to be in a perpetual state of longing and loss, always having to say goodbye to one family in order to rejoin the other. No wonder children pine for their parents to get back together. They're yearning for wholeness in their constantly fragmenting little worlds. In a Conscious Uncoupling, there is only *one* family that endures a recalibration and expansion, and it demands that the parents accomplish the necessary growth and emotional maturation to elegantly execute such a transition, rather than expecting the children to do so.

I admit it is growth by gunpoint, but welcome to parenthood.

Dr. Ahrons even gave us a name for this new family structure: *binuclear families.* Rather than a nuclear family that revolves around one physical location, you now have a binuclear family that revolves around two. When you think about it, it's not that new a concept. When Aunt Sue finally gets her own apartment and leaves her parents' home after living there for over two decades, she doesn't stop being part of the family, even if her continual fighting with her mother instigated her move. She simply moves into a new home and everyone remains one family. Her mother may have to adjust to Aunt Sue's rebellious insistence that she now run her own life, but adjust she will, for it is the nature of families to accommodate the growth and life changes of its members.

It's never easy to disappoint our children. Yet, the opportunity to develop wisdom and depth begins when we're young. Children can't be shielded from the inevitable losses of life; instead, they need to be offered a tremendous amount of love and support as they go through them, as well as wise guidance to help make empowered meaning of what's happening, lest they blame themselves. Another dear friend and colleague, parenting expert and author of *Parenting with Presence,* marriage and family therapist Susan Stiffelman, offers this sane advice:

One of the most difficult things about being a parent is allowing for the fact that our children may have different experiences than we want them to have. When they're angry or hurt, we want to help them feel better. When they're blaming us for their sadness ("If you had been nicer to Mommy, we'd all still be together in the same house!"), we want to defend ourselves. When they withdraw, we may desperately want to cheer them up. We may be tempted to help them numb their sadness with special treats. We might even try to convince them that things are going to be better in this new family configuration.

The fact is, what children need most from us in these challenging moments is for us to be a steady pair of loving, comforting arms they can fall into when their hearts are heavy with sadness. This is not easy to do when we ourselves are struggling with grief and loss, but if we're to help our children know that they *will* be okay, then Mommy and Daddy have to be present for the times when things *aren't* so okay. Only then can they trust us with their emotional truth so that we can help them heal.

> In times of stress, the best thing we can do for each other is to listen with our ears and our hearts and to be assured that our questions are just as important as our answers.
>
> **FRED ROGERS**

Rather than try to minimize your child's loss, help her to name it by mirroring what you sense she might be feeling. "I can see that you're sad." Be sad with her, but let your sorrow be contained. We never want our children to have to parent us, and so it will be important for you to have places to go where you can get the emotional support you'll need in order to be this deeply present and available to them. Reassure your kids and help them understand what's happening by clearly stating that it's not their fault, that you're still a family, they're not going to lose either one of you, you both still love them, and you're all going to be okay.

I know I'm making it all sound so cool, calm, and collected. It's not. It's awkward and disappointing and painful and hard and heart-wrenching. Some days you may just want to scream and other days you'll wish you could run away. But I promise you this: in the long run, it'll all be worth it. At the end of the day, what we all want most are kids who grow up to be well-adjusted, healthy, resilient, good-hearted adults. People who feel fundamentally safe in their own skin, who know they're loved without having to think too much about it, who feel confident that they belong in this beautiful world of ours, and who, when it's time, are fully equipped to bond with others and form loving, stable families of their own.

And that, my friend, is possible with a Conscious Uncoupling.

Dividing Hearth and Home

I used to live in a beautiful four-bedroom house with a sunroom where I would sit and read the morning paper, an elegant fireplace in the living room where I'd curl up to read my mountains of books, and a Zen-like garden out back where I enjoyed watching the clouds go by. Currently, I live in a lovely, yet moderate two-bedroom apartment in a tall building that overlooks a park. In the center of the park is a huge fountain that is a magnet for playing children, who love to chase each other around its contours and throw pennies in to make a wish. All day long I hear the sound of running water along with shrieks of delight through my open windows, which stream bright light into my spacious and handsome living room. Five stories below, Mark and Alexandria live in an apartment that mirrors my own, making it easy for our daughter to go up and down the elevator to see us both as often as she likes, and affording Mark and me ample opportunity to collaborate on her upbringing. While I miss my big house and look forward to the day when I can buy a new one, I happily let it go in favor of our current more user-friendly and wholesome structure for raising a happy, healthy child whose challenges in life have little to do with the fact that Mark and I are no longer married to one another. I realize it's almost anti-American to suggest that downsizing might be a good thing, yet I firmly believe that quality of life over quantity of possessions should determine how we live, particularly when our children's developing psyches are at stake.

> The happiest people don't have the best of everything. They just make the best of everything.
> ANONYMOUS

Much of the shock of losing a long-term partnership is the hope it held for a better life—specifically, for a *financially* better life. The happily-ever-after myth includes the expectation of upward, not downward, mobility. Yet when a couple dissolves their union, the harsh reality is that the same amount of money that once supported one home now needs to support two. In fact, studies show that a drop in economic status is the norm for most divorcing families, lasting on average five years. Few prospects frighten us more. Or cause us to behave in sociopathic ways, such as insisting the kids spend more time with us than their other parent in order to qualify for a bigger piece of the financial pie, hiding important assets, stealing from joint accounts, or bending the numbers to try to get more than our fair share. It's easy to lose sight of the forest for the trees when we're frightened.

Smoldering hatred and rage can also become deeply intertwined in the process of divvying up the assets, and instigate malicious moves generated by a vindictive soon-to-be-former spouse who may have completely lost perspective. Divorce-reform advocate Joseph Sorge relays a horror story in his book *Divorce Corp.,* told to him by Judge Thomas Zampino from a New Jersey family court. During a particularly contentious divorce, an expert witness testified to the value of a marital asset that he estimated to be $60,000. The judge was surprised, for he had been informed that the witness was being paid $70,000 for his testimony. "Why on earth would you charge $70,000," he asked from the bench, "when you know that the most your client could possibly get from this asset is half of $60,000—less than half your fee?" The witness shrugged and looked at the resentful wife who'd hired him. "Because she wanted me to," he replied.

It seems ludicrous that anyone should behave in such a self-destructive way. Yet scientist David Rand from Harvard University spearheaded an interesting experiment called the Ultimatum Game that gives us a clue as to what might motivate someone to burn through their child's college fund as though it were pocket change in an effort to retaliate against a former spouse. The game involves two players who bargain over a pot of money. Player One makes a proposal to Player Two on how she wants to split the money. If Player Two agrees, they both receive the split as suggested. If the offer is declined, neither player receives anything. It's only logical, then, that Player One should offer Player Two the least amount possible and that Player Two should accept that offer, as any money is better than no money at all. Yet, roughly half of those offered an unfair split will reject it. Many of us would rather pay to get even with our former partner for offering an unfair split—even if it is to our own detriment—than settle for less than what we think is fair. Another study conducted by Golnaz Tabibnia and Matthew D. Lieberman at UCLA further demonstrates that perceived fairness is more vital to resolution than the amount one actually receives. Monitoring the brains of their subjects, the researchers were able to verify that receiving 50 cents of a dollar created more of a reward response in the brain than receiving $10 of $50.

Let's hope you've calmed down by now and can enter this critical negotiation with a sane mind and with the intent of leaving it with a clear conscience. Because untying the knot is not nearly as simple as tying it was, you want to carefully consider the relationship you desire on the other side of this setback, and doggedly work to protect that possibility by making the effort to keep things fair. One couple I know, Lizzie and Phil, had been married for nearly thirty years when they joined the ranks of the fastest-growing segment of the divorcing population in America—those over fifty. They were quite supportive and generous to one another throughout the sale of their home and possessions, splitting everything down the middle without thinking much about it. Occasionally, they would argue, but only because one of them felt the other deserved to keep more than 50 percent of an asset for one reason or another—an argument that was usually lost. One day, after they were no longer living together, Phil called Lizzie, uncharacteristically huffing and puffing. He informed her in no uncertain terms that he was keeping the bulk of the passive income generated from the network marketing company they'd built together. Lizzie was so stunned by this sudden bullying behavior that she quietly replied, "Okay, if that's what you really want," and quickly got off the phone. Yet minutes later, Phil called to apologize. He wanted to take back what he'd said, mumbling something about losing perspective and becoming temporarily confused. "What happened?" Lizzie asked. "You talk to an attorney?"

"Yep," he replied sheepishly. "Sorry about that."

It's important to get good legal advice so you understand what you're legally entitled to. But please don't give your power away to anyone to determine who you're going to be in this negotiation, even if that "expert" has fancy credentials after his or her name. At the end of the day, you want to behave in ways that are going to shepherd your relationship to a healthy new form, without the burden of the nasty emotional residue that can come from taking ungenerous actions that may be hard to recover from. Because we human beings have biology that can so quickly move us into attack mode, you'll want to be conscious of what your actions are generating in yourself and in your former partner, and keep in mind the high cost of unfair, stingy behaviors.

Years ago, I lived with a lover for a couple of years. During that time, we invested in a few pieces of furniture and, when we broke up, we split those possessions down the middle, each of us taking one of two matching dressers we'd bought for the bedroom. Months later, he asked for the dresser back. Frankly, it was fair of him to do so, given that he'd actually paid for it. But I was using it in a spare bedroom at the time and I didn't want to let it go. I liked how it looked in the room and I'd become attached to it. I told him he couldn't have it, and without giving it much thought, I kept the dresser for myself. In hindsight, I see that moment as a missed opportunity for generosity that may have preserved our friendship. That choice came with a price; for though I saw him intermittently for years after our breakup, we were never friends. There was always a chasm that lay awkwardly between us that was too wide to cross. It would have been so easy to generate the goodwill that might have made evolving into authentic friendship possible. Yet, I chose the dresser instead. A few years later I sold that dresser for $25 in a yard sale. It was a lesson I've not forgotten.

Just because you *can* get something doesn't mean you *should.* Many divorce laws in America are just plain stupid and unfair. Consider the bizarre New York law that makes a professional degree or license earned while married community property. Tanya Finch and Kenneth Quarty were married in the year 2000, just as Tanya began her

> *Too many people today know the price of everything and the value of nothing.*
> ANN LANDERS

nursing training. They divorced in 2009, by which time she'd completed her degree. As part of their divorce settlement, Kenneth insisted he was entitled to receive up front a percentage of the monies Tanya *could potentially earn* as a result of the degree she now possessed. Whether or not she ever actually secured employment as a nurse was irrelevant to his case. Never mind that Kenneth did not work the entire time they were married and hadn't contributed anything financially to her education. It was Tanya who worked multiple jobs to support them both while she earned her degree. Yet, because he'd babysat her daughter on those evenings when she was in school, the courts thought it fair that he receive 25 percent of her *projected* lifetime earnings as part of their divorce settlement, requiring her to turn over $155,372 to Kenneth in order to obtain a divorce. This, from the now-single mother of two whose earning capacity as a registered nurse was roughly $70,000 a year.

With horror stories like this, it's no mystery why fewer and fewer Americans are choosing to marry; they make marriage seem more like tying a noose than tying the knot. While many of us look to the courts to help us divide our assets fairly, fairness can't always be legislated. For the law is absolute, and not contextual. What's right in one case may not be right in another. The case that instigated the New York courts to adopt the above-mentioned law was a situation in which a wife had financially supported her husband through medical school, only to be left by him soon after he graduated and was about to cash in on all of *her* hard work.

Fairness is a mindset and it demonstrates that, when push comes to shove, one values people over profits—a key principle for those whose relationships remain stable and healthy over time. Just how selfless you should be in the dissolution of your marriage will be organic to the nuances of your unique situation. Yet, wrestling with the many complex decisions that must now be made from an ethic of fairness, rather than the emotion of fear, will go a long way toward setting you up for the next healthy stage of your relationship.

Fairness is also fluid, meaning that what may seem fair in one moment may over time reveal itself to be not fair at all. When Mark and I were negotiating the division of our property, the ongoing royalties of my first book, *Calling in "The One,"* came into question. While our mediator informed Mark of his right to a portion of those royalties, Mark wanted none of it, as he felt it only fair that these royalties belong completely to me, given that I was the creator of that work. At the time, I was genuinely moved by his generosity. Two years later, however, I found myself uneasy each time a check came in. While Mark had never mentioned it again, I began to feel that we'd made an unfair decision. Surely he had invested his energy in the book's creation by painstakingly reading and critiquing each section as I wrote it, and by financially doing more than his fair share at a time when I was bringing less income into the family in order to write the book. One afternoon, several years after our divorce was final, I called our mediator and asked him what amount Mark might have gotten had he asked for what was rightfully his. I then called Mark and explained to him why I was reversing the decision we'd made, and repaid him the monies due him dating back to our divorce, and granting him his rightful percentage moving forward.

Did I have a devil on my shoulder screaming in my ear about how foolish I was to do this? Of course I did. But I've come to understand that integrity feels a whole lot better than a trip to Italy or a new Infiniti ever could. A clean conscience is worth more than money can ever buy.

> *Live so that when your children think of fairness, caring, and integrity, they think of you.*
>
> H. JACKSON BROWN JR.

Legalizing the Loss of Love

In 1969, Ronald Reagan, then governor of California, made what he would later call one of the greatest mistakes of his political career. He signed into law America's first no-fault divorce bill. Historians speculate that he may have done so because his first wife, Jane Wyman, had accused him of "mental cruelty" to obtain their divorce in 1948. No-fault divorce allowed couples to end their marriage for any cause, without having to prove to a judge they'd been cheated on, abused, or abandoned to obtain permission to separate. In the decade that followed, every state in the Union followed suit and adopted a no-fault divorce law of its own, paving the way for the divorce revolution that swept the country like wildfire.

Divorce is now big business in America. According to Joseph Sorge, author of *Divorce Corp.*, we spend roughly $50 billion a year on a vast and decentralized network of judges, lawyers, psychologists, consultants, expert witnesses, private investigators, and others who make their living in the family court system. In fact, more money passes through family court than all other courts in America combined. It's a system that encourages war, fosters acrimony, and is designed to drag out the process of divorce often far longer than the marriages being dissolved even lasted.

An absurdly complex system, America's family court was created roughly four decades ago in an attempt to expedite the tens of thousands of divorces flooding the courts as the result of the divorce boom. Originally meant to be a kinder, gentler court, family law has since ballooned from a few pages of basic code into a two-thousand-page volume of fine print, demanding the participation of counsel who often charge as much as $700 per hour. It's not hard to see why divorce is now listed as the third cause of bankruptcy in America.

According to Judge Michele Lowrance, author of *The Good Karma Divorce,* you and I might expect to pay about $30,000 for a litigated divorce—or $50,000, if it's contested, which for many Americans is an entire year's salary. Yet, in some civilized parts of our world, people manage to dissolve their unions for the cost of a mere postage stamp. Joseph Sorge tells of meeting with Alexandra Borg, a twenty-something divorced Swedish citizen. When he asked her how much her divorce cost, she seemed genuinely confused by the question, before finally remembering that she spent five kronor on the stamp for the envelope. Like all those she knew who'd gotten divorced, she did not need an attorney. Nor had she paid exorbitant fees for psychological evaluations to determine who would keep custody of their son. Instead, Borg simply went on the Internet, found the court website, downloaded a simple form, and sent it in. Six months later, she and her husband were divorced. What made it so easy? First, there is no such thing as alimony in Sweden. Divorce effectively ends all economic obligations between two people, except for the potential $150 per month one might receive to care for the child of that union (which is what the government stipulates to be the cost of a child's food and clothing). One telling practice of the Scandinavian government's life-affirming policies concerning divorce is their procedure for collecting child-support payments directly from the parent who is ordered to pay, and sending it to the recipient parent. In this way, the children never know if the money was sent late, or if it has even gone unpaid. It spares the children the agony of watching their mother wait for the check to arrive, so she can buy them schoolbooks or take them shopping for clothes.

Talk about conscious.

I'm not about to enter the hornet's nest of alimony debate in America, recognizing it as a huge issue for women's right advocates, who want to provide economic protection for those tens of thousands of stay-at-home mothers who may have spent decades not working while caring for the kids. The biggest thing that impresses me about the Scandinavian system is the utter absence of rancor between separating spouses, as well as concern for the well-being of the children. I mean, with nothing to fight over, why bother waging war? While Iceland boasts one of the highest divorce rates in the world, the people there are also reported to be some of the happiest on earth. As well as some of the smartest and most productive, with Iceland's kids outperforming American kids in standardized math and science tests, as well as ranking sixth in the world's per-capita GDP (gross domestic product), one of the main indicators of financial vitality in any society.

I share all this not to convince you to move to Scandinavia, as tempting as that may be, but to awaken you from the trance that divorce is inherently hateful. That you must fight with your boxing gloves firmly in place and your fists held high. The vindictiveness to which we've become accustomed may have as much to do with the gnarly knot of our legal system as it does with our biology. Interestingly enough, however, it's not just therapists who are coming to the rescue. It's also lawyers themselves. For while attorneys bear the brunt of a thousand jokes that assume they'll do anything to win a case, ethical or not, many are actually dedicated advocates of divorce reform and are actively creating better and less hostile ways to transition our families.

Wevorce founder Michelle Crosby is one such holistically inclined attorney who, in response to her parents' devastating divorce when she was nine, when she was put on the stand and forced to choose between her mother and father, is devoted to transforming the landscape of divorce in America. Recently, she was named a "Legal Rebel" by the American Bar Association in their national *ABA Journal,* which recognizes those attorneys who "are strivers, pushing change and rejecting the rule book to . . . serve clients and improve access to justice." Ms. Crosby has spent the past decade of her life developing an empowering process that is a hybrid of mediation and collaborative divorce practices, and currently has offices in twenty states.

Ms. Crosby is just one of the thousands of legal professionals in America who are working hard to improve things both emotionally and financially, as they seek to create less expensive alternatives to litigation. Another is collaborative divorce attorney Lisa Forberg, founder of the Forberg Law Office in New Hampshire, who is an advocate for an all-inclusive approach to divorce that takes into account each family's unique needs. Recently, Ms. Forberg shared with me about "Paul and Jesse," a gay couple who'd been married for several years when they decided to divorce. Because they'd adopted two sons, they were motivated to have an amicable end to their union. Jesse feared, however, that coming to a legal agreement would not be easy. Paul had been the main earner while Jesse stayed home to raise the children. He anticipated that Paul would not want to pay alimony or divide their assets equally. He had not wanted the breakup and felt betrayed by Jesse, a response that was impacting their ability to end things on good terms. In a collaborative divorce, a separating couple is given a team of professionals to work with. Each party gets his or her own attorney, as well as shares a financial adviser and divorce coach to help realize an outcome that everyone can live with. The divorce coach helped the couple to align on shared values as parents, supporting Paul to move beyond his anger and begin to appreciate how much money Jesse would need to provide a good home for the children. Jesse understood that financial status was more important to Paul than to him, believing that Paul would be a better co-parent if he were able to retain more of the assets. As long as he was adequately provided for, Jesse did not feel the need to split their assets down the middle. All he really wanted was an acknowledgment from Paul that his contributions had been appreciated and valued. Once he received that, they were able to begin negotiating a settlement that felt fair to both. To help them reach this resolution, their financial adviser was able to demonstrate to Paul, using objective charts and graphs, how much support Jesse was going to need to avoid running at a deficit each month. The expert also worked with Jesse's projected monthly expenses to make sure they were realistic and reasonable, and could be justified based on the shared goals of cooperative co-parenting. By having these numbers in front of him, Paul was able to be less emotionally reactive and think more rationally about what was the right thing to do.

> *I do not at all understand the mystery of grace—only that it meets us where we are but does not leave us where it found us.*
>
> ANNE LAMOTT

The most important reason to avoid litigation is the potential loss of control that can happen once the courts get involved. Which is particularly alarming if you're a parent and the custody of your children is at stake. You, along with your co-parent, want to be the ones making decisions about how your children will be raised, not some larger-than-life judge wearing an intimidating black robe, who doesn't even know you or your family but who will lay down the law you'll all need to live with for years to come. You and your co-parent understand the needs of your kids better than any judge or custody adviser ever could.

If you give in to a fantasy that somehow taking your former partner to court will bring about the justice you crave, you risk making a grave mistake. There are hundreds, if not thousands, of parents who have to live with the consequences of unfair court edicts who wish with all their hearts that they had never stepped foot in a courtroom. Countless people leave the system feeling violated and cheated, in terms of both the process they endured and the outcome they received. Even if you and your former partner don't share children, by litigating the loss of love you're likely to fatten the retirement accounts of high-priced attorneys while depleting your own.

Please remember that, though you're sure you're right, and though you're adamant that you have rights, when all is said and done, what will be most essential is that everything *is* actually right. Alternatives to litigation such as mediation, collaborative divorce, or some peace-building variation on that theme are what will help you come to agreements that will set everyone up to win moving forward.

Note: If you suspect your husband or wife of lying and hiding significant assets and income; if he or she has a history of threatening you or your children with physical violence; if you have been dominated and bullied throughout your relationship or if there is active drug or alcohol addiction involved, then you may wish to consider hiring an attorney to advocate on your behalf. A more collaborative approach requires at least some authentic interest in doing the right thing for the right reasons by both parties.

Every end is a new beginning.
PROVERB

Conscious Uncoupling Rituals

When performance artists Marina Abramovic and Ulay (Uwe Laysiepen) ended their twelve years spent as lovers and artistic partners, they honored the event by painstakingly walking the Great Wall of China, she starting at one end and he at the other to meet in the middle, embrace, and go their separate ways—an event that lasted ninety days and covered 2,000 miles.

They did not see one another again for twenty-three years when, as a surprise, Ulay showed up at a performance that Marina was giving at the Museum of Modern Art in Manhattan, called *The Artist Is Present.* For six days a week, seven hours a day, Marina would sit stoic and still under hot lights at an empty wooden table and stare across into the eyes of a stranger. One after another, those who were willing to wait on line, sometimes for hours, would finally get their privileged few moments to be with her. Between each guest, Marina would close her eyes to wait for the next person to be seated. When Ulay slipped into the chair across from her, you could hear a pin drop as the audience waited for her to open her eyes and see who sat before her. When she did, her eyes lit up first, then a slight smile crept across her face. And then silent tears began streaming down her cheeks before she finally broke her pose and reached across the table to take his hands in hers. The audience went wild, shouting and applauding with vigor—and more than a few tears were shed. Few things move us more than the affirmation of love that survives separation and estrangement.

Rituals that mark the end of love are often quite emotional. Yet, we do not cry because we are sad; we cry because we are moved. We are touched by the recognition that love can survive even when the form of a relationship changes. You might think the term "divorce celebration" to be an oxymoron, yet more and more people are finding ways to say goodbye that honor the relationship that was shared. For we are enriched by the opportunity to witness two people soberly acknowledging an end, while humbly asking for forgiveness, validating the beauty of their time spent together, and offering a sincere blessing of happiness to the person who has disappointed them the most. There are few more tender or poignant experiences.

While some may think that a divorce party means a trip to Vegas with friends, getting plastered, and dancing on tabletops singing "I Will Survive" till the wee hours of the morning, most people who are forward-thinking enough to mark the end of their long-term union with some sort of ceremony usually create a deeply personal and soulful experience that helps everyone heal and move forward with love.

As ceremonies and customs mark the beginning of our relationships—from Valentine's Day rituals, to the marriage proposal, to engagement festivities, to the bachelor and bachelorette parties, to the wedding ceremony, and to the honeymoon—why not honor the end of our most important unions with a ceremony as well? Doing so symbolizes the end of an era and paves the way for healthy closure to occur.

One couple who'd been together for forty years created a simple ceremony held in a labyrinth close to an apartment they once shared. With several close family members and friends there to witness the undoing of their vows, they walked together into the center, shared some good memories of their life together, wished one another well, and hugged goodbye, before walking out separately to signify the coming apart of their union.

> *Divorce becomes a holy moment when you choose to use it as a catalyst for having an extraordinary life.*
> DEBBIE FORD

Another young couple invited their close circle of friends to the spot on the beach where they'd been married some five years before, to witness their bringing closure to their relationship. Sharing from their hearts, the couple acknowledged each other and the goodness and growth their relationship had provided. They exchanged rings, each of them taking the ring from the finger of their partner and placing it tenderly in a box they'd brought for the occasion. Their plan was to donate the rings to a charity they both cared about. They then invited their friends to speak words of encouragement, inspiration, and hope from their hearts, giving them the opportunity to express their love for the couple, and to bless their decision to part ways. And when it was over, they all went to a local restaurant to share a meal and drink to the future.

Not everyone will feel comfortable with an actual ceremony such as these, and some won't have partners who are willing participants. However, there are many simple, more common rituals that can help create completion for the two of you, as well as for the community of people who have been invested in your relationship. Such as hosting a dinner party to which you invite your former partner and those close to you both to gather together to share a meal. As you sit down to dinner, you begin with a toast to all the good memories you share, and invite others to toast to your new lives moving forward. If you are in a religious community, you might invite some friends over to pray with you both, to bless you as you go your separate ways. Or you might create a moving party when one of you moves from the home you've shared, inviting some friends to help,

> Getting over a painful experience is much like crossing monkey bars. You have to let go at some point in order to move forward.
>
> C. S. LEWIS

and offering housewarming gifts to bless his or her new home, such as food, plants, or bottles of wine.

For those who were not married to the ones they loved and lost, my good friend, relationship expert Lauren Frances, recommends staging a relationship funeral. The death of love for singles is often an unbearably lonely experience, particularly if you were having an affair or were in an unhealthy relationship that your family and friends did not support. Lauren suggests inviting some friends to your home while you reminisce about what the relationship meant to you, showing and burning old photos of the two of you together, giving away reminders of your romance, and toasting to happier days moving forward.

While all of the above-mentioned rituals include family and friends, it's just as meaningful to have a private ceremony between the two of you. Or even one you can do on your own, such as a Soul-to-Soul Communication (see Step 3), if it is not possible or desirable for you to be in direct contact with your former partner.

For free written and/or audio downloads of several Conscious Uncoupling rituals to choose from, please go to www.ConsciousUncoupling.com/StepFiveRituals.

Onward and Upward

One of my favorite passages in the Bible was written by the Psalmist: "Weeping may endure for a night, but joy cometh in the morning." For all the tears you've shed, you're long overdue for a heaping portion of joy. While it may not be the joy that comes from having those things you'd hoped for in life, it is the lightness of heart that comes from living closely to your truth,

> *At the height of
> laughter, the universe
> is flung into a
> kaleidoscope of new
> possibilities.*
> JEAN HOUSTON

and leaning in, on the edge of your seat, to listen for the possibilities calling you from the future that is seeking to emerge.

As you prepare to close this book, dear reader, may you also close this chapter of your life, leaving loss behind and reaching toward the new life, and new love, that await you on the other side of sorrow. The great actor and film director Orson Welles put it this way: "If you want a happy ending, that depends of course on where you stop your story." While one part of your story may have ended, a new part has only just begun. May you continue to live your own wondrous and unique adventure with resilience, creativity, and courage, as well as with an unshakable faith in the overall goodness of your life.

STEP 5 SELF-CARE SUGGESTIONS
(Take at least 2 each day)

1. **Take concrete steps to fulfill a lifelong dream,** such as taking an acting class, booking a trip to Italy, or starting work on that novel you've always dreamed of writing.
2. **Begin participating in social groups** and attending events, such as joining a book club, going to a wine tasting, signing up for a Sierra Club hike, or attending a local lecture on a subject that interests you.
3. **Attend a meditation retreat,** or enroll yourself in a spiritual class to develop and explore the deeper dimensions of who you are.

4. **Take on your physical health,** up-leveling your daily well-being and self-care practices like never before. Join a gym, begin working with a holistic nutritionist, go raw, or start training for a 5K or maybe even a marathon.

5. **Thank all those who helped** get you through this experience. Write thank-you notes, send flowers, buy thoughtful gifts, or just send an e-mail to offer a heartfelt acknowledgment of what it has meant to you to have their love and support.

6. **Make a list of the many ways you are a wiser,** more mature, and more loving human being because of this experience and determine to show up as this more evolved version of yourself from here on.

NOTE TO COUPLES DOING THE PROGRAM TOGETHER

In this fifth and final step of your Conscious Uncoupling program, I suggest you look for ways to become less and less dependent upon one another, with each of you consciously striving to develop new support systems that can assist you in managing those details of life that you used to turn to each other for handling. Yet, for those areas where you may continually need to engage with one another, strive to be fair and honorable in ways that communicate respect and generate a formal friendliness between you. Listen to one another, try to see things from each other's perspectives, and learn to think holistically about the needs of all involved. Put into practice all that you've learned by behaving in ways that are responsible and mature, and strive to use the new skills you've been learning that have the potential to generate greater levels of health and well-being between you, such as boundary setting and courteous communication.

At the end of the day, you want to part ways with a

blessing in your heart, rather than a curse. Do your best to express your appreciation and cultivate a growing sense of well-being between you by choosing to engage in self-responsible ways and making an effort not to repeat the hurtful and destructive behaviors of the past. Strive to keep your conscience clear, your mind open, and your heart soft so that you can leave one another enriched, expanded, and enhanced for having known each other.

evolving love

Look at the world around you. It may seem like an immovable,
implacable place. It is not. With the slightest push—
in just the right place—it can be tipped.
MALCOLM GLADWELL

In the United States, we live with an intriguing tension between our strong belief in marriage and our love affair with self-expression and personal development. While 90 percent of us will, at some point in our lives, pledge lifelong devotion to one person with the intention of settling down to build a family, our nation was founded upon the ideals of self-actualization and the pursuit of individual happiness, as tens of thousands of early settlers left behind their loyalties to family, friends, and governments in search of a better life. Is it any wonder, then, that we would find ourselves somewhat torn between these two ideals—one, which would compel us to honor our commitments with an unwavering and steadfast devotion, and the other, which might urge us to leave the ties that bind us behind

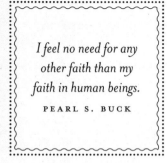

I feel no need for any other faith than my faith in human beings.

PEARL S. BUCK

to courageously venture forth into the unknown in the hope of finding a more fulfilling and authentic life.

I would be disappointed if, after reading this book, that you, dear reader, assumed that Conscious Uncoupling only advocated for the latter, casually throwing away long-term love for the next enthralling adventure. Because I, just like you, am moved when I hear stories of those who sacrifice their own personal happiness for the well-being of their families. I get choked up when people do the right thing for the right reasons, letting their conscience and not their current cravings dictate their decisions. My faith in the human race is restored each time I witness an act of loyalty and fidelity to a cause, particularly if that cause is one's own clan. Marriage and long-term, committed unions are the beauty and backbone of our society. I'm as disturbed as anyone by our tendencies to leave our partners behind when they no longer fit the vision of where we think we'd like to go next in life. As though partners were Pontiacs that one could easily just trade in when bored or tired, swapping an old model for a new one without much thought.

I do not purport to have all of the answers on how we should navigate the strains of modern-day mating, which include so many factors that can easily undermine long-term love—from longer life spans (a recent cover of *Time* magazine asserts that babies born today could live to 142 years old. . . . Imagine a time when a fiftieth wedding anniversary is considered to be just the beginning of marriage, when a couple is still in the blush of love!), to increased expectations of what we want from our unions, to living in a culture that in many ways values personal development over permanence, to living in a mobile society where we might not have extended family around to help keep us together when things get hard.

However, there are a few things I know for sure: That regardless of whether we stay together or come apart, we want to learn to value our relationships more and to hold them as precious, even when they disappoint us and fail to fulfill our expectations. That our commitments to each other matter, and that when we break or change them, it's important to do so in a way that shows accountability, contrition, respect, and amends. And finally, that how our collective story unfolds from here on is really up to us. Our long, dark history with deeply destructive breakups and divorces does not mean that we are bound to continue with our primitive, damaging, and soul-crushing ways of behaving. We have the power to consciously evolve how we treat each other at the end of love. And it's my hope we use it, not just for our own sake, but also as a contribution to future generations.

> *The new world will be created by people who know better than to be realistic. . . . We will learn what is possible by struggling for the world we desire.*
>
> RABBI
> MICHAEL LERNER

Whatever our views on divorce, whether we think it good or bad, right or wrong, moral or immoral, is irrelevant. Divorce is happening. And it will continue to happen. As much as we like to imagine that our current high level of divorce is the worst it's ever been, the truth is that anytime in recorded human history when woman have risen to hold equal power with men, divorce rates rise to about what they are today. It's just a fact. When women can leave bad and mediocre marriages, they often do. As I can't see the women of America going back to being dependent and disempowered any time too soon, I think we can safely

> *The history of love's evolution is the history of groups of individuals who dare to embrace a new expression of love, persevering in the face of opposition until the new form of love is accepted by society at large.*
>
> JEFF CARREIRA

say that our high divorce rates are probably going to stay put for a while.

By offering an alternative to antagonistic, hostile separations, Conscious Uncoupling can't help but make it easier for some to leave their long-term unions. For that, I am deeply grieved. And, as a relationship expert, I suspect I will spend the next few years devoted to developing better ways to save relationships and make them happier as penance for this inescapable fact. Yet ironically, while Conscious Uncoupling may make leaving long-term love even more feasible, it may also make it more unlikely. For many who engage the process I offer will find themselves markedly more equipped to love and be loved in healthier, happier ways moving forward. And it's safe to assume that the Conscious Uncoupling process will even revive some relationships—because of its emphasis on maturation and growth, which better equips people to repair the unions they're trying to leave.

Nothing would make me happier because, at the end of the day, whether we stay or whether we go, the bottom line is love. And if we can find ways to transform our heartaches into headway on the challenging journey of

> *God has no hands but ours.*
>
> DEBRA PONEMAN

learning to better love ourselves and each other, then all we've been through, dear reader, will well be worth it.

the conscious
uncoupling creed

We aspire to have a life-affirming breakup or divorce characterized by the sincere effort to leave each other and all involved
well, healthy, and whole, and enhanced by the love that's been
shared, rather than diminished or damaged by the way the relationship ends.

Instead of shaming and blaming each other, we look to be
self-responsible.

Instead of inflicting retaliation and revenge, we seek to forgive ourselves and each other.

Instead of indulging in greed, we aspire to be considerate
of the needs of all involved, fair-minded and generous in ways
that generate goodwill between us.

In the midst of fear, we choose to have faith.

In the midst of grief, we choose to affirm the goodness
of life.

In the midst of challenging problems, we choose to look
for positive solutions where everyone is set up to win moving
forward.

We do our best to supersede any impulse we may have to lash

out and do harm by making decisions and taking actions with the sole intent of bringing healthy completion and fostering hope and healing for all involved.

While promises may have been broken, and hearts hurt in the process, we still fundamentally value, honor, and appreciate the time spent together as a couple.

While we acknowledge the relationship's shortcomings, we also recognize the overall sanctity of human relationships and choose to focus on the good that came of this union rather than dwell on the negative.

During this tender transition, we aspire to do the least amount of damage to ourselves, each other, our children, and the extended community of family and friends who have supported this union.

We avoid pulling on others to take sides and, when appropriate, support our circle of loved ones to cultivate a healthy relationship with each of us individually.

When children are involved, we put their needs first and foremost, and work to create a new, holistic family system that allows for everyone to remain one expanded family, rather than two fragmented ones that children can easily be torn between.

When looking for solutions to the breakdowns we face, we aspire to long-term growth over short-term gain by investing in the creation of new agreements and structures that can nurture the development and emergence of the next healthy, healed stage of the relationship.

When considering how best to divide assets and debts, we strive to be fair, reasonable, and open-minded, remembering the goal is not to punish, but to preserve and protect existing assets.

We avoid unnecessary and costly litigation that could do irreparable damage and drain resources, and work instead to solve our problems with professionals who can help us do so with integrity, fairness, honesty, and even-handedness.

Most of all, in the midst of our pain, we strive to do the right thing for the right reasons, allowing our ethics to triumph over our emotions. We recognize the power we hold to consciously evolve our collective behavior at the end of love to be reflective of the kinder world we aspire to create for ourselves, our children, and future generations.

DEEP GRATITUDE GOES TO . . .

I don't believe I can adequately express the depth and breadth of my gratitude for the support I've received that has allowed me to birth this work into the world. First and foremost, to my dear friend and brilliant teaching partner of ten years, Claire Zammit, whose extraordinary capacity for clarity, along with her deep devotion to making a positive contribution to the evolution of culture, has had tremendous influence on the creation of this work. I thank you, Claire, from the bottom of my heart for the hundreds of ways you have supported and inspired me over the years to bring forth the highest and the best I have within me. And to Craig Hamilton, for generously supporting me to develop these ideas by offering a program at Evolving Wisdom.

To my Conscious Uncoupling team at Evolving Wisdom, Juliana Farrell, Khristina Kravis, Brian Hamilton, Ashley Fuller, Ben Schick, Katy Rawson, Christine Kriner, Katharine McCarthy, Therese Factora, Sylvie Curran, Cami Elen, Sese Abejon, and the many others who supported the development of this work for years before it became this book.

To my brilliant literary agent, Bonnie Solow, who has mentored this work each step of the way and, by setting the bar high, inspired me to bring forth the best I had in me. To my talented editor, Heather Jackson, who is an author's dream come true. Thank you for your patience and for gracing this project with your many gifts. Thank you, too, to my entire team at Crown, who are my partners in bringing this work into the world.

A great big thank-you to my brilliant research assistant, Dr. Karey Pohn, who has influenced this book more than I can say; and to Ellen Daly, Blu Cohen, Jenny Gladding, Lisa Steele, Lindy Franklin, and Marci Levin for your support in the trenches.

To my glorious tribe of great girlfriends who showed up with an extraordinary amount of sisterhood and support: Alanis Morissette, Marianne Williamson, Marci Shimoff, Debra Poneman, Arielle Ford, Geneen Roth, Janet Attwood, Susan Stiffelman, Jen Kleiner, Deborah Ward, Dianna Burdick, Wendy Zahler, Meredith Scott Lynn, Chris Faulconer, Karen Abrams, Carol Allen, Lauren Frances, Amy Edelstein, and (can I put my mom in the girlfriend category, too?) Sandra Pullman.

And to the loving men in my life who fed me a steady diet of encouragement: Mark Thomas, Jeff Carreira, Jay Levin, Bob Kersch, Jeff Brown, Michael Beckwith, Brian Hilliard, Jeremiah Abrams, Bill Farber, Hank Grupe, Todd Grupe, Richard France, and Kit Thomas, whose magical turn of a phrase initiated a global conversation.

To my wonderful, bright publicist, Emily Lawi; my brilliant mentor, Dr. Don Beck; and my generous and gifted coach, Joel Roberts. To Rose Rossi, Carey Campbell, Nita Rubin, and Maria Flores for your great attitudes and helpful deeds.

To the Conscious Uncoupling certified coaches who've been

working with me side by side all along the way, and most especially to those who've supported thousands to move through the online five-week program: Dr. Jana Smith, Janet Webber, Lyndra Hearn Antonson, Mary Rizk, Melissa Erin Monahan, Senami Fred, Victoria Rose, Sara Wilson, Rochelle Edwards, Susan Reiner; and most particularly Lina Shanklin, Jeanne Byrd Romero, and Marilyn Hager, who have been there, strong and steadfast from the beginning.

Thank you, too, to my Calling in "The One" and Feminine Power certified coaches, most especially those of you in the "core," who have so generously offered so much of yourselves: Prem Glidden, Judy Waters, Juli Stone, Keren Clark, and Jane Velten, as well as the Feminine Power Mastery sisters, particularly Jen Conkie and Sue Little, from whom I'm continually inspired. I thank you all for the honor of being your teacher.

I am also deeply grateful to Gwyneth Paltrow and Chris Martin, who so generously introduced this work to the world.

And finally, to my happily-even-after family: Mark, Alexandria, Sandi, Don, Bob, Barbara, Hank, Scott, Todd, Anne, Sarah, Kay, and Kelli. I love you all and am so very grateful to be a part of this good-hearted clan of ours.

HELP FOR HEARTACHE

ConsciousUncoupling.com The virtual home of the Conscious Uncoupling process, this site provides an array of free offerings to ease your suffering and grief, as well as support to create your happily-*even*-after life. Included is a directory of certified Conscious Uncoupling coaches, as well as all free downloads that serve as written and audio companions to this book.

TheAnatomyOfLove.com Bestselling author and world-renowned expert on romantic love Dr. Helen Fisher and her research partner, Dr. Lucy Brown from the Albert Einstein College of Medicine, have put together an exceptionally engaging website to educate us about what's going on in our brains at all stages of a relationship. Particularly helpful are the sections on heartbreak. Interesting articles and videos abound, helping us to understand why we feel the way we feel when our hearts are hurting and what we can do about it.

HelpGuide.org A wonderful free resource for those dealing with a range of emotional challenges related to grief. Created by Dr. Jeanne Segal and her husband in honor of their late daughter, Morgan, this website offers a cornucopia of wise and helpful advice for anyone going through heartbreak. However, the two sections I recommend most are

"Grief & Loss," found under the Mental Health tab, and the "Family & Divorce" section, found under the Children & Family tab.

TheTappingSolution.com/HealYourHeart On this webpage you will find guided tapping audios offered by Nick Ortner that will help minimize trauma symptoms of a broken heart and provide emotional relief, as well as a video of Jessica Ortner providing basic tapping instructions for those of you new to this powerful practice.

Just for Parents

SusanStiffelman.com Susan Stiffelman is the bestselling author of *Parenting with Presence,* as well as a licensed marriage and family therapist. Her user-friendly website offers a host of helpful resources and tips on how to deal with difficult parenting situations, including co-parenting advice and support for single parents. You will find videos, blogs, and Q&A on everything from power struggles to depression to anger to poor grades to blended families.

EmpoweringParents.com A comprehensive resource for general parenting issues, particularly if your child is displaying signs of a behavioral problem. Toward the bottom of the home page, you will find a section entitled "Browse Articles." It's here you'll find many articles for divorced parents, blended and step families, and other nontraditional families.

Help for Your Relationship

ConsciousRecoupling.com A sister site to ConsciousUncoupling .com dedicated to helping couples who choose to stay together, offering various resources and tools on how to repair past hurts, rebuild trust, and learn to move toward whole new levels of healthy, happy, and flourishing love.

DrSueJohnson.com Bestselling author of *Love Sense,* Dr. Sue Johnson's website offers some wonderful talks during which Dr. Johnson explains what it really takes to make a relationship work. Look for the Videos tab on the home page of her site to find a wealth of information on creating healthy, secure relationships that last over time.

TherapistLocator.net A listing of over 15,000 marriage and family therapists throughout the United States offered by the American Association of Marriage and Family Therapists. Just put in your zip code, and the website will locate marriage and family therapists in your area.

ImagoRelationships.org Imago Therapy was introduced to us through Dr. Harville Hendrix in his book *Getting the Love You Want*. This website is offered by Imago Relationships International, a nonprofit organization that supports therapists who are trained in this modality and offers a free referral service to help you find a therapist in your area who can assist you in learning more about this highly acclaimed process to help turn your relationship around.

GottmanReferralNetwork.com A referral service for those looking for help from a Gottman-trained therapist. The therapists recommended have received training in Gottman Method Couples Therapy, an approach developed by Dr. John Gottman over a forty-year period of research with thousands of couples.

Relationship Skills Building

Hendricks.com Drs. Gay and Katie Hendricks have been developing their Conscious Loving teachings for decades, and they lavishly share what they know about how to create joyful relationships on this content-rich website. They offer many free and highly informative articles and audios, as well as share some helpful advice that can support you to have happy, healthy relationships in your future.

MarsVenus.com Dr. John Gray and his daughter, Lauren Gray, provide an abundance of free resources on this bounteous website, from a daily video blog, to advice columns, to a community forum, to nutritional suggestions. John has been a pioneer in helping people have more satisfying love lives, and he continues to provide leadership from the leading edge of his own development and research.

HarvilleHendrix.com Drs. Harville Hendrix and his wife, Helen LaKelly Hunt, kindly offer a tremendous amount of free content on this site that can help you improve your relationship skills, whether you're in a relationship right now or not. What better time to prepare yourself for your next opportunity to love and be loved than now?

CREATING NEW LOVE

CallingInTheOne.com Featuring the time-tested 7-step process that has worked for thousands of people throughout the world on how to break old painful patterns in love, and magnetize in happy, healthy love. You are invited to download a free 75-minute audio seminar, How to Identify and Release Your Hidden Barriers to Love and Become Magnetic to Your Soulmate.

SoulMateSecret.com Bestselling author Arielle Ford has an array of offerings on this helpful website, all designed to enhance your happiness in love. Included is her free 75-minute seminar, The Soulmate Secret: The 3 Keys to Manifesting True Love.

RE-CREATING YOUR LIFE

FemininePower.com My friend and colleague Claire Zammit and I spent nearly a decade co-developing a powerful transformative program for women, Feminine Power, to support women to realize their higher potentials in life, love, and livelihood. Join hundreds of thousands of women from around the world who have awakened their feminine power by visiting this site for your free download of the 75-minute audio The Three Keys to Feminine Power and connect with the power you hold to realize your full potentials.

RickHanson.net Bestselling author and fellow at the Greater Good Science Center at UC Berkeley, Dr. Rick Hanson offers a content-rich site that is abundant in free articles and videos, as well as multiple practices to help increase your fundamental well-being and psychological health.

INTRODUCTION: LANDING ON THE WRONG SIDE OF LOVE

6 **relationships have changed**: Stephanie Coontz, *Marriage, A History: How Love Conquered Marriage* (New York: Penguin, 2006), 4.

6 **"cultural creative"**: Paul H. Ray and Sherry Ruth Anderson, *The Cultural Creatives: How 50 Million People Are Changing the World* (New York: Harmony Books, 2000).

CHAPTER 1: SHAME, BLAME, AND THE FAILURE OF LOVE

16 **"Till death do us part"**: [Originally, "till death us departe."] Francis Procter and Walter Frere, "Chapter XV, The Occasional Services: Section 1 Solemnization of Matrimony," in *A New History of the Book of Common Prayer with a Rationale of Its Offices* (London: Macmillian, 1910), www.justus.anglican.org/resources/bcp/Procter&Frere/ch15.htm#note19.

17 **root of the word *shame***: *Online Etymology Dictionary*, 2014, http://www.etymonline.com/index.php?term=shame&allowed_in_frame=0.

18 **shame differs from guilt**: Gregory McNamee, "Shame vs. Guilt," *Virginia Quarterly Review* 91, no. 1 (2015), http://www.vqronline.org/essays-articles/2015/01/shame-vs-guilt. See also Marilyn Ivy,

"Benedict's Shame," *Cabinet* 31 (Fall 2008), http://cabinetmagazine .org/issues/31/ivy.php.

18   **violating external rules and expectations:** Michael Lewis, "Shame: The Exposed Self," in *Zero to Three* 12, no. 4 (April 1992), 6–10.

19   **Our brains much prefer it when:** David Rock, "A Hunger for Certainty: Your Brain Craves Certainty and Avoids Uncertainty Like It's Pain," *Psychology Today: Your Brain at Work,* October 25, 2009, https://www.psychologytoday.com/blog/your-brain-work/ 200910/hunger-certainty.

19   **studies with the Neuroleadership Institute:** Dr. Karey Pohn, e-mail to author May 7, 2014, based on Dan Radecki, "Expectations," presentation, Certificate in Foundations of Neuroleadership, New York, 2011.

21   **"lived happily ever after":** "Once Upon a Time," Wikipedia, http://en.wikipedia.org/wiki/Once_upon_a_time (last modified January 17, 2015).

21   **fairy tales themselves only emerged:** Ruth B. Bottigheimer, *Fairy Tales: A New History* (Albany: State University of New York Press, 2009),16–17.

22   **extreme life conditions:** Ibid., 20–25, 93–94.

23   **Giovanni Francesco Straparola:** Ibid.

25   **serial monogamy has now become:** Helen Fisher, *Anatomy of Love* (New York: Ballantine Books, 1994), 279.

25   **over 40 percent of first marriages:** "Second, Third Marriages: Divorce Rate Explained," *Huffington Post,* March 6, 2012, http:// www.huffingtonpost.com/2012/03/06/second-third-marriages -divorce-rate_n_1324496.html (video clip of *Today Show* interview with Gail Saltz). See also David Popenoe and Barbara Dafoe Whitehead, "The State of Our Unions 2007: The Social Health of Marriage in America" (Piscataway, NJ: National Marriage Project, 2007), 18–19; Matthew D. Bramlett and William D. Mosher, "Cohabitation, Marriage, Divorce, and Remarriage in the United States," *Vital and Health Statistics* 23, no. 22 (2002), 17–19.

26   **more people over fifty:** Sam Roberts, "Divorce After 50 Grows More Common," *New York Times,* September 20, 2013, http://www

.nytimes.com/2013/09/22/fashion/weddings/divorce-after-50
-grows-more-common.html?_r=1&.

26   **"Silver Seekers" over sixty**: Sadie Whitelocks, "Silver Surfers:
        Over 60s the Fastest Growing Group to Tap Into Online Dating,"
        Daily Mail, February 13, 2012, http://www.dailymail.co.uk/femail/
        article-2100568/Silver-surfers-Over-60s-fastest-growing-group
        -tap-online-dating.html.

27   **in spite of having one**: Andrew J. Cherlin, *The Marriage-Go-Round:
        The State of Marriage and the Family in America Today* (New York: Vintage
        Books, 2010).

27   **90 percent of us are predicted to marry**: Fisher, *Anatomy of Love,*
        298.

CHAPTER 2: BITTER BREAKUPS, NASTY ENDINGS, AND THE ART OF LIVING *UN*HAPPILY EVER AFTER

28   **Burt Pugach and Linda Riss**: Raoul Felder and Barbara Victor,
        Getting Away with Murder: Weapons for the War Against Domestic Violence (New
        York: Touchstone Books, 1996), 133–34.

29   **In a recent TED Talk**: Helen Fisher, "The Brain in Love," YouTube
        (uploaded on July 15, 2008), https://www.youtube.com/watch?v
        =OYfoGTIG7pY.

30   **During this initial protest stage**: Judith Horstman, *The Scientific
        American Book of Love, Sex and the Brain: The Neuroscience of How, When, Why
        and Who We Love* (San Francisco: Jossey-Bass, 2011), 166–68 (refer-
        ring to Fisher's work).

30   **Consider Christina Reber**: Douglas Walker, "Indiana Woman to
        Claim Self-Defense in Torn Scrotum Case: Christina Reber Is
        Charged with Aggravated Battery in Alleged Attack on Former Boy-
        friend," *USA Today,* http://www.usatoday.com/story/news/nation/
        2014/02/25/woman-self-defense-torn-scrotum/5813897/.

31   **Alanis Morissette's song**: Alanis Morissette and Glen Ballard,
        "You Oughta Know," *Jagged Little Pill* (Maverick/Reprise, 1995).

33   **Dr. Fisher comes to the rescue**: Helen Fisher, "Lost Love: The
        Nature of Romantic Rejection," in *Cut Loose: (Mostly) Older Women Talk*

About the End of (Mostly) Long Term Relationships, ed. Nan Bauer-Maglin (New Brusnwick, NJ: Rutgers University Press, 2006), 182–95.

35 **Dr. Louis Cozolino:** Personal communication with the author, May 2, 2014.

36 **In a study done at UCLA:** Matthew D. Lieberman and Naomi I. Eisenberger, "The Pains and Pleasures of Social Life: A Social Cognitive Neuroscience Approach," *Neuroleadership* 1 (2008), 38–43, http://www.scn.ucla.edu/pdf/Pains&Pleasures%282008%29 .pdf.

37 **"Broken Heart Syndrome":** Horstman, *The Scientific American Book of Love, Sex and the Brain,* 172. See also "'Broken Heart' Syndrome: Real, Potentially Deadly but Recovery Quick," *Johns Hopkins Medicine,* February 9, 2005, http://www.hopkinsmedicine.org/Press _releases/2005/02_10_05.html.

39 **One of my favorite songs:** *Mack and Mabel,* Stephen Citron, *Jerry Herman: Poet of the Showtune* (New Haven, CT: Yale University Press, 2004), 194.

40 **diminished capacity to love:** Ginette Paris, *Heartbreak: New Approaches to Healing: Recovering from Lost Love and Mourning* (Minneapolis, MN: Mill City Press, 2011), 9.

40 **movement in the therapeutic community:** Holly G. Prigerson et al., "Prolonged Grief Disorder: Psychometric Validation of Criteria Proposed for *DSM-V* and *ICD-11,*" *PLoS Medicine* 6, no. 8 (2009). doi: 10.1371/journal.pmed.1000121.

40 **described by the Mayo Clinic:** "Complicated Grief: Symptoms," Mayo Clinic, http://www.mayoclinic.org/diseases-conditions/ complicated-grief/basics/symptoms/con-20032765. See also Daniel Goleman, *Social Intelligence: The New Science of Human Relationships* (New York: Bantam Books, 2006), 113.

40 **treat your broken heart:** Naomi I. Eisenberger et al., "An Experimental Study of Shared Sensitivity to Physical Pain and Social Rejection," *Pain* 126 (2006): 132–38, http://www.scn.ucla.edu/pdf/ Eisenberger,Jarcho,Lieberman,Naliboff%282006%29.pdf.

42 **In the immortal words:** Leonard Cohen, "Anthem," 2015 Sony Music, http://www.leonardcohen.com/us/music/futureten-new -songs/anthem.

CHAPTER 3: A NEW POSSIBILITY BETWEEN US: INTRODUCING CONSCIOUS UNCOUPLING

44   **"It is with hearts full of sadness"**: Gwyneth Paltrow and Chris Martin, *Goop*, March 25, 2014, http://goop.com/journal/be/conscious-uncoupling?utm_source=goop+issue&utm_campaign=e01b658d69-A_Note_From_GP_3_25_2014&utm_medium=email&utm_term=0_5ad74d5855-e01b658d69-45659 (page taken down).

46   **This attachment circuitry causes**: Louis Cozolino, *The Neuroscience of Human Relationships: Attachment and the Developing Social Brain* (New York: W. W. Norton, 2014).

46   **Dr. Cozolino demonstrates**: Personal communication with author, May 2, 2014.

54   **Dr. Ginette Paris**: Ginette Paris, *Heartbreak: New Approaches to Healing: Recovering from Lost Love and Mourning* (Minneapolis, MN: Mill City Press, 2011), xvii.

54   **the concept of karma**: "What Is Karma?" *Unfettered Mind: Pragmatic Buddhism,* 2015 posting, http://www.unfetteredmind.org/karma-genesis-conditions.

56   **The word *generous***: *Etymology Online,* http://www.etymonline.com/index.php?term=genus&allowed_in_frame=0.

58   **"The Sun Never Says"**: Hafiz, in *The Gift,* trans. Daniel Ladinsky (New York: Penguin Compass, 1999), 34.

58   **Futurist Buckminster Fuller**: Daniel Quinn. *Beyond Civilization: Humanity's Next Great Adventure* (New York: Broadway Books, 2000), 137.

59   **New phrases and words**: "Wasband," *Wiktionary,* http://en.wiktionary.org/wiki/wasband; *Wevorce,* http://www.wevorce.com/about.html; "binuclear families," "About Dr. Ahrons," http://www.constanceahrons.com/about (last updated 2014); "stepwives," Lynne Oxhorn-Ringwood and Louise Oxhorn, with Marjorie Vego Krausz, *Stepwives: Ten Steps to Help Ex-Wives and Stepmothers End the Struggle and Put the Kids First* (New York: Touchstone, 2002).

CHAPTER 4: HOW AND WHEN TO DO THIS PROGRAM

63 **hellish end will soil**: Daniel Gilbert, *Stumbling on Happiness* (New York: Vintage Books, 2007), 223–25.

67 **over 90 percent of communication**: Albert Mehrabian, *Silent Messages: Implicit Communication of Emotions and Attitudes* (Belmont, CA: Wadsworth, 1981).

69 **"The State of Our Unions"**: David Popenoe and Barbara Dafoe Whitehead, "The State of Our Unions: The Social Health of Marriage in America, 1999," Piscataway, NJ: National Marriage Project. Cited in Laura Kipnis, *Against Love: A Polemic* (New York: Vintage Books, 2004), 149. See also Sandra Tsing Loh, "Let's Call the Whole Thing Off," *The Atlantic*, July 1, 2009, http://www.theatlantic.com/magazine/archive/2009/07/lets-call-the-whole-thing-off/307488/.

69 **three most common reasons**: Laura A. Wasser, *It Doesn't Have to Be That Way: How to Divorce Without Destroying Your Family or Bankrupting Yourself* (New York: St. Martin's Press, 2013), 24.

STEP 1: FIND EMOTIONAL FREEDOM

85 **Dr. Judith Herman**: Judith Herman, *Trauma and Recovery: The Aftermath of Violence—from Domestic Abuse to Political Terror* (New York: Basic Books, 1992, 1997).

85 **midst of a painful breakup**: Suzanne Lachmann, "How to Mourn a Breakup to Move Past Grief and Withdrawal," *Psychology Today*, June 4, 2013, https://www.psychologytoday.com/blog/me-we/201306/how-mourn-breakup-move-past-grief-and-withdrawal; see also Arif Najib et al., "Regional Brain Activity in Women Grieving a Romantic Relationship Breakup," *American Journal of Psychiatry* 161, no. 12 (December 2004): 2245–56, http://ajp.psychiatryonline.org/doi/abs/10.1176/appi.ajp.161.12.2245.

85 **We are relational creatures**: Thomas Lewis, Fari Amini, and Richard Lannon, *A General Theory of Love* (New York: Vintage, 2001); see also Helen Fisher, *Anatomy of Love* (New York: Ballantine Books, 1994).

86 **registers rejection:** Naomi I. Eisenberger et al., "The Pain of Social Disconnection: Examining the Shared Neural Underpinnings of Physical and Social Pain," *Nature Reviews Neuroscience* 13, no. 6 (June 2012): 421–34.

86 **by disturbing physical symptoms:** Ginette Paris, *Heartbreak: New Approaches to Healing: Recovering from Lost Love and Mourning* (Minneapolis, MN: Mill City Press, 2011), 40.

91 **restore a sense of safety:** Herman, *Trauma and Recovery*, 3.

91 **reactive part of our brain:** Daniel Goleman, *Emotional Intelligence: Why It Can Matter More Than IQ* (New York: Bantam Books, 1995), 113.

92 **Social psychologist Dr. Matthew Lieberman of UCLA:** Matthew D. Lieberman et al., "Putting Feelings into Words: Affect Labeling Disrupts Amygdala Activity in Response to Affective Stimuli," *Psychological Science* 18, no. 5 (2007) 421–28.

97 **Effective grieving:** Stephen Gilligan, *The Courage to Love: Principles and Practices of Self-Relations Psychotherapy* (New York: W. W. Norton, 1997).

99 **It plunges us into a fight-or-flight:** Paris, *Heartbreak*.

99 **likened anger to garbage:** Thich Nhat Hanh, *Anger: Wisdom for Cooling the Flames* (New York: Riverhead Books, 2001), 29–31.

101 **synchronizing with those we're closest:** "Lovers' Hearts Beat in Sync, UC Davis Study Says," *UC Davis News and Information,* February 8, 2013, http://news.ucdavis.edu/search/news_detail.lasso?id =10494.

101 **with a "breathing bear":** Lewis, Amini, and Lannon, *General Theory of Love,* 157.

101 **Dr. Jaak Panksepp:** Kat McGowan, "The Second Coming of Sigmund Freud," *Discover,* March 6, 2014, http://discovermagazine .com/2014/april/14-the-second-coming-of-sigmund-freud.

102 **Neuropsychologist Mark Solms interprets:** Ibid.

103 **Elisabeth Kübler-Ross:** *National Library of Medicine* [National Institutes of Health], 2013 biographical posting, http://www.nlm .nih.gov/changingthefaceofmedicine/physicians/biography_189 .html.

109 **try numbing your discomfort:** Robert Weiss, "Self-Soothing: How We Balance Ourselves," *The Therapist,* November/December

2013, http://www.camft.org/Content/NavigationMenu/Resource Center/ReadTheTherapist/NovemberDecember13/default.htm.

110 **Dr. Lawrence Calhoun:** Mark Miller, "Surviving the Jolt," *AARP Magazine*, April 2014, 62, http://pubs.aarp.org/aarptm/20140405 _NC?sub_id=1HyCsDRRPuvA#pg60.

110 **Well-known Buddhist nun:** Pema Chodron, *When Things Fall Apart: Heart Advice for Difficult Times* (Boston: Shambhala, 2000).

112 **Winston Churchill once said:** George Loftus, "If You're Going Through Hell, Keep Going—Winston Churchill," *Forbes*, May 9, 2012, http://www.forbes.com/sites/geoffloftus/2012/05/09/if-youre -going-through-hell-keep-going-winston-churchill/.

STEP 2: RECLAIM YOUR POWER AND YOUR LIFE

117 **drawn toward pinning blame:** Lauren Bryant, "The Blame Game," *Ohio University Research Newletter*, November 7, 2011, http://www.ohio.edu/research/communications/blamegame.cfm.

124 **seeing things about *yourself*:** Debbie Ford, *Spiritual Divorce: Divorce as a Catalyst for an Extraordinary Life* (New York: HarperOne, 2006).

124 **creating a breakup narrative:** Diane Vaughan, *Uncoupling: Turning Points in Intimate Relationships* (New York: Vintage, 1990). See also Matthew Lieberman, "Diaries: A Healthy Choice," *New York Times*, November 25, 2012, http://www.nytimes.com/roomfordebate/ 2012/11/25/will-diaries-be-published-in-2050/diaries-a-healthy -choice.

134 **foremost experts on forgiveness:** Frederic Luskin, *Forgive for Good* (New York: HarperOne, 2003).

134 **great Austrian psychiatrist:** Viktor E. Frankl, *Man's Search for Meaning*, trans. Isle Lasch (Boston: Beacon Press, 2006); and Carolyn Gregoire, "This Man Faced Unimaginable Suffering, and Then Wrote the Definitive Book About Happiness," *Huffington Post*, February 4, 2014, http://www.huffingtonpost.com/2014/02/04/this -book-youve-probably-_n_4705123.html.

STEP 3: BREAK THE PATTERN, HEAL YOUR HEART

139   **sheer insult it can be:** Diane Vaughan, *Uncoupling: Turning Points in Intimate Relationships* (New York: Vintage, 1990).

141   **beliefs we formed:** Stephen Wolinsky, *The Way of the Human, Volume II: The False Core and the False Self* (Capitola, CA: Quantum Institute Press, 1999).

141   **"We see life not as it is":** Anaïs Nin, *The Seduction of the Minotaur* (Athens, OH: Swallow Press, 1961), 124.

144   **Drs. John and Julie Gottman's:** John Gottman and Nan Silver, "What Makes Marriage Work? It's How You Resolve Conflict That Matters Most," *Psychology Today*, March 1, 1994, https://www.psychologytoday.com/articles/200910/what-makes-marriage-work.

153   **is simply *not true*:** Wolinsky, *The Way of the Human*.

154   **"It may take years":** Stephen Gilligan, *The Courage to Love: Principles and Practices of Self-Relations Psychotherapy* (New York: W. W. Norton, 1997), 12.

STEP 4: BECOME A LOVE ALCHEMIST

180   **Dr. Glenn Seaborg:** "The Philosopher's Stone: The Magic of Harry Potter That Turned Celluloid into Gold for Robert Matthews," *The Telegraph*, December 2, 2001, http://www.telegraph.co.uk/news/science/science-news/4767654/The-Philosophers-Stone.html. See also Wikipedia entry for "Glenn T. Seaborg," http://en.wikipedia.org/wiki/Glenn_T._Seaborg.

183   **Recent studies:** Jeremy Dean, "Reconstructing the Past: How Recalling Memories Alters Them: The First Experiment to Show the Enhancing and Distorting Effect of Recall," *PsyBlog: Understanding Your Mind*, February 19, 2013, http://www.spring.org.uk/2013/02/reconstructing-the-past-how-recalling-memories-alters-them.php. See also Peggy L. St. Jacques and Daniel L. Schacter, "Modifying Memory: Selectively Enhancing and Updating Personal Memories for a Museum Tour by Reactivating Them," *Psychological*

Science, February 13, 2013, http://pss.sagepub.com/content/24/4/
537; Constantine Sedikides and Jeffrey D. Green, "On the Self-
protective Nature of Inconsistency/Negativity Management: Using
the Person Memory Paradigm to Examine Self-referent Memory,"
Journal of Personality and Social Psychology 79 (2000): 906–92.

184 **"The question becomes":** Marianne Williamson, *A Year of Miracles:
Daily Devotions and Reflections* (New York: HarperOne, 2013), 8.

185 **late Reverend Roberta Herzog:** Roberta Herzog, "Forgiveness
Prayer," *Interspiritual Mindfulness and Meditation Study Group—Circle of Friends,*
July 16, 2010, http://cof-interspiritual-mindfulness.blogspot
.com/2012/07/forgiveness-prayer-as-offered-by.html.

186 **ancient Hawaiian prayer *Ho'oponopono:*** Sita Khasla, "Morrnah Nalamaku Simeona, Hawaiian Healer," Amazing Women
in History, http://www.amazingwomeninhistory.com/morrnah
-nalamaku-simeona-hawaiian-healer/.

187 **Self-forgiveness will usually require:** Colin Tipping, *Radical Forgiveness: A Revolutionary Five–Stage Process to Heal Relationships, Let Go of Anger
and Blame, Find Peace in Any Situation* (Boulder, CO: Sounds True,
2009).

193 **physicist Niels Bohr:** Brian Dodson, "Quantum 'Spooky Action at a Distance' Travels at Least 10,000 Times Faster Than
Light," *Gizmag,* March 10, 2013, http://www.gizmag.com/quantum
-entanglement-speed-10000-faster-light/26587/.

193 **journalist turned thought leader:** Lynne McTaggart, *The Bond:
How to Fix Your Falling-Down World* (New York: Free Press, 2011), 12.

202 **philosophy behind Kintsugi:** Blake Gopnik, "'Golden Seams:
The Japanese Art of Mending Ceramics' at Freer," *Washington
Post,* March 3, 2009, http://www.washingtonpost.com/wp-dyn/
content/article/2009/03/02/AR2009030202723.html.

STEP 5: CREATE YOUR HAPPILY-*EVEN*-AFTER LIFE

212 **As the Sufi poet Rumi once said:** Rumi, "When I Die," trans.
Nader Khalili, May 18, 1992, *Allspirit, Death, Dying, Grief,* http://
allspirit.co.uk/poetry/death-dying-grief/.

214 **maintaining the right expectations:** David Rock, *Your Brain at*

Work: Strategies for Overcoming Distraction, Regaining Focus, and Working Smarter All Day Long (New York: HarperCollins, 2009), 140.

218 **Dr. Naomi Eisenberger from UCLA:** Naomi I. Eisenberger, "The Pain of Social Disconnection: Examining the Shared Neural Underpinnings of Physical and Social Pain," *Nature Reviews Neuroscience* 13, no. 6 (June 2012): 421–34, http://www.nature.com/nrn/journal/v13/n6/full/nrn3231.html.

218 **Dr. Eisenberger reports:** David Rock, "Status: A More Accurate Way of Understanding Self-Esteem," *Psychology Today,* October 18, 2009, https://www.psychologytoday.com/blog/your-brain-work/200910/status-more-accurate-way-understanding-self-esteem.

221 **inside the happily-ever-after myth:** Ruth B. Bottigheimer, *Fairy Tales: A New History* (Albany: State University of New York Press, 2009).

229 **negative effects that divorce had:** Judith S. Wallerstein, "The Long-Term Effects of Divorce on Children: A Review," *Journal of the American Academy of Child & Adolescent Psychiatry* 30, no. 3 (May 1991): 349–60. See also Alison Clarke-Stewart and Cornelia Brentano, *Divorce: Causes and Consequences* (New Haven, CT: Yale University Press, 2006), 106.

229 **high levels of conflict and strife:** Lynn Fainsilber Katz and John M. Gottman, "Buffering Children from Marital Conflict and Dissolution," *Journal of Clinical Child Psychology* 26, no. 2 (1996): 157–71.

230 **Resolution, an organization:** "Exam Results 'Suffering,'" *Resolution,* November 24, 2014, http://www.resolution.org.uk/news-list.asp?page_id=228&page=1&n_id=251.

232 **pioneering bestseller** ***The Good Divorce:*** Constance Ahrons, *The Good Divorce: Keeping Your Family Together When Your Marriage Comes Apart* (New York: Harper Perennial, 1995).

232 ***binuclear families:*** "About Dr. Ahrons," http://www.constanceahrons.com/about.

233 **family therapist Susan Stiffelman:** E-mail to the author, February 2, 2015.

235 **drop in economic status:** Clarke-Stewart and Brentano, *Divorce: Causes and Consequences,* 68.

236 **Judge Thomas Zampino:** Joseph Sorge and James Scurlock, *Divorce Corp.* (Jackson, WY: DC Books, 2013), 4.

236 **Ultimatum Game:** Peter Reuell, "When Fairness Prevails: Harvard Research Shows How Uncertainty Affects Behavior," *Harvard Gazette,* January 30, 2013, http://news.harvard.edu/gazette/story/2013/01/when-fairness-prevails/.

237 **Golnaz Tabibnia and Matthew D. Lieberman:** Golnaz Tabibnia and Matthew D. Lieberman, "Fairness and Cooperation Are Rewarding Evidence from Social Cognitive Neuroscience," *Annals of the New York Academy of Science* 1118 (2007): 90–101. See also David Rock, "SCARF: A Brain-Based Model for Collaborating with and Influencing Others," *NeuroLeadership* 1 (2008), 78–87, www.davidrock.net/files/NLJ_SCARFUS.pdf.

237 **those over fifty:** Sam Roberts, "Divorce After 50 Grows More Common," *New York Times,* September 20, 2013, http://www.nytimes.com/2013/09/22/fashion/weddings/divorce-after-50-grows-more-common.html.

239 **bizarre New York law:** Sophia Hollander, "After Divorce, a Degree Is Costly: New York, Unlike Most States, Treats Education Achievements and Even Talents as Property to Be Divided Between Spouses," *Wall Street Journal,* December 23, 2012, http://www.wsj.com/articles/SB10001424127887324481204578180132637628330.

241 **In 1969, Ronald Reagan:** Bradford Wilcox, "The Evolution of Divorce," *National Affairs,* Fall 2009, http://www.nationalaffairs.com/publications/detail/the-evolution-of-divorce.

242 **$50 billion a year:** Ibid., xvii.

242 **ballooned from a few pages:** Sorge and Scurlock, *Divorce Corp.,* 26.

242 **third cause of bankruptcy:** Ibid., xxxiii.

242 **pay about $30,000:** Michele Lowrance, *The Good Karma Divorce: Avoid Litigation, Turn Negative Emotions into Positive Actions, and Get On with the Rest of Your Life* (New York: HarperOne, 2010), 53.

243 **Alexandra Borg:** Sorge and Scurlock, *Divorce Corp.,* 82.

244 **Wevorce founder Michelle Crosby:** Victor Li and Stephanie Francis Ward, "Legal Rebels 2014," *ABA Journal,* September 1, 2014, http://www.abajournal.com/magazine/article/legal_rebels_2014/.

245 **divorce attorney Lisa Forberg:** Personal communication and follow-up e-mail with the author, May 27, 2014.

247 **Marina Abramovic and Ulay:** Abby Ellin, "Untying the Knot, and

Bonds, of Marriage," *New York Times*, April 27, 2012, http://www .nytimes.com/2012/04/29/fashion/weddings/leaving-a-spouse -behind-for-good.html?pagewanted=all&_r=0.

248 ***The Artist Is Present:*** Matthew Akers, director, *The Artist Is Present*, June 16, 2012, Music Box Films, http://www.musicboxfilms.com/ marina-abramovic-the-artist-is-present-movies-3.php.

251 **relationship funeral**: Lauren Frances, "How to Stage a Relationship Funeral! Lauren on *The Ricki Lake Show*" (video), YouTube, https://www.youtube.com/watch?v=GhbZ6MGpErM.

POSTSCRIPT: EVOLVING LOVE

255 **live with an intriguing tension**: Andrew Cherlin, *The Marriage-Go-Round: the State of Marriage and the Family in America Today* (New York: Vintage Books, 2010), 4.

255 **90 percent of us will**: Helen E. Fisher, *Anatomy of Love: The Natural History of Monogamy, Adultery and Divorce* (New York: W. W. Norton, 1992), 298.

256 **a recent cover of *Time:*** Laura Carstensen, "The New Age of Much Older Age," Special Health Double Issue, *Time*, February 23, 2015, http://time.com/3706775/in-the-latest-issue-23/.

257 **When women can leave**: "Who Initiates the Divorce More Often, the Wife or the Husband?" Divorce Lawyer Source, http://www .divorce-lawyer-source.com/faq/emotional/who-initiates-divorce -men-or-women.html. See also Fisher, *Anatomy of Love*, 104–107.

BIBLIOGRAPHY

Ahrons, Constance. *The Good Divorce: Keeping Your Family Together When Your Marriage Comes Apart.* New York: Harper Perennial, 1995.

———. *We're Still Family: What Grown Children Have to Say About Their Parents' Divorce.* New York: Perennial Currents, 2005.

Akers, Matthew, director. *The Artist Is Present.* Music Box Films, June 16, 2012. http://www.musicboxfilms.com/marina-abramovic-the-artist-is-present-movies-3.php.

Beck, Don Edward, and Christopher C. Cowan. *Spiral Dynamics: Mastering Values, Leadership, and Change.* Malden, MA: Blackwell, 2009.

Birnbach, Lawrence, and Beverly Hyman. *How to Know If It's Time to Go: A 10-Step Reality Test for Your Marriage.* New York: Sterling Ethos, 2010.

Blau, Melinda. *Families Apart: Ten Keys to Successful Co-Parenting.* New York: Perigee, 1995.

Bottigheimer, Ruth B. *Fairy Tales: A New History.* Albany: State University of New York Press, 2009.

Bramlett, Matthew D., and William. D. Mosher. "Cohabitation, Marriage, Divorce, and Remarriage in the United States." *Vital and Health Statistics* 23, no. 22, 2002.

"'Broken Heart' Syndrome: Real, Potentially Deadly but Recovery Quick." *Johns Hopkins Medicine,* February 9, 2005. http://www.hopkinsmedicine.org/Press_releases/2005/02_10_05.html.

Brown, Brené. *Daring Greatly: How the Courage to Be Vulnerable Transforms the Way We Live, Love, Parent, and Lead*. New York: Gotham Books, 2012.

——. *The Gifts of Imperfection: Let Go of Who You Think You're Supposed to Be and Embrace Who You Are*. Center City, MN: Hazeldon, 2010.

Bryant, Lauren. "The Blame Game." *Ohio University Research Newletter,* November 7, 2011. http://www.ohio.edu/research/communications/blamegame.cfm.

Carstensen, Laura. "The New Age of Much Older Age." Special Health Double Issue, *Time,* February 23, 2015, 185. http://time.com/3706775/in-the-latest-issue-23/.

Cherlin, Andrew J. *The Marriage-Go-Round: The State of Marriage and the Family in America Today*. New York: Vintage Books, 2010.

Chodron, Pema. *When Things Fall Apart: Heart Advice for Difficult Times*. Boston: Shambhala, 2000.

Citron, Stephen. *Jerry Herman: Poet of the Showtune*. New Haven, CT: Yale University Press, 2004.

Clarke-Stewart, Alison, and Cornelia Brentano. *Divorce: Causes and Consequences*. New Haven, CT: Yale University Press, 2006.

Cohen, Andrew. *Evolutionary Enlightenment: A New Path to Spiritual Awakening*. New York: Select Books, 2011.

Colgrove, Melba, Harold H. Bloomfield, and Peter McWilliams. *How to Survive the Loss of a Love*. Los Angeles: Prelude Press, 1991.

Collins, Tara. J., and Omri Gillath. "Attachment, Breakup Strategies, and Associated Outcomes: The Effects of Security Enhancement on the Selection of Breakup Strategies." *Journal of Research in Personality* 46, no. 2 (2012): 210–222. doi:10.1016/j.jrp.2012.01.008.

"Complicated Grief: Symptoms." Mayo Clinic. http://www.mayoclinic.org/diseases-conditions/complicated-grief/basics/symptoms/con-20032765.

Coontz, Stephanie. *Marriage, a History: How Love Conquered Marriage*. New York: Penguin Books, 2006.

Cozolino, Louis. *The Neuroscience of Human Relationships: Attachment and the Developing Social Brain,* 2nd ed. New York: W. W. Norton, 2014.

Dean, Jeremy. "Reconstructing the Past: How Recalling Memories Alters Them: The First Experiment to Show the Enhancing and Distorting Effect of Recall." *PsyBlog: Understanding Your Mind,* February 19, 2013.

http://www.spring.org.uk/2013/02/reconstructing-the-past
-how-recalling-memories-alters-them.php.

Dodson, Brian. "Quantum 'Spooky Action at a Distance' Travels at
Least 10,000 Times Faster Than Light." *Gizmag*, March 10, 2013.
http://www.gizmag.com/quantum-entanglement-speed-10000
-faster-light/26587/.

Dworkin, Andrea. *Heartbreak: The Political Memoir of a Feminist Militant*. New
York: Basic Books, 2002.

Eisenberger, Naomi I. "The Pain of Social Disconnection: Examining the Shared Neural Underpinnings of Physical and Social
Pain." *Nature Reviews Neuroscience* 13, no. 6 (June 2012). http://www
.nature.com/nrn/journal/v13/n6/full/nrn3231.html. doi:10.1038/
nrn3231.

Eisenberger, Naomi I., et al. "An Experimental Study of Shared Sensitivity to Physical Pain and Social Rejection." *Pain* 126 (2006).
http://www.scn.ucla.edu/pdf/Eisenberger,Jarcho,Lieberman,
Naliboff%282006%29.pdf.doi:10.1016/j.pain.2006.06.024.

Ellin, Abby. "Untying the Knot, and Bonds, of Marriage." *New York Times*,
April 27, 2012. http://www.nytimes.com/2012/04/29/fashion/
weddings/leaving-a-spouse-behind-for-good.html?pagewanted
=all&_r=0.

Elliott, Susan J. *Getting Past Your Breakup: How to Turn a Devastating Loss into the
Best Thing That Ever Happened to You*. Cambridge, MA: Da Capo Press,
2009.

"Exam Results 'Suffering.'" *Resolution*, November 24, 2014. http://www
.resolution.org.uk/news-list.asp?page_id=228&page=1&n_id=251.

Felder, Raoul, and Barbara Victor. *Getting Away with Murder: Weapons for the
War Against Domestic Violence*. New York: Touchstone Books, 1996.

Fisher, Helen E. *Anatomy of Love: The Natural History of Monogamy, Adultery and
Divorce*. New York: Ballantine Books, 1994.

———. "The Brain in Love." YouTube, TED Talk video. Uploaded July 15,
2008. https://www.youtube.com/watch?v=OYfoGTIG7pY.

———. "Lost Love: The Nature of Romantic Rejection." In *Cut Loose:
(Mostly) Older Women Talk About the End of (Mostly) Long Term Relationships*,
edited by Nan Bauer-Maglin, 182–95. New Brunswick, NJ: Rutgers University Press, 2006.

bibliography

Ford, Arielle. *Wabi Sabi Love: The Ancient Art of Finding Perfect Love in Imperfect Relationships.* New York: HarperOne, 2012.

Ford, Debbie. *Spiritual Divorce: Divorce as a Catalyst for an Extraordinary Life.* New York: HarperOne, 2006.

Forward, Susan, with Donna Frazier. *Emotional Blackmail: When the People in Your Life Use Fear, Obligation and Guilt to Manipulate You.* New York: Quill, 2001.

Frances, Lauren. "How to Stage a Relationship Funeral! Lauren on *The Ricki Lake Show*" (video), YouTube. https://www.youtube.com/watch?v=GhbZ6MGpErM.

Frankl, Viktor E. *Man's Search for Meaning.* Translated by Isle Lasch. Boston: Beacon Press, 2006.

Gilbert, Daniel. *Stumbling on Happiness.* New York: Vintage Books, 2007.

Gilbert, Elizabeth. *Committed: A Love Story.* New York: Penguin Books, 2010.

Gilligan, Stephen. *The Courage to Love: Principles and Practices of Self-Relations Psychotherapy.* New York: W. W. Norton, 1997.

Goleman, Daniel. *Emotional Intelligence: Why It Can Matter More Than IQ.* New York: Bantam Books, 1995.

———. *Social Intelligence: The New Science of Human Relationships.* New York: Bantam Books, 2006.

Gopnik, Blake. "'Golden Seams: The Japanese Art of Mending Ceramics' at Freer." *Washington Post,* March 3, 2009. http://www.washingtonpost.com/wp-dyn/content/article/2009/03/02/AR2009030202723.html.

Gottman, John, and Nan Silver. *The Seven Principles for Making Marriage Work: A Practical Guide from the Country's Foremost Relationship Expert.* New York: Harmony Books, 1999.

———. "What Makes Marriage Work? It's How You Resolve Conflict That Matters Most." *Psychology Today,* March 1, 1994. https://www.psychologytoday.com/articles/200910/what-makes-marriage-work.

Gray, John. *Mars and Venus Starting Over: A Practical Guide for Finding Love Again After a Painful Breakup, Divorce or the Loss of a Loved One.* New York: Perennial Currents, 2005.

Gregoire, Carolyn. "This Man Faced Unimaginable Suffering, and

Then Wrote the Definitive Book About Happiness." *Huffington Post*, February 4, 2014. http://www.huffingtonpost.com/2014/02/04/ this-book-youve-probably-_n_4705123.html.

Hafiz. "The Sun Never Says." In *The Gift*, translated by Daniel Ladinsky. New York: Penguin Compass, 1999.

Hanh, Thich Nhat. *Anger: Wisdom for Cooling the Flames*. New York: Riverhead Books, 2001.

Hay, Louise L., and David Kessler. *You Can Heal Your Heart: Finding Peace After a Breakup, Divorce, or Death*. Carlsbad, CA: Hay House, 2014.

Hendrix, Harville. *Getting the Love You Want: A Guide for Couples*. New York: Harper Perennial, 1990.

Herman, Judith Lewis. *Trauma and Recovery: The Aftermath of Violence—from Domestic Abuse to Political Terror*. New York: Basic Books, 1992, 1997.

Herzog, Roberta. "Forgiveness Prayer." *Interspiritual Mindfulness and Meditation Study Group—Circle of Friends*, July 16, 2010. http://cof-interspiritual -mindfulness.blogspot.com/2012/07/forgiveness-prayer-as -offered-by.html.

Hollander, Sophia. "After Divorce, a Degree Is Costly: New York, Unlike Most States, Treats Education Achievements and Even Talents as Property to Be Divided Between Spouses." *Wall Street Journal*, December 23, 2012. http://www.wsj.com/articles/SB10001424127 8873244812045781801326376528330.

Horstman, Judith. *The Scientific American Book of Love, Sex and the Brain: The Neuroscience of How, When, Why and Who We Love*. San Francisco: Jossey-Bass, 2012.

Houston, Jean. *Jump Time: Shaping Your Future in a World of Radical Change*. Boulder, CO: Sentient, 2004.

Ivy, Marilyn. "Benedict's Shame." *Cabinet*, Fall 2008. http://cabinet magazine.org/issues/31/ivy.php.

Johnson, Sue. *Love Sense: The Revolutionary New Science of Romantic Relationships*. New York: Little, Brown, 2013.

Katz, Lynn Fainsilber, and John M Gottman. "Buffering Children from Marital Conflict and Dissolution." *Journal of Clinical Child Psychology* 26, no. 2 (1996): 157–71.

Kersey, Cynthia. *Unstoppable Women: Achieve Any Breakthrough Goal in 30 Days*. Emmaus, PA: Rodale Books, 2005.

Khasla, Sita. "Morrnah Nalamaku Simeona, Hawaiian Healer." Amazing Women in History. http://www.amazingwomeninhistory.com/morrnah-nalamaku-simeona-hawaiian-healer/.

Kingma, Daphne Rose. *Coming Apart: Why Relationships End and How to Live Through the Ending of Yours*. San Francisco: Conari Press, 2012.

Kipnis, Laura. *Against Love: A Polemic*. New York: Vintage Books, 2004.

Kirshenbaum, Mira. *Too Good to Leave, Too Bad to Stay: A Step-by-Step Guide to Help You Decide Whether to Stay In or Get Out of Your Relationship*. New York: Plume, 1997.

Lachmann, Suzanne. "How to Mourn a Breakup to Move Past Grief and Withdrawal." *Psychology Today*, June 4, 2013. https://www.psychologytoday.com/blog/me-we/201306/how-mourn-breakup-move-past-grief-and-withdrawal.

Lesser, Elizabeth. *Broken Open: How Difficult Times Can Help Us Grow*. New York: Villard Books, 2005.

Levine, Amir, and Rachel S. F. Heller. *Attached: The New Science of Adult Attachment and How It Can Help You Find—and Keep—Love*. New York: Jeremy P. Tarcher/Penguin, 2011.

Lewis, Michael. "Shame: The Exposed Self." *Zero to Three* 12, no. 4 (April 1992): 6–10.

Lewis, Thomas, Fari Amini, and Richard Lannon. *A General Theory of Love*. New York: Vintage Books, 2001.

Li, Victor, and Stephanie Francis Ward. "Legal Rebels 2014." *ABA Journal*, September 1, 2014. http://www.abajournal.com/magazine/article/legal_rebels_2014/.

Lieberman, Matthew. "Diaries: A Healthy Choice." *New York Times*, November 25, 2012. http://www.nytimes.com/roomfordebate/2012/11/25/will-diaries-be-published-in-2050/diaries-a-healthy-choice.

Lieberman, Matthew D., and Naomi I. Eisenberger. "The Pains and Pleasures of Social Life: A Social Cognitive Neuroscience Approach." *Neuroleadership* 1 (2008). http://www.scn.ucla.edu/pdf/Pains&Pleasures%282008%29.pdf.

Lieberman, Matthew D., et al. "Putting Feelings into Words: Affect Labeling Disrupts Amygdala Activity in Response to Affective Stimuli." *Psychological Science* 18, no 5 (2007).

Loftus, George. "If You're Going Through Hell, Keep Going—Winston Churchill." *Forbes*, May 9, 2012. http://www.forbes.com/sites/geoffloftus/2012/05/09/if-youre-going-through-hell-keep-going-winston-churchill/.

"Lovers' Hearts Beat in Sync, UC Davis Study Says." *UC Davis News and Information*, February 8, 2013. http://news.ucdavis.edu/search/news_detail.lasso?id=10494.

Lowrance, Michele. *The Good Karma Divorce: Avoid Litigation, Turn Negative Emotions into Positive Actions, and Get On with the Rest of Your Life*. New York: HarperOne, 2010.

Luskin, Frederic. *Forgive for Good: A Proven Prescription for Health and Happiness*. New York: HarperOne, 2003.

May, Simon. *Love: A History*. New Haven, CT: Yale University Press, 2011.

McGhee, Christina. *Parenting Apart: How Separated and Divorced Parents Can Raise Happy and Secure Kids*. New York: Berkley, 2010.

McGowan, Kat. "The Second Coming of Sigmund Freud." *Discover*, March 6, 2014. http://discovermagazine.com/2014/april/14-the-second-coming-of-sigmund-freud.

McNamee, Gregory. "Shame vs Guilt." *Virginia Quarterly Review* 91, no. 1 (2015). http://www.vqronline.org/essays-articles/2015/01/shame-vs-guilt.

McTaggart, Lynne. *The Bond: Connecting Through the Space Between Us*. New York: Free Press, 2011.

Mehrabian, Albert. *Silent Messages: Implicit Communication of Emotions and Attitudes*. Belmont, CA: Wadsworth, 1981.

Miller, Mark. "Surviving the Jolt." *AARP Magazine*, April 2014. http://pubs.aarp.org/aarptm/20140405_NC?sub_id=1HyCsDRRPuvA#pg60.

Moore, Thomas. *Care of the Soul: A Guide for Cultivating Depth and Sacredness in Everyday Life*. New York: Harper Perennial, 1994.

Nadler, Relly. "What Was I Thinking? Handling the Hijack," *Business Management*, July 1, 2009. http://www.busmanagement.com/issue-16/what-was-i-thinking-handling-the-hijack/.

Najib, Arif, et al. "Regional Brain Activity in Women Grieving a Romantic Relationship Breakup." *American Journal of Psychiatry* 161, no. 12 (December 2004): 2245–56. doi:10.1176/appi.ajp.161.12.2245.

Nin, Anaïs. *The Seduction of the Minotaur*. Athens, OH: Swallow Press, 1961.

Oxhorn-Ringwood, Lynne, and Louise Oxhorn, with Marjorie Vego Krausz. *Stepwives: 10 Steps to Help Ex-Wives and Stepmothers End the Struggle and Put the Kids First*. New York: Fireside, 2002.

Paris, Ginette. *Heartbreak: New Approaches to Healing: Recovering from Lost Love and Mourning*. Minneapolis, MN: Mill City Press, 2011.

Phillips, Roderick. *Untying the Knot: A Short History of Divorce*. New York: Cambridge University Press, 1991.

"The Philosopher's Stone: The Magic of Harry Potter That Turned Celluloid into Gold for Robert Matthews." *The Telegraph,* December 2, 2001. http://www.telegraph.co.uk/news/science/science-news/4767654/The-Philosophers-Stone.html.

Phipps, Carter. *Evolutionaries: Unlocking the Spiritual and Cultural Potential of Science's Greatest Idea*. New York: Harper Perennial, 2012.

Popenoe, David, and Barbara Dafoe Whitehead. "The State of Our Unions 2007: The Social Health of Marriage in America." Piscataway, NJ: National Marriage Project, 2007.

Prigerson, Holly G., et al. "Prolonged Grief Disorder: Psychometric Validation of Criteria Proposed for *DSM-V* and *ICD-11*." *PLoS Medicine* 6, no. 8 (2009). doi: 10.1371/journal.pmed.1000121.

Procter, Francis, and Walter Frere. "Chapter XV, The Occasional Services: Section 1 Solemnization of Matrimony." In *A New History of the Book of Common Prayer with a Rationale of Its Offices*. London: Macmillian, 1910. http://www.justus.anglican.org/resources/bcp/Procter&Frere/ch15.htm#note19.

Quinn, Daniel. *Beyond Civilization: Humanity's Next Great Adventure*. New York: Broadway Books, 2000.

Ray, Paul H., and Sherry Ruth Anderson. *The Cultural Creatives: How 50 Million People Are Changing the World*. New York: Harmony Books, 2000.

Reuell, Peter. "When Fairness Prevails: Harvard Research Shows How Uncertainty Affects Behavior." *Harvard Gazette,* January 30, 2013. http://news.harvard.edu/gazette/story/2013/01/when-fairness-prevails/.

Roberts, Sam. "Divorce After 50 Grows More Common." *New York Times,* September 20, 2013. http://www.nytimes.com/2013/09/22/fashion/weddings/divorce-after-50-grows-more-common.html.

Rock, David. "A Hunger for Certainty: Your Brain Craves Certainty and Avoids Uncertainty Like It's Pain." *Psychology Today: Your Brain at Work*, October 25, 2009. http://www.psychologytoday.com/blog/your-brain-work/200910/hunger-certainty.

———. "SCARF: A Brain-Based Model for Collaborating with and Influencing Others." *NeuroLeadership* (2008). www.davidrock.net/files/NLJ_SCARFUS.pdf.

———. "Status: A More Accurate Way of Understanding Self-Esteem." *Psychology Today*, October 18, 2009. https://www.psychologytoday.com/blog/your-brain-work/200910/status-more-accurate-way-understanding-self-esteem.

———. *Your Brain at Work: Strategies for Overcoming Distraction, Regaining Focus, and Working Smarter All Day Long.* New York: HarperCollins, 2009.

Rumi, "When I Die" [Ghazal Number 911]. Translated by Nader Khalili. In *Allspirit: Death, Dying, Grief*. http://allspirit.co.uk/poetry/death-dying-grief/.

Sanchez, Sharon. "Working with Difficult Emotions: Shame's Legacy." *The Therapist*, November/December 2013. http://www.camft.org/Content/NavigationMenu/ResourceCenter/ReadTheTherapist/NovemberDecember13/default.htm.

"Second, Third Marriages: Divorce Rate Explained." *Huffington Post*, March 6, 2012. http://www.huffingtonpost.com/2012/03/06/second-third-marriages-divorce-rate_n_1324496.html [video clip of *Today Show* interview with Gail Saltz].

Sedikides, Constantine, and Jeffrey D Green. "On the Self-Protective Nature of Inconsistency/Negativity Management: Using the Person Memory Paradigm to Examine Self-Referent Memory." *Journal of Personality and Social Psychology* 79 (2000): 906–92.

Shimoff, Marci, with Carol Kline. *Happy for No Reason: 7 Steps to Being Happy from the Inside Out.* New York: Free Press, 2008.

Solomon, Marion F., and Daniel J. Siegel, eds. *Healing Trauma: Attachment, Mind, Body, and Brain.* New York: W. W. Norton, 2003.

Sorge, Joseph, with James Scurlock. *Divorce Corp.* Jackson, WY: DC Books, 2013.

St. Jacques, Peggy L., and Daniel L. Schacter. "Modifying Memory: Selectively Enhancing and Updating Personal Memories for a

Museum Tour by Reactivating Them." *Psychological Science*, February 13, 2013. http://pss.sagepub.com/content/24/4/537. doi: 10.1177/0956797612457377.

Sussman, Rachel A. *The Breakup Bible: The Smart Woman's Guide to Healing from a Breakup or Divorce*. New York: Three Rivers Press, 2011.

Tabibnia, Golnaz, and Matthew D. Lieberman. "Fairness and Cooperation Are Rewarding Evidence from Social Cognitive Neuroscience," *Annals of the New York Academy of Science* 1118 (2007): 90–101. doi: 10.1196/annals.1412.001.

Taylor, Barbara Brown. *Learning to Walk in the Dark*. New York: HarperOne, 2014.

Tesler, Pauline H., and Peggy Thompson. *Collaborative Divorce: The Revolutionary New Way to Restructure Your Family, Resolve Legal Issues, and Move On with Your Life*. New York: Harper, 2007.

Tipping, Colin. *Radical Forgiveness: A Revolutionary Five-Stage Process to Heal Relationships, Let Go of Anger and Blame, Find Peace in Any Situation*. Boulder, CO: Sounds True, 2009.

Tsing Loh, Sandra. "Let's Call the Whole Thing Off." *The Atlantic*, July 1, 2009. http://www.theatlantic.com/magazine/archive/2009/07/lets-call-the-whole-thing-off/307488/.

Vaughan, Diane. *Uncoupling: Turning Points in Intimate Relationships*. New York: Vintage Books, 1990.

Viorst, Judith. *Necessary Losses: The Loves, Illusions, Dependencies, and Impossible Expectations That All of Us Have to Give Up in Order to Grow*. New York: Free Press, 2002.

Voo, Jocelyn. "Love Addiction—How to Break It." CNN, October 16, 2007. http://www.cnn.com/2007/LIVING/personal/10/09/end.relationship/.

Walker, Douglas. "Indiana Woman to Claim Self-Defense in Torn Scrotum Case: Christina Reber Is Charged with Aggravated Battery in Alleged Attack on Former Boyfriend." *USA Today*, February 25, 2014. http://www.usatoday.com/story/news/nation/2014/02/25/woman-self-defense-torn-scrotum/5813897/.

Wallerstein, Judith S. "The Long-Term Effects of Divorce on Children: A Review." *Journal of the American Academy of Child & Adolescent*

Psychiatry 30, no. 3 (May 1991): 349–60. doi: 10.1097/00004583
-199105000-00001.

Wasser, Laura A. *It Doesn't Have to Be That Way: How to Divorce Without Destroying Your Family or Bankrupting Yourself.* New York: St. Martin's Press, 2013.

Weiss, Robert. "Self-Soothing: How We Balance Ourselves." *The Therapist,* November/December 2013. http://www.camft.org/Content/NavigationMenu/ResourceCenter/ReadTheTherapist/NovemberDecember13/default.htm.

"What Is Karma?" Unfettered Mind: Pragmatic Buddhism. 2015 posting. http://www.unfetteredmind.org/karma-genesis-conditions.

Whitelocks, Sadie. "Silver Surfers: Over 60s the Fastest Growing Group to Tap Into Online Dating." *Daily Mail,* February 13, 2012. http://www.dailymail.co.uk/femail/article-2100568/Silver-surfers-Over-60s-fastest-growing-group-tap-online-dating.html.

"Who Initiates the Divorce More Often, the Wife or the Husband?" Divorce Lawyer Source. http://www.divorce-lawyer-source.com/faq/emotional/who-initiates-divorce-men-or-women.html.

Wilcox, Bradford. "The Evolution of Divorce." *National Affairs,* Fall 2009. http://www.nationalaffairs.com/publications/detail/the-evolution-of-divorce.

Williamson, Marianne. *Enchanted Love: The Mystical Power of Intimate Relationships.* New York: Simon & Schuster, 2001.

———. *The Law of Divine Compensation: On Work, Money and Miracles.* New York: HarperOne, 2012.

———. *A Year of Miracles: Daily Devotions and Reflections.* New York: HarperOne, 2013.

Wolinsky, Stephen. *The Way of the Human, Volume II: The False Core and the False Self.* Capitola, CA: Quantum Institute Press, 1999.

Abramovic, Marina, 247–48
Adams, Scott, 37
affect labeling, 92–93, 96, 162
"After a While" (Shoffstall), 138
agreements, 213–16
Ahrons, Constance, 232
Al-Anon, 137
Albom, Mitch, 52
Alcoholics Anonymous (AA), 124
Alexandria (author's daughter), 224,
    230–31, 235
Amanda and Benita, 72–73
American Bar Association, 244
Andersen, Susan, 223
Angelou, Maya, 2, 98
anger, 48, 56, 92, 98–101, 186–89, 245
Aristotle, 226
Artist Is Present, The, 248
art therapy, 124
Aslay, Jonathan, 220–21
assumptions, 105–10, 147–48
    see also beliefs, core
attachment theory, 231
attention deficit hyperactivity disorder
    (ADHD), 65–66

Attwood, Chris, 175–77, 227
Attwood, Doris, 176
Attwood, Janet Bray, 175–77,
    227
Atwood, Margaret, 17
avoidant attachment style, 145

Bach, Richard, 140
Ballard, Glen, 32n
Beck, Martha, 15
Beckwith, Michael, 177
beginner's mind, 164
beliefs, core, 51–52, 138–41, 146–49,
    153–55, 161
Benedict, Ruth, 18
binuclear families, 232
blessings, 56–57, 73, 159–60, 180, 214,
    249–51
Bond, The (McTaggart), 193
bonding:
    attachment theory and, 231
    negative, 34–38
    parent-child, 145, 153
    predisposition to, 85
Book of Common Prayer, 16

index

brain chemistry:
  emotions and, 19–20, 29–32, 35–36,
    45–46
  rational thinking and, 47
  social rejection and, 218
breakup narratives:
  identifying your, 124–25, 137–41,
    146–48
  perpetuating your, 150–52, 222
  worldviews and, 115, 121
breakups:
  assumptions underlying, 105–10,
    147–48
  as catalysts for change, 249
  closure and, 194–95, 199
  communication and, 205–8
  as crossroads, 9–10, 42, 111
  emotions and, *see* emotions
  language of, 59
  personal change and, 41–43, 49–51,
    83–84, 166
  physical symptoms of, 86
  process of, 4, 8–11, 44–45, 49
  remaining friends after, 176, 225–28
  revenge and, 29–36
  self-responsibility for, 50–52,
    115–18, 128, 222
  shame of, 7–8, 59
  shock of, 85–87
  social circles and, 221, 249–50
  stress of, 3
Broken Heart Syndrome, 37
Brown, Brené, 18, 164
Brown, H. Jackson, Jr., 241
Brown, Jeff, 115, 171
Buck, Pearl S., 99, 256
Burt and Linda, 28–30

Calhoun, Lawrence, 110
Calling in "The One" (Thomas), 1, 146n,
    191, 198n, 240
Carreira, Jeff, 258

case studies:
  Amanda and Benita, 72–73
  Christina, 30–31
  Claudia and Andrew, 65–67
  Dara, 90–91
  Diana and Brian, 48–54
  Doju and Lucio, 57–58
  Emily, 213–14
  Emily and Rick, 149–50
  Janet, 37–38
  Kate and Jack, 125–28
  Leslie, 17–18
  Lily and Jason, 131–32
  Lizzie and Phil, 237–38
  Melissa, 225–27
  Monique and Larry, 121–23
  Paul and Jesse, 245–46
  Ralph and Richard, 172–74
  Rita, 32–33
  Robin and Gary, 195–97
  Sarah, 154, 162–63
  Sarah and Andrew, 142–46
  Sophie and Mary, 216–18
  Tania, 91–92
centering, 84, 93–95, 147, 157–58
change:
  breakups as catalyst for, 41–43,
    49–51, 166, 249
  using emotions to inspire, 83–114
Cherlin, Andrew J., 26–27
child development, 162–63
children, and divorce:
  "broken homes" and, 8, 229
  custody of, 2–3, 123
  extended families and, 211,
    230–31
  impact on, 49, 52–53, 195
Chodron, Pema, 106, 110
Christina, 30–31
Christmas, 231
Churchill, Winston, 112, 197
classic movies, 16

index

Claudia and Andrew, 65–67

Coelho, Paulo, 75, 231

Cohen, Leonard, 42–43

communication:

  agreements and, 215–16

  breakups and, 205–8, 251

  conflicts in, 88–89

  healthy relationships and, 161–63, 253

  making amends and, 129–30

  platonic relationships and, 228

  reconciliations and, 70, 201

  resolving the past and, 191–92

  soul-to-soul, 156–60

  styles of, 69–70

conflict resolution, 130, 142–44, 161, 167

Congreve, William, 32, 98–99

conscious uncoupling:

  ceremony for, 211

  coaches for, 78

  committing to, 62

  creed for, 259–61

  definition of, 45

  doing alone, 75–77

  doing together, 74–75

  future intentions and, 177–80, 206, 218–19

  goal of, 55–56

  guidelines for, 61

  introduction of, 44, 59

  process of, 48–54, 60

  program length, 77–78

  rituals for, 247–51

  see also breakups, process of

Cook, Barbara, 39

Coontz, Stephanie, 6

couples counseling, *see* marriage counseling

Courage to Love, The (Gilligan), 154

Cozolino, Louis, 35, 45–46

Crosby, Michelle, 244–45

crossroads, 9–10, 42, 111

Crowley, Mary C., 172

Dara, 90–91

"dark night of the soul," 11, 61, 189

Debussy, Claude, 35

de la Bruyère, Jean, 161

depression, 101–5

Diagnostic and Statistical Manual of Mental Disorders (DSM), 40

Diana and Brian, 48–54

divorce:

  children and, *see* children, and divorce

  child support and, 202–3

  decision to, 8, 36, 48, 57, 65

  division of assets and, 4, 58, 211, 219, 234–41, 260

  family life after, 7, 53, 178–80, 223–25, 260

  finances and, 36, 235, 240, 242

  holidays and, 230–31

  legal system and, 242–44

  self-responsibility for, 50–52

  shame of, 7–8, 20

  statistics of, 1, 9, 25–27, 228, 244, 257

  see also breakups

divorce, common reasons for:

  addictions or alcoholism, 4, 69

  communication problems, 69–70

  different core values and, 5, 57

  domestic violence, 4, 71

  emotional unavailability, 195–97

  financial problems, 4, 69

  infidelity, 4, 48, 69

  no-fault divorce and, 242

  power imbalances, 4, 65

Divorce Corp. (Sorge), 236, 242

divorce parties, 249

Doju and Lucio, 57–58

domestic violence, 71

Edelmann, Marian Wright, 26
Edison, Thomas A., 20
Einstein, Albert, 193
Eisenberger, Naomi, 36, 218
Emerson, Ralph Waldo, 127, 140
Emily, 213–14
Emily and Rick, 149–50
Emotional Intelligence (Goleman), 91
emotions:
    anger, 48, 56, 92, 98–101, 186–89,
        245
    awareness of, 147
    brain chemistry and, 19–20, 29–32,
        35–36, 45–46
    children and, 233
    fueling change and, 83–114
    healing of, 39–41, 109, 138–39
    joy, 10, 40, 53, 251
    resolving the past and, 189–93
    sadness, 39, 44, 50, 220, 233
    see also fear; grief; rage; shame
Enchanted Love (Williamson), 184
entanglement, 193
Epictetus, 141
Erhard, Werner, 177
Erikson, Kai, 144
Erickson, Milton, 24
Eugenides, Jeffrey, 145
Euripides, 35
expectations, 213–15, 256–57

fairy tales, 21–24
faith, 90–91, 184, 259
family counseling, 195
family law, 58, 238–40, 246–47
family life:
    binuclear families and, 232
    children and, 5, 48, 143
    after divorce, 7, 53, 178–80,
        223–25, 260
fear:
    assumptions and, 105, 108
    breakups and, 36, 89–92, 149, 170,
        240
    communication and, 69–70, 100
    of criticism and judgment, 20, 135
    as motivation, 112
    regulation of, 46–47
    self-reflection and, 40–42, 139
finances, 36, 235, 240, 242
Finch, Tanya, 239–40
Fisher, Helen, 25, 29–30, 33
Forberg, Lisa, 245
Ford, Debbie, 249
forgiveness exercises, 185–89
Fowles, John, 58
Frances, Lauren, 109, 251
Frank (author's ex-boyfriend), 3,
        190–94
Frankl, Viktor, 24, 123, 134
Freud, Sigmund, 140
friends:
    breakup narratives and, 121, 216–21
    former lovers as, 77, 103, 175–77,
        225–28
    lack of, 37, 126
    making new, 210
    support from, 18, 52, 172, 249–50
Frost, Robert, 39
Fuller, Buckminster, 58
Fuller, Millard, 110

Gandhi, Mahatma, 34
gay partnerships, 9, 72–73, 172–74,
        216–18, 245–46
generosity, 54–58, 203–4, 239–41, 259
Gibran, Kahlil, 72, 85
Gilbert, Elizabeth, 1, 77
Gillies, Isabel, 133
Gilligan, Stephen, 93n, 154
Gladwell, Malcolm, 255
Gold, August, 160
Goleman, Daniel, 91
Good Divorce, The (Ahrons), 232

Good Karma Divorce, The (Lowrance), 242
Goodman, Ellen, 214
Gottman, John, 144, 229
Gottman, Julia, 144
Grandma and Grandpa (author's
    parents), 218–19, 223–24
gratitude, 11, 208, 253
Great Wall of China, 248
Green, John, 202
grief:
    death of child and, 22–23
    depression and, 103
    effective vs. ineffective grieving and,
        97
    faith and, 90
    healing and, 109, 138–39
    of lost love, 9, 32–33, 73, 90, 190
    prolonged and unprocessed, 3,
        39–40
    source-fracture wound and, 105–6
    stages of, 60, 63, 103–4, 133
    working through, 173
Gudmundson, Grant, 132

Hafiz, 58, 155
Hamilton, Craig, 54
"happily *even* after," 27, 176, 210–54
"happily ever after" myth, 21–22
Happy for No Reason (Shimoff), 185
healing, 38–41, 84–85, 137–68, 221,
    258
healthy relationships, 160–66, 169–71,
    204, 238–40, 260
heartbreak:
    baggage from, 63, 71
    healing from, 38–41, 84–85, 137–68,
        221, 258
Heartbreak (Paris), 54
Hemingway, Ernest, 112
Hendrickson, Kevis, 33
Herman, Jerry, 39
Herman, Judith, 85

Herzog, Roberta, 185
Hillesum, Etty, 97
Holm, Constance, 65
Holy Bible, 251
Ho'oponopono prayer, 186–87
Houston, Jean, 24
human potential movement:
    beginnings of, 24
    breakups as catalyst for, 43, 111–12
    core values and, 6–7, 70–71
    stability of marriage vs., 27, 57, 255

Inge, Dean, 174

James, William, 24
Janet, 37–38
journaling, 78–79, 113, 128
Jung, Carl, 143

karma, 54–55, 242
Kate and Jack, 125–28
Keller, Helen, 194
King, Martin Luther, Jr., 111
Kintsugi, 202
Koran, 62
Krause, Jennifer, 215
Kübler-Ross, Elisabeth, 60, 103, 212

Lamott, Anne, 246
Landers, Ann, 181, 239
Laysiepen, Uwe, 247–48
legal system:
    American, 242, 244
    avoiding litigation and, 246–47, 260
    European, 243–44
legislation:
    family law and, 58, 238–40, 246–47
    on marriage, 5, 9, 23
    no-fault divorce bill, 241–42
Lennon, John, 182
Lerner, Michael, 257
Leslie, 17–18

Lesser, Elizabeth, 207
Lewis, C. S., 250
Lieberman, Matthew D., 92, 237
Lily and Jason, 131–32
limbic regulation, 101
literature, 21–24, 30, 191
litigation, avoiding of, 246–47, 260
Lizzie and Phil, 237–38
Lord's prayer, 185
love addiction, 28–30, 46, 119, 228
Lowrance, Michele, 242
Luskin, Frederic, 134

McLeod, Ken, 54–55
McTaggart, Lynne, 193
Malloy, Merrit, 199
Mandela, Nelson, 181
mantras, 107–10, 118
Maraboli, Steve, 120, 180
Mark (author's ex-husband):
    child support and, 202–3
    division of assets and, 234–35,
        240–41
    divorce and, 3–6
    holidays and, 230–31
    intention of healthy future and,
        218–19, 223–25
    manifesting love and, 191–92
    shame of failed marriage and, 15–16
marriage:
    anniversaries of, 16
    as backbone of society, 256
    core values and beliefs, 5, 51–52,
        70–71, 88
    divorce and, see divorce
    gays and, 9, 72–73, 172–74, 216–18,
        245–46
    history of, 5–9, 22–25
    intimacy and, 17, 26, 144
    legislation on, 5, 9, 23; see also family
        law
    race and, 5
    statistics and, 27, 69
    upward mobility and, 235
    vows and rituals of, 16, 213–14, 219,
        249
marriage counseling, 50, 69
Marriage-Go-Round, The (Cherlin),
    27
Martin, Chris, 44
Maslow, Abraham, 24
Matisse, Henri, 57
Mead, Margaret, 24
Meir, Golda, 103
Melissa, 225–27
Melton, Glennon Doyle, 210
Meyers, Sheri, 220–21
mindfulness, 96, 135
    see also beginner's mind
Monique and Larry, 121–23
Moore, Thomas, 27
Morgen, Cherralea, 9
Morissette, Alanis, 31–32
movies, classic, 16
Munch, Edvard, 124
Museum of Modern Art, 248

Neruda, Pablo, 226
Neuroscience of Human Relationships, The
    (Cozolino), 35
Nietzsche, Friedrich, 122
Nin, Anaïs, 141

Oh, Sandra, 42

Paltrow, Gwyneth, 44
Panksepp, Jaak, 101–2
Parenting with Presence (Stiffelman), 233
Paris, Ginette, 54
Parks, Rosa, 173
Passion Test, The (Attwood and Attwood),
    176
Paul and Jesse, 245–46
Plato, 211

platonic relationships, 225–28
Pohn, Karey, 19
Poneman, Debra, 258
Popenoe, David, 69
power, personal, 115–36, 184
power struggles, 170
prayer:
    forgiveness and, 184–87
    of gratitude, 11
    Ho'oponopono prayer, 186–87
    Lord's prayer, 185
    relationships and, 173, 180, 217
    religious community and, 250–51
    searching for meaning and, 2
primate behavior, 33, 46
Prolonged Grief Disorder, 40
Pugach, Burt, 28–29

quantum mechanics, 193
Quarty, Kenneth, 239–40
Qubein, Nido, 213

race, 5
Radner, Gilda, 131
rage:
    betrayals and, 98, 110
    breakups and, 3, 170, 236
    Burt and, 28–30
    Christina and, 30–31
    facilitating change and, 98–100,
        186–88
    journaling about, 79, 113, 128
    letting go of, 50, 163
    Rita and, 32–33
Ralph and Richard, 172–74
Rand, David, 236
Rawlings, Marjorie Kinnan, 87
Reagan, Ronald, 241
Reber, Christina, 30–31
reconciliations, hoping for, 72–74, 131,
    136, 201
red flags, 89, 116

relationship endings, see breakups;
    divorce
relationship funerals, 251
relationship patterns:
    breaking, 137–68
    core beliefs and, 50–52
    love addiction and, 28–30, 46, 119,
        228
    transforming, 10, 64, 70, 76, 83–84
relationships:
    expectations of, 213–15, 256–57
    healthy, 160–66, 169–71, 204,
        238–40, 260
    letting go of, 175, 212
    platonic, 225–28
    public vs. private, 219
    recommendations for saving, 67–72
    stages of, 170, 260
repetition compulsion, 140
Resolution, 230
respect, 222–23, 227, 253, 257
revenge:
    Adams on, 37
    Congreve on, 32
    Euripides on, 35
    Gandhi on, 34
    Hendrickson on, 33
    Shakespeare on, 28
Riss, Linda, 28–29
Rita, 32
Roberts, Julia, 227
Robin and Gary, 195–97
Rock, David, 214
Rogers, Carl, 24
Rogers, Fred, 233
romantic love:
    classic movies about, 16
    fantasy vs. reality, 15, 19, 25–26, 220
    origins of, 22–24
    rejection and, 28–30, 36
    Romeo and Juliet, 191
Rumi, 97, 212

sadness, 39, 44, 50, 220, 233
Sarah, 154, 162–63
Sarah and Andrew, 142–46
Sartre, Jean-Paul, 169
"schema fracture," 91
Scott (author's brother), 223
Scream, The, 124
Seaborg, Glenn, 180–81
self-actualization, *see* human potential
    movement
self-care, 109–10, 113–14, 135–36, 166,
    208, 252–53
self-reflection, 118–20, 124, 128
self-responsibility, 50–52, 115–18, 128,
    167, 222, 259
Seven Principles of Making Marriage Work, The
    (Gottman), 229
sexual vitality, 26
Shakespeare, William, 28, 63, 86
shame:
    definition of, 17
    of failed relationships, 7–8, 15–17,
        118–19
    of our behavior, 32
    societal expectations and, 19–20,
        221
    vs. guilt, 18
Shimoff, Marci, 185–86
shock, 3, 85–87
Shoffstall, Veronica, 138
"Silver Seekers," 26, 237
Smith, Jaclyn, 196
social rejection, 218
"sociostasis," 46
solitude, 104
Solms, Mark, 102
Sophie and Mary, 216–18
Sorge, Joseph, 236, 242
"source-fracture story," *see* breakup
    narratives
Southard, John E., 204
Stafford, William, 6

"State of Our Unions, The" (Popenoe
    and Whitehead), 69
Stephanie, 48–49, 52–53
Stiffelman, Susan, 233
Straparola, Giovanni Francesco,
    23–24
stress, 3
suicide, 105
"Sun Never Says, The" (Hafiz), 58
survival, 22–23
Symposium (Plato), 211

Tabibnia, Golnaz, 237
Tania, 91–92
Taylor, Barbara Brown, 83
Terence (poet), 30
Thanksgiving, 230
Thich Nhat Hanh, 99
Thomas, Kit, 59
"Time Heals Everything" (Herman),
    39
Tizon, Robert, 55
Tolle, Eckhart, 117
tragedies, 30, 191
Trauma and Recovery (Herman), 85
Trungpa, Chögyam, 111

Ulay, 247–48
Ultimatum Game, 236–37
Under the Tuscan Sun (film), 42

Valentine's Day, 249
values, core:
    authentic living and, 212
    disparity of, 5, 193
    fairness as, 240–41
    shifts in, 70–71, 88, 221–22
Venice, 21–24
vision boards, 225

Walker, Alice, 122
Ward, J. R., 19

Warhol, Andy, 40
Wevorce, 244
When Things Fall Apart (Chodron), 110
Whitehead, Barbara Dafoe, 69
Wilber, Ken, 195
Williamson, Marianne, 184
Wyman, Jane, 242

"You Oughta Know" (Morissette and Ballard), 31–32
Your Brain at Work (Rock), 214

Zach, Miles, and Emma, 195
Zachary, 121
Zammit, Claire, 93, 107, 146, 189, 198
Zampino, Thomas, 236

yellow
kite

books to help you live a good life

Join the conversation and tell
us how you live a #goodlife

@yellowkitebooks
YellowKiteBooks
Yellow Kite Books
YellowKiteBooks